One Hundred Lengths
of the Pool

One Hundred Lengths of the Pool

Julia Roberts

preface

Published by Preface 2013

10 9 8 7 6 5 4 3 2 1

First published in Great Britain in 2013 by Preface Publishing
20 Vauxhall Bridge Road
London, SW1V 2SA

An imprint of The Random House Group Limited

www.randomhouse.co.uk
www.prefacepublishing.co.uk

Addresses for companies within The Random House Group Limited
can be found at www.randomhouse.co.uk

The Random House Group Limited Reg. No. 954009

A CIP catalogue record for this book is available from the British Library

ISBN 978 1 84809 427 7

'Unwritten' written by Natasha Bedingfield, Danielle Brisebois and Wayne Rodriguez.
Reproduced by kind permission of Sony/AVT Music Publishing and Kobalt Music Group Ltd.

The Random House Group Limited supports the Forest Stewardship Council®
(FSC®), the leading international forest-certification organisation. Our books
carrying the FSC label are printed on FSC®-certified paper. FSC is the only
forest-certification scheme supported by the leading environmental organisations,
including Greenpeace. Our paper procurement policy can be found at:
www.randomhouse.co.uk/environment

Typeset in Centaur by SX Composing DTP, Rayleigh Essex
Printed and bound in Great Britain by Clays

One of my earliest memories was sitting with my maternal grandmother 'Gaga at Green Street', watching the Miss World competition on our black-and-white television set.

'I want to be Miss World when I grow up,' I said.

Gaga just smiled at me, knowing that it was highly unlikely that a four-year-old with a pronounced limp would ever be able to walk a catwalk in stiletto heels. She was right, of course. I can't walk in stilettos, and anyway, as I grew older, I had self-image issues particularly regarding my body, but that moment almost certainly defined my destiny.

Introduction

You may be wondering how I arrived at the title of this book and some of you may even think it is a book about fitness. Let me assure you it's not, although the idea for the book came about whilst I was engaged in my own personal fitness regime.

I was taught to swim at the age of four as part of a physiotherapy programme to help me regain strength in my left leg, which had been weakened by a life-threatening illness three years earlier.

I have maintained my relationship with swimming throughout my life as it is the most manageable form of exercise for me. When I was finally fortunate enough to own a holiday home with a pool I set myself the challenge of swimming a hundred lengths of it every day of each visit, weather permitting. I should probably mention at this point that the pool is only twelve metres long, not Olympic size, so it's not quite as impressive as it may have initially sounded.

The trouble is, swimming lengths can be really tedious, particularly swimming a hundred of them in a session. I found the whole process more achievable if I associated the number of each length of the pool with something that had taken place in my life.

Here's an example. In 1972 I left school, a fairly momentous occasion, so, when I get to length 72, I think of things associated with that time. I had made the decision that I didn't want to stay on at West Bridgford Comprehensive School (formerly Grammar School) to study for A levels despite pleas from my dad, who was keen for me to go to university. All students who had taken this decision had to have a meeting with the careers advisor.

'So, Julia,' he asked, 'What are you going to do when you leave school?'

'I'm going to be a dancer,' I replied.

'Yes, but what are you going to do to earn a living?'

Within twelve months of that question I had my first professional dancing job and was earning the Equity minimum wage, which at the time was twelve pounds a week.

Ironically, many years later I was asked to give a talk at Caterham School in Surrey, which both my children attended, about a career in television. I'm happy to say I was able to offer realistic advice but also practical help in the form of work experience at QVC, where I have worked as a presenter for over nineteen years, for a couple of interested pupils.

One of the questions I was asked was, 'What is it like to be famous?' I found that one difficult to answer as I don't consider myself famous. Sometimes I am recognised when I'm out shopping or at the airport and I genuinely enjoy people coming up to me for a chat, but I wouldn't want the sort of fame associated with being a movie star like my namesake, the 'other' Julia Roberts. I like doing normal things like supermarket shopping, or going out to dinner or the cinema without being mobbed or bothered by the paparazzi trying to catch me without my make-up on, which in my case wouldn't be difficult as I rarely wear make-up unless I am working or going for an evening out. I do my own cooking and cleaning and gardening, and I've even been known to mix cement! Apparently I am a dab hand at this as I treat it like a cake mixture and fold everything in to make it the perfect consistency.

No, I never wanted to be really famous but I think I always knew I was destined for something a little different in my life. Maybe I was meant to survive being born with the umbilical cord around my neck and then contracting a killer disease at fourteen months old.

It's funny, but I have always had the feeling that I might not have a very long life, so I wanted to make the most of the time I have. I never thought I would make it past fifty so in a way I'm in 'time added on for injury' to use a football analogy, which is appropriate as I am a fan of the beautiful game. I have said on many occasions,

'If I die tomorrow I can honestly say I have lived'

and I truly mean it, not that I'm planning on going anywhere just yet if I can help it.

Not all the lengths of the pool related to years though, otherwise there would have been nothing to preoccupy my mind until I got to the mid-50s. I started to associate addresses I had lived at, my age when certain things happened in my life, and even the position I finished in the 'Song for Europe' competition.

So pairing up lengths of the pool with events in my life didn't start out as an idea for a book; it was merely to alleviate boredom and, to be honest, it also helped me keep count. I'm sure on some occasions I have swum fewer or extra lengths without realising it! The light-bulb moment of turning my memories into a book with a hundred chapters struck whilst I was on holiday in July 2011, as you will read more about in *chapter 11*.

I got home and started planning the content of the book but I hadn't actually written anything when a chance encounter spurred me to action. Following a party at a friend's house in Hertfordshire, Kealan, one of our QVC producers, and his girl-friend Zoe, who I had not previously met, needed a lift back to

London. We volunteered. An hour and a half in a car with two people you barely know could have descended into long periods of silence, but Zoe was gregarious and I love to talk, after all I do it for a living. She asked me what I had done prior to starting work at QVC and I told her about being a dancer, having a record deal and being a hostess on *The Price is Right*. She seemed genuinely interested and quizzed me further, expressing surprise that I had also been a club DJ and appeared in numerous television advertisements.

I then mentioned that I was planning to put it all in a book and she said, 'Well, I'll buy it.'

I hope she does.

One

It is official, I am Number One . . .
in numerology that is.

I have always been interested in astrology, tarot cards, even Chinese Horoscopes, as you will find out in *chapter 60*, so, as this book is all about numbers, I was very keen to find out what number I am in numerology, and it's actually a lot easier than you might think.

All you do is write down your day, month and year of birth and then put a plus sign in between the individual numbers. I will use me as an example. I was born on the 10th of June 1956 so my equation is: $1+0+0+6+1+9+5+6 = 28$.

If, like me, it comes out as two numbers you reduce it again in the same way, so $2+8 = 10$, and again $1+0 = 1$. There you have your birth or life force number. 'Simples', as the meerkats would say!

But it doesn't stop there. We are also influenced by our day force number, which is simply adding together the two numbers of your birth date without including the month or year, so once again using me as an example, the tenth is $1+0 = 1$.

So both my birth force and day force number is 1. If you are born before the tenth of the month you only have a single digit anyway so your day force number is already worked out.

The only exceptions to these calculations are when at any point the double-digit number is 11 or 22 (or 33 or 44) then you don't add them together because they are Master Numbers in their own right.

So we've established how you work out your number in numerology, but what does it mean? Well for that you will have to treat yourself to a book on the subject. Mine is called *Zillionz* by Titania Hardie, and it's a pretty comprehensive introduction to the subject. However, I will just share a few of the 'Number One' characteristics with you in case you are one, and to help you understand me better. Bear in mind though that, as my birthday is the tenth, it increases some of the 'number 1' tendencies tenfold – my poor family and friends.

Apparently I am independent and self-reliant, sometimes bossy, and naturally assume the lead. My energies are aggressive in the best sense and I will never be walked over. Able to stand alone, other people may lean on me and seek me out for advice but are less able to help me. I prefer to do the job myself rather than rely on others and discover my mistakes through hard-earned knocks. Even as a child I would have been required to stand on my own two feet and show adult tendencies. I'm idealistic, full of clever ideas and initiate change both at home and at work. I sometimes need to be alone to think and create and to unwind from my own energy. I need (and fortunately have) a very understanding partner, who is patient, independent and good at reading between the lines.

As you might imagine, I have also worked out the numerology for my family members, and as you are going to be meeting them in the pages of this book, I thought I would introduce them now.

My partner of thirty-four years is Chris. His birth force and day force are both number 3.

My son is Daniel. His birth force is 8 but his day force is 9.

My daughter is Sophie. Her birth force and day force are both 8. She was born on the eighth in the year 1988, so lots of eights surround her, which is supposed to be very lucky!

In my numerology book there are also letters associated with the number I and these are A, J and S, all of which are in my name. The letter J, particularly at the beginning of a name, suggests profound honesty and inventive ability, the latter of which is quite useful when writing a book!

Before I move on from the subject of numerology, there is just one more calculation that you might find useful and in my case has been inspirational. You can work out what numerology year you are currently in and how that may influence you. You add together the numbers from your day and month of birth as before, but substitute your birth year with the current year. For me this is: $1+0+0+6+2+0+1+1 = 11$. So when I started to write this book I was in a year eleven, which started on my birthday in 2011 and ended on my birthday in 2012.

As I mentioned before, 11 is a Master Number and in this year you must be prepared for harder work with greater demands, but with the possibility of greater rewards. There are excellent prospects for success during this time but **much** hard work is needed. (Are you noticing a trend here?) **Don't waste** time troubling over what you cannot change. Be **prepared** to move forward. If you can grasp this truth, the sky is now the limit. If you dig deep into your bag of talents you may surprise yourself by what you can do. You have nothing to lose, and everything to gain, so don't be lazy or shy. Go for it!

This has inspired me to finally start and finish a book, something I have been trying to do for years, but maybe the numbers have been against me until now.

Two

In 1966, at the age of ten, I came second in a
story-writing competition.

They say there are no prizes for coming second, but actually there was. It was a book token to the value of twelve shillings and sixpence, which in 1966 was quite a lot of money. I spent it very wisely on books about ballet!

I had been entered for the competition, along with several other members of my class at the Jesse Gray County Primary School, by our teacher, Mr Syson. You will read more about Mr Syson in *chapter 47*.

I still have the original handwritten copy of my story, which caused great amusement amongst my family when I read it to them after all these years. I toyed with the idea of reproducing it at this point but decided against it, as I want you to read the rest of this book and I didn't want you to think that my writing style is in any way similar to how it was in 1966!

Here though is a brief synopsis. I was writing the story through the eyes of a dog. His mistress gets called away to deal with a sick aunt and subsequently brings her back to stay at their house. The aunt doesn't like dogs so 'I' and another dog live 'rough' until the aunt goes home. I think I had seen the film *The Incredible Journey* and that had certainly influenced my choice of subject matter.

What was much more surprising was the language I used and

my ability to bring world politics into a story about two dogs! Everything from the war in Vietnam to the problems in Rhodesia, now known as Zimbabwe. The latter I can understand because my parents were very serious about emigrating to Rhodesia around this time, so it must have been discussed at length around the dinner table. I also did a geography project on the country so all the information leaflets were not wasted when, in the end, my parents decided against the move. As it turns out, with all the problems in Zimbabwe now, it was a wise move not to move!

If you do want to read this 'work of art', I have included it at the back of the book, just don't read it now.

This wasn't my first attempt at writing. I had already written a play, loosely based on the story of 'The Princess and the Pea', which my then teacher, Mr Corner, had allowed me to put on as a school production. I held the auditions, wrote the script, produced, directed and probably appeared in it as well. I was ten and it was a feat I didn't repeat until I was forty-seven, when I did my first piece for Sky Sports. That is still my proudest piece of work, Sky Sports not the school play, as you will read about in *chapter 94.*

So my writing took a very long break, unless you include writing lyrics for songs, which I have done since the 1980s.

It wasn't until I was working at a cable television channel that I got 'into print'. I used to write a short piece for the *Cable Guide* magazine entitled 'From The Presenter's Chair' about what was coming on the local show in the forthcoming month. Half the time it was guesswork, as the bookings were often very last minute, so I had to be quite ambiguous.

It was also whilst I was working at the cable channel that I started to write a piece about Crystal Palace Football Club for the *Palace News*, a free paper that was distributed with the *Croydon Advertiser* at the time. It was called 'A Bird's-Eye View', a title I came up with, which was very appropriate as Crystal Palace are the 'Eagles'. Birds, eagles, you see my train of thought, and I am female, so a double entendre!

When it was first suggested a couple of years back that the presenters at QVC should write a weekly blog for the QVC website, I was definitely up for it. It is not intended to push products; it is a way for the viewers to become more familiar with our lives on and off air. I don't 'tell all' because I think some things should be kept private, but I do enjoy sharing snippets of news and the odd recipe here and there. I am pleased to say I have a lot of 'hits' each week on my blog and also loads of comments which I do my best to reply to.

I have been threatening to write a book for years . . . and years . . . and years, and in fact I have started but not finished two other factual books and at least three novels. It is a case of being strict with myself and making the time to sit down and write uninterrupted. It's not always easy to find the time, particularly when I'm busy at QVC and with the other projects I am working on, but if I want to write, I have to make sacrifices, and who needs eight hours' sleep anyway?

Depending on the success of this book, no pressure here guys, there could be sequels to this one. Bring on the black coffee!

Three

This is the number of green purses
I have owned.

If you are thinking I just have a penchant for green you are partly correct. However, there is a significance to owning a green purse and it is all to do with Feng Shui.

I was introduced to it courtesy of my best friend Denise, who, as you will discover in *chapter 34*, I met whilst we were filming *The Price is Right*. We have remained friends over the years and although we don't see each other that often it's not important. I know that she is there for me, and I will always be there for her, no matter what the problem.

Denise works for a company called Talkback Thames, and on one occasion when we met for lunch we began talking about Feng Shui because we were going to be selling some products on QVC. She was really into it and had brought me some I Ching coins to carry in my purse, and promised to make me a purple star to put in the career area of my house. I wasn't sure where that was, so the next time Denise visited she brought her compass with her to identify the different areas of my house. She also brought me a three-legged toad, sitting on a pile of money, to position near my front door, but not facing outwards, and some more I Ching coins to place in the bottom of my spaghetti jar, so that we would never go short of food.

As I mentioned, she had already given me some I Ching coins

for my purse when we had met up for lunch, but apparently for the best results you need a green purse.

Well, Christmas was around the corner, so guess what was on my Christmas list?

It wasn't easy finding a green purse in the late 1990s; it simply wasn't a fashionable colour. I'm pleased to say the family persevered and I was really delighted with my first green leather purse.

In truth I think it was a bit on the dark side for Feng Shui purposes but it was a really good purse and lasted me the best part of six years. Hold the jokes about it lasting so long because it never sees the light of day!

Anyway, it was replaced by a slightly lighter green purse, also in leather, but neither of these two purses had the zip coin section on the outside of the back of the purse, that forms an elongated triangle shape when you unzip it. However, my latest green purse does.

I was out with my family at Bluewater Shopping Centre in Kent, shopping for clothes for work, when my eyes alighted on a gorgeous bright green, patent leather purse with a shocking pink lining. We were in Ted Baker, and I was in lust. It was a bit on the expensive side but, as luck would have it, we were only a month away from my birthday. Deal done, birthday present bought. I absolutely love my purse and often get comments about it when I get it out to pay at the checkout. As I said, it has the zip pocket at the back which is where I keep my I Ching coins, along with any £1 coins I have in my possession.

Does Feng Shui work? It's not for me to say. A lot of it makes a great deal of sense, and, if you are interested, I would suggest investing in a book on the subject. I have a handbag-sized book called, *Lillian Too's Little Book of Feng Shui*, which has a few basic guidelines in it.

I also have another little book that I wouldn't recommend if you are serious about the subject. My partner Chris bought it for me as a joke! It is called *Feng Shite,* and is for the non-believer!

What I do know, is that I will be hanging on to my Ted Baker purse until it falls apart.

Four

This is the number of cats I have had: Dylan,
Charlie, Poppy and Daisy.

The funny thing is, I was never really a cat person, as we had always had dogs when I was growing up.

I didn't set out to become a cat owner, it just sort of happened. Chris and I were living in a top-floor flat, which I will tell you more about in *chapter 52*. It was Christmas time and we had only moved in a few weeks before so we didn't know any of the other tenants very well.

I was working as a dancer in a pantomime at the Palace Theatre in Watford, and on Christmas Eve we only had an afternoon show, so I arrived home in the early evening. As I went up the stairs to the top floor, I noticed a kitten crouched down on one of the steps. It looked scared and hungry but obviously I didn't have any cat food to give it, so I improvised with a saucer of milk and some chopped-up pork luncheon meat. The following morning the kitten had gone and so had the milk but, unsurprisingly, the pork luncheon meat was untouched!

I later found out that the owners of the kitten, who was called Dylan, had gone away for Christmas. They had left food in a bowl outside for him, but he had come into the house to keep warm. He survived that Christmas all right, but a couple of years later, when his owners moved out, they didn't take him with them. I bought a cardboard pet carrier from the pet shop and drove him to their new address but, to my horror, they hadn't left him behind because they had forgotten him, as I had assumed; they simply didn't want him any more, as they now had a toddler and twins to look after. There really was no option, I had to adopt him.

At first Dylan was very timid, but we heaped affection on him and soon he came to realise that he had fallen squarely on all four feet. When we visited relatives in Nottingham or Lincolnshire, Dylan went with us in his cat basket. He was actually quite a good traveller and got on pretty well with other cats.

On one occasion we had gone to visit my mum and dad and Dylan had gone out exploring. There was a massive thunderstorm and, despite calling for him to come, there was no sign. We had to leave without him as we were both working the next day. I was absolutely distraught. I rang my mum repeatedly during the course of the next day, but he was still a no-show, so I had to drive my old MGB roadster all the way back to Lincolnshire in the hope that I would be able to find him.

When I arrived my mum took me up to their bedroom and there was Dylan curled up on the bed. Apparently he had sauntered in, just after my last frantic phone call, totally oblivious to the distress he was causing, and there was no way my mum could let me know as there were no mobile phones in those days.

He was a truly amazing cat and very intuitive. If I was upset he would come and brush against me to let me know that he was there. If I didn't respond by stroking him, he would sit down at my side and wait until I was ready to include him in my woes. He would allow me to pick him up and hold him like a baby without ever struggling, and he never ever scratched any of us.

We had no intention of getting a second cat but, again, circumstances dictated. We were still living in the top-floor flat in Upper Norwood and on the middle floor one of the tenants owned a female cat called Pancho. She had become pregnant — nothing to do with Dylan, I might add, as we'd had him neutered.

One evening, I opened the front door to our flat and a movement caught my eye. I screamed as I thought it was a rat but, on closer inspection, it was one of the tiniest kittens I had ever seen. Just at that moment Pancho rounded the turn in the staircase with another tiny kitten in her mouth. I have no idea why she was bringing them up to our flat. We carefully gathered the kittens up and Pancho followed us downstairs to our neighbour. We only just caught him as he was leaving for a business trip. He took the little kittens and their mum to his girlfriend's to be looked after while he was away.

The next morning I started to wonder if we had interrupted Pancho in the middle of transporting her family and began to worry that there might be other kittens. Chris and I had a good look round outside but found nothing. However, later that morning I was putting some rubbish in the dustbins at the side of the house and I thought I heard a very faint miaow. Again I looked around, but I couldn't see any other kittens. I told Chris what I thought I had heard and, although we both thought I must have been imagining it, he went for one final look. He came back a few minutes later.

'No,' he said, 'there was nothing . . . except this.'

Sitting in the palm of his hand was a tiny black-and-white kitten whose eyes were barely open. I immediately rang our vet and they told me to take the kitten straight there. He was so small he actually sat in the middle of a Danish Cookies biscuit tin with loads of woollen fabric around him. It looked like a nest.

The vet was not very hopeful that he would survive without his mother to nurse him but, as Pancho had been sent away with her other kittens, we had no choice but to attempt to bottle-feed him.

We were given a special formula, which we had to make up

with water and a drop of cooking oil, a tiny feeding bottle and instructions to feed him every couple of hours. It really was touch and go for the first few days but he was a fighter, and with the care we gave him he pulled through. When it was clear he was going to survive we named him Charlie.

Dylan was a fantastic surrogate mother, cleaning and cuddling him. He also showed him how to use the litter tray, although for the first couple of weeks he was so tiny that he couldn't even climb into it himself, but had to be lifted in.

Charlie even became a minor celebrity. I was just about to start filming the second series of *The Price is Right* and my friend from the show, Denise, who I mentioned in the previous chapter, rang a photographer she knew, who was always on the look out for 'feel-good' stories. She told him of Charlie's lucky rescue and, at the age of eight weeks, he and I were pictured together and his story told in a national newspaper. Maybe you even read it at the time?

Six months after finding Charlie we moved from the flat into our first house and of course Dylan and Charlie moved with us. Eighteen months later we started our family with the arrival of our son Daniel, followed by Sophie thirteen months after that.

Both of the cats were really good with the children, even though from time to time they had their tails pulled. Daniel was particularly fond of Charlie and they used to race up the stairs to his bedroom – Charlie usually won!

We moved again nine and a half years later to a village in Surrey called Woldingham. Although it was a quieter area, we lived on the main road through the village. We had only been there three months when, one night, Charlie failed to come in for his supper. Sadly he had been knocked down by a car just a few days before Christmas. We buried him in the woodland across the road from our house, and erected a little wooden cross in his memory. For months after his death, the children were subdued as we passed the site of the accident on their walk to school each morning.

At first I wasn't keen on having another cat but, as the months passed, I did wonder if Dylan was lonely on his own, particularly as he was getting older. We had visited the local pet shop a few times to see the various kittens on offer, but it wasn't until the June that a particular kitten stole our hearts. The cage had two kittens in it, a brother and sister. One was all black and the other was black and white, not dissimilar to Dylan. The black cat was the boy and he was miaowing and reaching his paws through the bars of the cage. The black-and-white cat was the girl, and she just sat quietly looking at us with appealing eyes. It was the black-and-white female who we all fell in love with, although I did have a few pangs of guilt over leaving her brother all by himself. We called her Poppy.

Dylan wasn't terribly impressed with Poppy at first. She was a kitten and was always leaping around wanting to play. He was eighteen, which made him a very old man in cat years, round about ninety! She used to do that vertical jumping thing you see cartoon cats do and he would bop her on the head to try and calm her down if she hassled him too much. She was so lovely though, particularly if she wanted attention and I was busy at my desk in my little home office. She would jump up onto my desk, scattering papers around, and then climb up me and lie across the back of my neck while I worked. I found it very comforting, almost like a living, breathing hot water bottle.

Dylan and Poppy each had a basket to sleep in at night, which were located in the storm porch. When I came in late at night I would unlock the outside door into their little area and they would look up at me sleepily as I then unlocked the front door to let myself into the house. I knew Dylan had completely accepted Poppy when I came home on a freezing winter night and they were curled up together in Dylan's basket for warmth.

Soon after this Dylan's health started to deteriorate. He began to lose weight and his beautiful sleek coat started to fall out in clumps. The vet wasn't too concerned with his condition and seemed to put it down to old age. He still liked to go out in the garden for a wander and I didn't want to stop him as I thought it would be unfair to take away something he enjoyed. Then one day he simply didn't come home. Memories of the night Charlie had gone missing came flooding back and I think we all feared the worst. We walked up and down our road calling him and looking to see if he had been knocked down, but nothing. He just seemed to have disappeared.

I had read somewhere that cats sometimes do this when they are ready to die. They go off and find themselves a safe place and just go to sleep. I was beside myself with grief. Dylan was my first 'baby' before I had my children. I tried to comfort Sophie, who was also in floods of tears, but it was a dreadful time, particularly as we couldn't 'say our goodbyes'.

Five days after Dylan's disappearance I was driving into work when my car phone rang. It was Chris.

'You had better pull in to the side of the road,' he said. 'I think we've found Dylan.'

I started to cry as I assumed he meant that they had found his body.

'Where?' I asked.

'At the RSPCA in Putney,' he replied.

It turned out that Chris had been walking back from taking the children to school and had seen a note pinned to a telegraph pole which read:

IF YOU ARE THE OWNER OF A BLACK-AND-WHITE CAT WITH A GREEN SPARKLY COLLAR IT HAS BEEN TAKEN TO THE RSPCA.

This was followed by a phone number.

The people who had posted the note thought that Dylan was being mistreated because of his weight and the poor condition of his fur, so they had called the RSPCA, who had taken him off to their 'pet hospital'.

As I was working Chris went to fetch him home. It was quite amusing actually, as the hospital was a location for the TV show *Animal Hospital*, starring Rolf Harris, and they were filming when Chris arrived to collect Dylan. Fortunately they didn't include him in the show, as Chris is not a fan of the limelight, although Dylan would have looked the part with his emerald green sparkly collar!

They had given Dylan a thorough examination and had also given him an injection of some description. I don't know what the injection was, but it gave Dylan a new lease of life. He started to put on a little weight and his fur started to grow back.

We had at least two years of Dylan being quite well before his health started to deteriorate again. He began to get a little shaky on his feet and we had to stop letting him go out on his own in case he wandered into the road. Instead we used to put a little dog harness on him and walk him round the garden.

The vet assured me that Dylan wasn't in pain but I think we all knew he didn't have much longer to live. Tragically he died the day before we got back from a family holiday. My child minder, who was also my 'cat minder', had come to feed the cats and Dylan had collapsed and died in the litter tray. The vet thought it was most likely kidney failure. My cat minder had made him a little coffin and buried him in the garden, so at least we were able to have a little ceremony for him. It was heartbreaking to lose him, but twenty-three is some age for a cat.

Poppy seemed changed after that and became quite timid. We wondered if she was lonely being on her own or traumatised by what had happened to Dylan. We discussed whether it would be best for her if we got another cat but hadn't reached a decision.

It was my birthday and amongst my presents was a tin of cat food. On closer inspection, I realised it was a tin of kitten food, and a few minutes later the children carried in a box containing a beautiful tabby kitten. She really was very pretty, apart from her huge ears which I hoped she would grow into. Do you remember the film *Gremlins?* Well, there was a slight resemblance!

I called the kitten Daisy and she was a bit of a live wire from the start. The night before my birthday I had come home from work quite late and was quite surprised that the children had decided to 'camp' in the lounge to watch WWF – the World Wrestling Federation rather than a nature programme – only the television wasn't on when I got home. It turned out that they were babysitting Daisy, who was leaping around like a mad thing. When Sophie had heard my car pull into the drive she had pulled Daisy under her covers so the miaowing wouldn't give the game away. I didn't suspect a thing!

Daisy was much more sociable than Poppy and didn't mind being teased and played with by the children, but she was quite a naughty cat too. She would eat almost anything, including cheese, hummus, vegetables and even bread, so you couldn't leave anything out on the work surface in the kitchen, even if the kitchen door was closed. The reason for this? Daisy had worked out how to push the handle of the kitchen door down to open it! We discovered this after a trip to the supermarket. I had been unpacking the shopping and had been called away to do some-thing else. I went back to the unpacking a few minutes later to find Daisy munching on a piece of bread that she had removed from the plastic bag after tearing it open.

Her favourite titbit though was chocolate Maltesers. She would hear the Maltesers rattling around in the box and come running from wherever she was in the house. We would roll them for her to chase and then she would lick the chocolate before crunching the inside.

She liked crunching things, and unfortunately that included mouse bones. Daisy was a mouser and not averse to bringing us 'presents'. One time she brought a mouse into the house, I shouted at her, she dropped it and the mouse scuttled off. We went on a mouse hunt but couldn't find it anywhere until we spotted Poppy sitting by the French doors of the playroom looking at something. It was the mouse, and Poppy was just looking at it. Such a soppy Poppy! I think Daisy got the message eventually and stopped bringing things in, but she still used to catch mice and would sit crunching them under Sophie's bedroom window, ugh! Anyone would think we didn't feed her.

I wouldn't say Daisy and Poppy were friends. In fact, for the majority of the time Daisy had the run of the house and bullied Poppy a bit, but they tolerated each other. At meal times, though, the boot was on the other paw. The moment the door to the utility room, where they ate and slept, was closed, Poppy took charge and would happily whack Daisy if she attempted to take her food!

Poppy has always been more of house cat, but Daisy was an adventurer and that eventually led to her demise.

I was in the bathroom getting ready for an evening shift at QVC when Sophie came in and said, 'Mum, I've got something to tell you.'

Since the age of sixteen, whenever Sophie has said that, my response has always been the same: 'You're not pregnant are you?'

'Daisy has been knocked down by a car.'

I just looked at her in disbelief. It was less than two months since the death of my darling dad.

'Is she . . .?' The question just hung in the air.

'Yes, Mum, I'm so sorry.'

I was already in a fragile state and I just started to sob. Sophie was magnificent, as she always is in a crisis affecting someone else, and put her arms around me and just held me.

'Where is she?' I asked through my tears.

'Dad is just laying her out so that you can say goodbye to her.'

I went downstairs in a bit of a daze and Chris was by the open French doors. Daisy was lying at his feet on a towel. She looked so peaceful, like she was asleep. I kept waiting for her to twitch like she often did in her sleep, probably when she was imagining herself in pursuit of a mouse, but she was totally still.

I remember stroking her and saying, 'Are you sure she is dead?'

Sophie and Chris just exchanged glances. Some years later, when Sophie and I were talking about it, Sophie said that her dad had laid Daisy out in such a way that I couldn't see the impact of the car on her head. She must have died instantly.

I have no idea how I managed to work that evening. Automatic pilot, I guess. Sophie had to work as well and must have done the same. The next day we buried Daisy at the bottom of the garden and erected another little cross.

We had lost three cats while we had been living at The Downs Cottage so I guess Poppy was pretty relieved when we moved a couple of years later, although you wouldn't have known it from her behaviour!

She was always very unsettled when the suitcases came out for family holidays; in fact, sometimes she would sit in the empty cases looking mournful. In the weeks leading up to our house move, bearing in mind we had accumulated sixteen years of 'stuff', Poppy was clearly getting anxious. We had to empty the loft and the three garden sheds, the understairs cupboard and various other storage areas, and then we had to start boxing everything up. She was very confused.

Our house had sold before we had found a new house to buy, so we decided to rent for a while to prevent us from losing the sale. I hadn't realised that having a cat might be a problem with prospective landlords, particularly a cat like Poppy, but some places simply wouldn't entertain the idea of pets. There were already quite a few criteria to meet, so finding a house that suited all of us and with sufficient parking was becoming a bit of a nightmare, and we were running out of time. When the agent rang me with the details for the house we eventually moved into, everything was spot on, except that the landlord didn't want pets.

When we went to view we all agreed it was the perfect house for us, and we were only three weeks away from being homeless, but Poppy was potentially the deal breaker. No cat, no house! Fortunately the landlord took a liking to us.

We took the house we were moving into a couple of days before we had to move out of The Downs Cottage so we would have the opportunity to move some things ourselves before the removal lorry turned up. Even so it was a mammoth task and we had to keep Poppy locked in the attic room on 'moving day' with her bed, food and litter tray so that she wouldn't get spooked and run away.

After unloading the lorry at the new house, I went back to The Downs Cottage to fetch Poppy and the contents of the fridge/freezer and the food cupboards. She was very nervous when we set her carry basket down in the new house, even though she was surrounded by familiar things, familiar smells and familiar people. She moved around gingerly with her tummy very close to the floor, sniffing everything.

We were busy unpacking so left her to familiarise herself with her new surroundings, but when it came to supper time we couldn't find her. After a lengthy search we discovered her in the office, camped out in the filing cabinet, which had yet to have its drawers reinstated. We left the drawers out for a couple of days as she kept retreating there after meals, not that she ate much for the first few days. Once the cabinet was put back together, she had to make do with a new hiding place, behind the sofa in the family room.

It didn't take her long to settle in, particularly as the house had underfloor heating on the ground floor, and she started behaving in some quite kittenish ways, despite being sixteen years old. Her Christmas present included a catnip mouse which she loves to throw up into the air and pounce on, and she started racing Daniel up two flights of stairs to his room at the top of the house.

I hope I am that agile at eighty plus, the human equivalent of sixteen cat years!

Five

Some of you reading this book may well have bought
it because you know me from QVC but, without fate
stepping in, I wouldn't have had an audition,
and wouldn't have had to endure the
five-minute pencil test.

It was late on a Thursday afternoon in July 1993 and I had
just returned home from selling my flash new red Spacewagon
back to the garage I had bought it from just six months previously, because I couldn't meet the payments. You'll read more
about that and all my other cars in *chapter 16.*

As you can imagine, I was feeling rather sorry for myself. As
I put the key in the lock of the front door the phone started
ringing. It's that feeling of 'shall I hurry and try to get to the
phone before it stops ringing, or shall I just leave it because I
probably won't get there anyway?' Despite my negativity I rushed
and managed to answer the phone before it stopped ringing. It
was Jo from my agent's office.

'You're probably not going to be interested in this,' said Jo,
my agent's second-in-command, 'but you've been asked to go for
an audition for a new shopping channel tomorrow morning at
10 a.m.'

'Isn't it rather short notice?' I asked. It was 5.30 p.m. and Jo
would normally have left for the day.

'Well, apparently someone has dropped out and you were on

the reserve list after we sent them your showreel last week.'

'I'm not sure. What will I have to do?'

'You need to choose an object and sell it to them for approximately ten minutes. I know it isn't exactly what you're looking for, but it would be good experience and might get you noticed.'

'OK then, if you think it would be a good stepping stone. What's the address?'

And that was it. Out of the blue, I was a last-minute replacement to fill up the audition list.

That evening my partner Chris and I discussed what we thought would be a good product to spend ten minutes 'selling' – ten minutes is a very long time when it's just you talking. Eventually we decided on a mobile phone. I know what you are picturing – the tiny multi-functional gadgets that we all carry around these days. Not exactly; this was 1993, and the mobile phone we possessed, only because we were both freelance and didn't want to miss any offers of work, was affectionately referred to as a 'brick'! It was heavy and bulky, really not very mobile at all, but we decided that as well as pointing out what it does, I could also 'lifestyle' it. You know the sort of thing: 'If you break down on a country road you can ring the AA', 'if you're late for an appointment due to traffic, you can ring ahead and apologise.'

So it was decided that that would be my 'audition'.

The following morning I set off very early to get to the Sky Television Studios in Isleworth, where the auditions were being held.

I did my prepared piece on the mobile phone and I guess they must have liked it because, next thing I knew, I was being handed a pencil and the guy in charge said, 'Take a couple of minutes to get yourself ready and then we'd like you to sell us the pencil for five minutes'!

Apparently in America, where QVC had been up and running for the previous seven years, the 'five-minute pencil test' was famous. As a last-minute replacement I hadn't had the chance to do any research on QVC, and do remember this was well before you could just Google things and find out all you needed to know in a matter of minutes.

There was nothing spectacular about this pencil, just a regular HB that's used in a thousand offices and schools every day of the week. Well, out of nowhere, I managed to conjure up some stuff about the different types of lead in pencils used for drawing or writing – stuff I didn't even know I knew!

Then I started to chat on about the type of wood used, and how some wood makes pencils easier to sharpen, although I'm not actually sure if that's accurate or not, and how some pencils have erasers on the end. I think I might even have mentioned propelling pencils – you know the ones you used to get in pen and pencil sets but rarely used – just to fill a bit of time.

I'm not sure if I actually managed the five minutes before they stopped me but it felt like an eternity. I guess the idea was to see if you could 'think on your feet' and someone must have decided I could, as a couple of weeks later I was recalled for a second audition and to meet the American big bosses.

During this second audition I was asked if I had any retail experience. I told them about the Christmas job I had had many years earlier working in the men's knicker department of Marks & Spencer. I was also asked a very odd question: 'If you were a tin of soup, what flavour would it be?'

I later learnt that many of my future colleagues came up with answers like 'lobster bisque' or 'cock-a-leekie', but I said 'mushroom'! I have no idea why, as I don't even like mushroom soup. In fact I'm not that keen on mushrooms in anything!

I do remember them saying, 'Mushroom is so bland, that's not you at all!'

It couldn't have influenced their final decision too much, as three weeks later I started the job that altered the course of my life.

Incidentally, whilst we are on the number five, I also want to mention my children's favourite bedtime story when they were little.

It was called *Five Minutes' Peace*. It was about a mummy elephant and her three 'children', and was about her yearning for a few minutes of 'me' time while trying to bring up her youngsters. I used to put on all the voices of the characters to bring it to life.

I was so pleased with my 'performance' that I actually recorded it when I made a voice showreel, in the hope that I might get some work voicing characters for children's programmes. I didn't, so maybe it wasn't as good as I thought!

Still, at least my children loved it.

Six

The 6th of September is a very significant day for me,
but I didn't realise it until I started researching
for this book.

On the 6th of September 1971, I took my first and, as it transpired, only major Royal Academy of Dance ballet exam. For me this was a very big deal because at the age of six, when all the other little girls in my class at the Sissie Smith School of Dancing in Nottingham were taking their Primary exam, my mum was told I would never be able to take an RAD ballet exam of any description because I had a physical disability.

She subsequently took me away from Sissie Smith's at the age of seven, and when I started at Nora Morrison's dance school, two years later, nothing was said about my disability. If Miss Morrison noticed anything she made no comment, and within a year of starting there, I had taken my Grade 1 exam and passed Highly Commended. Grades 2, 3 and 4 followed, all passed with Honours, the highest accolade.

The RAD were changing their syllabus around this time and had replaced the old Grade 5 with Pre-Elementary, which was classed as a major exam, but for some reason I bypassed it and went straight to Elementary.

It was a very difficult exam for me, with a lot more control required than for the grade exams. You also had to do pointe work. For those of you who don't know, this is where a ballet dancer stands on her toes, and although the professionals make it look easy, it is anything but. It requires tremendous strength in your thighs to pull your weight away from the toes so that you don't 'skin' them. For me it was trickier because of the severe weakness in my left leg.

With the benefit of hindsight, I think Miss Morrison was nervous about entering me for the exam, after all, it was her reputation at stake too, but on the 6th of September 1971 it could be put off no longer.

I don't remember too much about the exam itself; however, I do remember waiting for the post over the next few days to find out the result. I still have the envelope the results arrived in that is postmarked the 13th of September, so I had waited at least a week and yet when the envelope dropped onto our doormat I could hardly bear to open it. I can still remember the feeling of trepidation as with shaking hands I pulled out the contents. There it was in black and white, I had passed. Not Honours, not Highly Commended or Commended, just a plain and simple Pass, but for me it was like reaching the summit of Mount Everest. The hard work, determination and dedication of Miss Morrison and my mum, who by this time was a dancing teacher with her own school, had helped me reach the top of my own personal mountain. I think we all knew that would be as far as I could go with the RAD exam process.

How funny then that just two short years later I should take another huge exam on exactly the same date. By this time I had become a professional dancer and was working in my first summer season on the Channel Island of Guernsey.

The moment I turned seventeen, I had arranged for my first driving lesson, and instantly loved it. I was in a very fortunate position as I had become friendly with a lad whose mum ran a car-hire business. Although it must have been strictly against the rules, which is why I shall name no names, he used to let me practise my driving in the hire cars. It helped enormously, and after only six lessons my instructor thought I was ready to take my test. Even so he suggested that I have a half-hour lesson prior to my test.

On the morning of the 6th of September 1973 I awoke to a thunderous banging on the front door of the house I shared with the other girl dancers in my show. I had slept through my alarm, and my driving instructor had been trying to rouse me from my slumbers!

I threw on a vest top, a pair of shorts and my flip flops and ran. There was no time for the last-minute lesson, no time even for a bite of breakfast, we went straight to the test centre.

You might think it was an easy option taking my driving test on a little holiday island, but I can assure you it wasn't. The island was full of hire-car drivers, or 'horror car' drivers as we used to call them, who hadn't always grasped how the rules were different than on the mainland. For example, at roundabouts you only let one car go at a time from each direction – totally alien for most experienced drivers from the UK mainland. You also had to reverse park between two cars, which at the time was not part of the mainland test. I really benefited from being taught to park properly and have always been a good parker, with the exception of one occasion.

I was picking my son Daniel up from school when he was about thirteen. There were cars all over the place and just one very small parking space. He was with a bunch of his friends and they were all doubting my ability to get into the available space. Daniel assured them that I could 'park on a postage stamp', which of course was the kiss of death. After hitting the kerb half a dozen times I eventually squeezed into the tiny space, but Daniel has never let me forget it. He is actually quite good at parking, but my daughter Sophie is not. She has been known to get out of the car and let her passenger park if the space is not big enough for a ten-ton truck, although in her defence she is improving!

So back to my driving test. After reversing round a corner, reverse parking between two cars and emergency stopping on the hill-climb road out of St Peterport without stalling, the examiner announced I had passed my test. I still have the certificate from my Royal Automobile Club Registered Instructor, Mr Cowling, stating that in his opinion I am a safe and competent driver, for those of you who know me and may have doubts!

One other 6th of September of note was in 1993. Although technically my first day working at QVC was the 4th of September 1993, that day was only for having our publicity photographs taken, both individually and as a group. That was a Saturday, so my first day of actually training to be a QVC presenter was . . . you guessed it, Monday the 6th of September 1993.

I wonder if anything momentous will happen on the 6th of September 2013? I do hope so, but only if it's good!

Seven

My first pantomime, Christmas 1973, was *Snow White
and the Seven Dwarfs* at the City Varieties Theatre
in Leeds.

I hadn't auditioned for the pantomime, but I had been spotted
by the show's choreographer when I attended an audition for
a Sunday-evening religious television programme called *Let's
Celebrate.*

It was a bit ambitious of me to audition for the TV show as
I had only done one professional dancing job in the summer of
1973, which I will tell you about in *chapter 73.* This meant I had
only completed twenty of the forty weeks required to become a
full Equity member, so I was only a provisional Equity member
– I had a red card instead of a blue card.

Equity is the entertainment industry's union and the rules were
in place to protect the members who had been in the profession
for longer and also so that the newcomers did a kind of 'appren-
ticeship'. Whilst most jobs were open to all Equity members,
provisional members were not allowed to work in London's West
End shows or on television. So you are probably wondering why
I went for the television job? Well I had heard there were 'ways
round the Equity issue' if you were the right person for the job.

The audition was held at The New Theatre in Birmingham
and my dad very kindly offered to drive me there. We arrived

at the theatre and I was shocked at the number of people who were auditioning. If I hadn't had my dad there for moral support I would probably have headed straight home again. Everyone was issued with a number and then we sat in the auditorium until our number was called, at which point we had to go up onto the stage. It was a two-part audition, as they were looking for singers who could dance, so there was a dancing audition, which we did as a group, and then we all had to sing a prepared song.

After the dancing audition, a lady came up to me and handed me her business card. She said if I didn't get the television job I should give her a call, as she was looking for dancers for a show.

Well, amazingly, when you consider that a) I was more of a dancer than a singer, b) I was only seventeen and c) I didn't have full Equity membership, I was recalled to a second audition the following week at the television studios. There were only eight of us recalled, four boys and four girls, and they were looking for six, so two of us were going to be disappointed. There was no dancing in the second audition, just singing and harmonising and in fairness I don't think my voice was 'trained' enough – probably because I'd never had a singing lesson in my life. Of course it was very disappointing to be one of the two that didn't get through the second audition but I did have a lovely letter of rejection (see page 36).

I have kept quite a few letters of rejection over the years, and trust me, not all of them are that lovely!

Well, all was not lost, of course, because as soon as I heard that I didn't get the television job, I was straight on the phone to the choreographer who had given me her card and I was offered the pantomime at Leeds City Varieties. If you are thinking the name of the theatre rings a bell, it was where they filmed *The Good Old Days* programme for the BBC.

The pantomime was *Snow White and the Seven Dwarfs*. Most

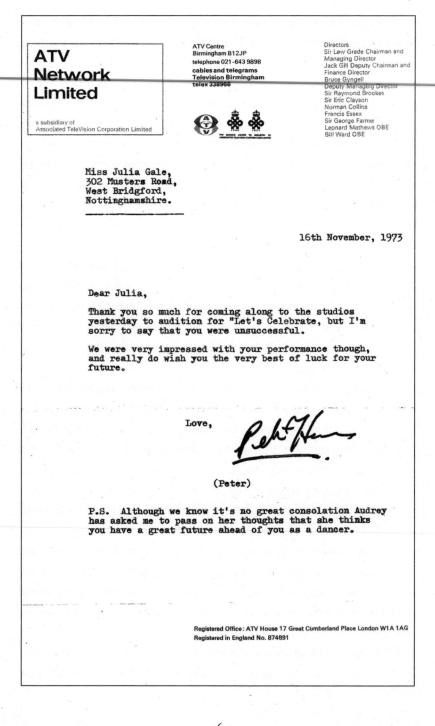

**ATV
Network
Limited**

a subsidiary of
Associated TeleVision Corporation Limited

ATV Centre
Birmingham B12JP
telephone 021-643 9898
cables and telegrams
Television Birmingham
telex 338966

Directors
Sir Lew Grade Chairman and
Managing Director
Jack Gill Deputy Chairman and
Finance Director
Bruce Gyngell
Deputy Managing Director
Sir Raymond Brookes
Sir Eric Clayson
Norman Collins
Francis Essex
Sir George Farmer
Leonard Mathews OBE
Bill Ward OBE

Miss Julia Gale,
302 Musters Road,
West Bridgford,
Nottinghamshire.

16th November, 1973

Dear Julia,

Thank you so much for coming along to the studios
yesterday to audition for "Let's Celebrate, but I'm
sorry to say that you were unsuccessful.

We were very impressed with your performance though,
and really do wish you the very best of luck for your
future.

Love,

(Peter)

P.S. Although we know it's no great consolation Audrey
has asked me to pass on her thoughts that she thinks
you have a great future ahead of you as a dancer.

Registered Office: ATV House 17 Great Cumberland Place London W1A 1AG
Registered in England No. 874891

pantomimes these days are lucky if they have a six-week run, and even back in 1973/74 the normal run was ten weeks, but this show was to run until the end of April! On the plus side, I would get another twenty weeks to give me my full Equity membership. The negative was that on occasions during the run there were as many people on the stage as there were in the audience, around thirty – and I'm not joking!

I must confess that I had assumed that the dwarfs would be played by stage school children, so I was very surprised on the first day of rehearsals to meet seven real-life little people. One of them, affectionately called 'Little Pete', became a great friend of all the dancers and used to go out clubbing with us after the show or should that be shows?

Where on earth did we get the energy to go out clubbing when they were working us so hard? At the beginning of the run it was two shows every day with three on Saturdays at 2 p.m., 5 p.m. and 8 p.m. There were also three or four occasions where we did an extra morning show on a Saturday at 11 a.m. and yet still went out afterwards, usually to Cinderella Rockerfellas, a newish venue run by Peter Stringfellow . . . what it is to be young!

My best friend in the show was a girl called Anita and we would probably have shared a flat together had she not been a local girl, so she was living at home. She introduced me to the delights of barley wine, which is not wine at all, more of a beer, and on payday either brandy and Babycham, or brandy and port.

When the pantomime eventually finished its run we went to Blackpool together to audition for a job in a South American circus and, although we both got it, she decided to return to Cleethorpes, where she had done her previous summer season, and I went back to the Channel Islands. I think we both made the right decision!

We kept in touch for a while but it wasn't so easy in the days before mobile phones and computers and I guess we both gave up eventually. I do still send 'Little Pete' and his family a Christmas card every year though.

When I first went to Leeds I was staying in 'digs' in Headingley near the Yorkshire cricket ground. I remember my mum and dad driving me up there and I know they were quite upset leaving me there alone. My room was at the top of the house and was quite nice, actually, but travelling to and from Leeds city centre by bus was a bit of a pain, particularly late at night on my own. When the offer of flat sharing with Debbie, one of the other girls in the show, came up I grabbed the chance to move. As it turned out this may have been a hasty decision.

The flat was off the Dewsbury Road in Leeds, which was not a particularly salubrious area. In fact, two weeks before the pantomime finished, an old lady was murdered in the local shop I used to go to. The phone box I used to call home from was next door to the shop and I became very nervous walking up there on my own. Everyone in the area was questioned, me included, and it must have looked very suspicious to the police when a couple of weeks later I upped sticks and went back to Nottingham, and then three or four weeks after that went to London for a couple of weeks before heading out to Jersey in the Channel Islands. Very suspicious indeed, as a week into the show at the Hotel de France, the owner of the hotel said the police were there to see me. I had to go to the police station and give them my fingerprints. I'm sure that created a great impression with my new employers!

So I moved out of my digs and into the flat with Debbie, but after a week or so Debbie got the flu and had to go home to her parents, so once again I was living on my own. Fortunately one of the other girls in the show, Christine, lived on the next street, so we used to get the bus home together. Our respective flats were in old Victorian terraced houses that had less of a back garden, more of a backyard – not that a garden would have been of much use in the depths of winter! Anyway, the backyards opened onto a cobbled lane that ran between the two rows of houses, so we would walk up the lane together and then I would stand by the back gate of my flat until Christine reached the back gate of hers, before going inside.

What we thought was flu turned into something worse, possibly glandular fever, and as far as I can remember Debbie never returned to the flat or the show. The only good thing was that, as we had taken the flat for three months together, her parents continued to pay her half of the rent until the pantomime finished. The bad news was that I was really lonely for a lot of the time, especially as we moved into March and April and we were doing fewer and fewer shows. Evenings were OK as Anita and Pete and I were still going out loads, and it was an evening out in Leeds that turned me into a football fan for the first time in my life.

The whole cast from *Snow White* was invited out to a do at a working-men's club as kind of minor celebrities. Also invited to the do was the Leeds United football team. If you know your football, you will know that Leeds United in the 1970s were the Manchester United of today in terms of winning things, but they were not the superstars that today's footballers are, nor were they paid anything like today's players . . . don't get me started on that!

Even so, it was quite a thrill to meet the members of the team that were there and, as you can probably imagine, there was a bit of flirting going on between the dancers and the footballers! It was still quite a surprise though when a bouquet of flowers arrived for me at the theatre the next night with a note attached asking me if I would like to go out to dinner.

I can't remember why I didn't go, maybe I had a crush on some one else, but I politely declined, and there went my opportunity to be a WAG!

Eight

Well, eightish, is the number of
GCE O levels I have.

Isay eightish because my certificate from the University of London states that I achieved seven passes, but I have always begged to differ. Let me explain.

I took ten GCEs: French, German, Maths, History, Biology, Food and Nutrition, Geography, English Literature, English Language and Spoken English. As you can see there are three English exams listed.

The way it worked was that you couldn't have Spoken English as a pass unless you also passed English Language. Well I did pass English Language, so I have always claimed eight O level passes, but that is not what it says on my certificate – it clearly states seven!

So you might be wondering why I am saying eightish rather than just eight. Well let's not forget my German oral, which incredibly I passed whilst failing miserably on the written paper. Surely that counts as a half, doesn't it? At least that's what I managed to persuade my parents when it came to the 'pay off'.

We had a deal, and for those days it was a pretty good one. They would give me £10 for every GCE I passed, and £85 went a lot further than £80 in 1972!

Some people may call this bribery, but I call it encouragement. Although bright, I was simply not interested in academia as I had already decided that my career path was in the world of entertainment generally, and dancing specifically. I know my dad in particular would have loved me to stay on at school and then go to university but I had other plans. So the deal was struck to encourage me to work hard for my exams.

Years later I did something very similar with my children, but as I recall the sums involved were considerably higher, and not to do with passing and failing but to do with the grades they attained. I'm pleased to say they both cost me a small fortune!

Anyway, obviously I didn't work quite hard enough because I failed biology, which I had always been good at. I think it had something to do with taking a chance that the bulk of the exam would be about the eye, which I had revised relentlessly. Imagine my horror when the main question was about the ear – no wonder I failed. I think I learnt a vital lesson though: always hedge your bets!

So technically I have seven O levels listed on my certificate from the University of London, but I still think it should be eight, if not eight and a half if you include my German Oral.

Speaking of which, eight is also the number of languages in which I can count from one to ten. Obviously in some of them, English for example, I can count a lot higher, which is just as well, as there are a hundred and one chapters in this book.

So English is my mother tongue, and I would hope that I could count before going to school at the age of four.

French I learnt from the age of seven, although considering how many years I studied it, you would have thought I would have been more accomplished at it than I am. Mind you, I'm not so sure I always paid full attention in class.

There was one time when I kept chatting to the girl next to me and, eventually, after a couple of warnings, my exasperated teacher Mr Thompson sent me out of the classroom. I was really shocked and to be honest felt a little foolish just standing there doing nothing so I decided that, rather than waste my time completely, I would do a little ballet practice. About ten minutes later I heard laughter from inside the classroom and then the door swung open and Mr Thompson, with a face like thunder, stormed off down the corridor. I hadn't realised that although the bottom of the glass separating the classroom from the corridor was opaque, so obscured me from view, the occasional arm wafting about, as I performed arabesques and grand jetés, was clearly visible and had the rest of my classmates in hysterics.

Despite my obvious lack of interest in the subject I did manage to pass my O level, but it wasn't a very good grade!

I learnt a little Urdu in my early childhood from my dad, who grew up in India, as his dad was in the army and stationed out there. I think I can still count to twenty and ask what the time is . . . maybe?

German came next. I studied it from the second year of senior school, and although I never really got the hang of the grammar, which is why I failed my written GCE paper, I can still remember some vocabulary and may even be able to count to a hundred at a push.

I tried very hard to study Italian when I was a dancer on the SS *Doric* in 1975, as I had an Italian boyfriend. My favourite phrase is '*non c'è male*', meaning 'not too bad', and I can definitely count to at least ten.

Spanish was next, which I picked up when I worked in Barcelona in 1976. I shared an apartment with one of the other girl dancers and her boyfriend's mother, who didn't speak a word of English. I didn't realise how much I had picked up until I bought my house in Spain, and found myself able to have conversations with tradesmen . . . sort of!

Next came Mandarin Chinese. I didn't really need to learn any Chinese when I worked in Hong Kong, as most of the people we mixed with spoke excellent English, but I wanted to at least be able to count to ten and say 'hello'.

And finally Greek. This was courtesy of my children, who learnt it when we went on holiday to Skiathos, and were eager that I should be able to count to ten in Greek too. I think I may also still know the Greek alphabet, which I taught myself from a book as a child . . . but don't test me on it!

Nine

In 2009, aged a mere fifty-three,
I became Great-Great-Aunt Julia.

Not just Great-Aunt Julia, no, I had been that for some time. Let me repeat: a great-great-aunt, who one normally imagines as a little old lady sitting knitting in an armchair, with her grey hair tied back in a tight little bun in the nape of her neck, and a pair of rimless glasses perched on the end of her nose. Actually, writing it down like that, I'm not that far off on several of those stereotypes!

Leo was born in August 2009 to my great-niece Tansy, who had just had her eighteenth birthday. Tansy is the only child of my niece Toogie, who was in her early twenties when she had her. Toogie is the second of my sister Lynda's five children, and like Tansy she gave birth shortly after her eighteenth birthday. So the maths does add up, and it is possible to be a great-great-aunt at age fifty-three, just rather improbable. Leo's arrival also made my mum a great-great-grandmother... or is there a different term used?

My sister and her family live in Scotland, and have done since the late 1960s, so we don't get to see them that often. In fact, I had only met Tansy on a couple of occasions prior to a big family wedding the summer that Leo was born.

The first time was when she was about three years old and Toogie came to visit us in Surrey with her boyfriend at that time.

My lasting memory was of Tansy specifically being instructed not to lock the bathroom door when she went to the loo, as the bolt was a bit dodgy. Tansy ignored the advice and, as you were probably expecting, got locked in the bathroom! Chris went to fetch his tool box as it looked likely that we were going to have to take the door off its hinges, but after much cajoling from her mum, Tansy slid the bolt and appeared, cool as a cucumber, none the worse for her temporary imprisonment.

The second visit Tansy made to our house was as a fifteen-year-old. She had come down to London to see a friend of hers and I think the trip had been allowed by her mum on the proviso that she stayed overnight with us, rather than at the friend's – not sure of the reason, but we just went along with it. We met her from the local station in the early evening, fed her and gave her a room for the night. Her ticket home was booked on the bus for the following day. The trouble was, Tansy seemed rather reluctant to go home.

I was working the next day, so the task of getting Tansy to the Victoria bus station fell to poor long-suffering Chris. Because of the reluctance she had shown, we didn't think that putting her on a train to Victoria was adequate in terms of her getting on the bus back to Scotland and we felt we had a certain responsibility towards her. So Chris drove her into London, parked his car and waited with her until the time came for her to board the bus.

Tansy kept saying, 'It's OK, you can go now,' but Chris hung around until the bus actually pulled out of the station just to be certain that she stayed put! I think there was a rest stop in the Midlands somewhere but we felt we had done our bit to get her home safely – by then, she was out of our jurisdiction!

So the next time we saw Tansy was at my niece Rachel's wedding in June 2009. The wedding was due to be held in the grounds of the Atholl Palace Hotel in Pitlochry but we weren't certain until about thirty minutes before the ceremony that we would be outside, due to the unpredictability of the British weather. It was actually one of the nicest weddings I have ever been to, not at all 'stuffy', and complete with all male members of the immediate family wearing kilts. Rachel even brought her pet rabbit so that she wouldn't miss out on the occasion . . . don't ask!

Toogie and Rachel's other sister Becky were both bridesmaids. I felt a bit sorry for Toogie though as I don't think she got to enjoy the wedding as much as she might have. She had spent the morning doing everyone's hair and make-up, as she is a professional make-up artist, but she was also having to keep one eye on her heavily pregnant daughter.

There was a sit-down meal after the ceremony and then a buffet at the evening reception. While the bride twirled on the dance floor in her wedding dress, holding her train in one hand and a pint of lager in the other, Chris and I went to get a few nibbles from the buffet. Tansy was stood there virtually resting her plate on her bump. Chris gestured to her tummy and in a jokey manner asked, 'So what have you got in there then?'

As Tansy was standing at the buffet, the inference was that maybe she had been indulging in too much of the food on offer.

Absolutely deadpan she answered, 'A baby'!

Ten

This is the number of times I have watched
my new favourite film at a very conservative
estimate!

I say new favourite film because, until five years ago, I would
never have thought anything could replace *Gone with the Wind* at
the top of my chart. So what is this masterpiece that replaces
such an iconic epic? Well, believe it or not, my new favourite
movie of all time is **Love Actually**.

I have watched it every Christmas for the last ten years and I
see something new with each viewing and love it more each time,
which is why it is now my favourite. On the surface it may seem
a lightweight, throwaway movie but watch it again, and in my
case again and again, and I'm sure you will appreciate the real
people in slightly exaggerated situations. The family can predict
with a great deal of accuracy the 'tear-jerker' moments and have
even been known to hand me the tissues prior to the said moments,
so that I am prepared!

I love the way the movie jumps from one story to another,
with each story having its own set of characters that occasionally
cross over fleetingly into a different storyline.

There is Sam, a young boy who has recently lost his mum
and lives with his step-dad, played by Liam Neeson. He falls
head over heels with an American girl at his school and decides

to learn to play the drums to try and impress her as part of her backing band when she performs 'All I Want for Christmas' in the school Christmas concert.

Colin Firth plays a not-very-successful writer who goes over to France each year to write his latest work of art. This particular year he has a young Portuguese girl, Aurelia, to clean and cook for him. He doesn't speak Portuguese and she doesn't speak English and we are treated to the subtitles of what they are both thinking. After she inadvertently lets the pages of his manuscript blow into the lake and then dives into said lake in her underwear to try and retrieve them, they both realise that they are growing fond of each other. Firth's character returns to England and begins learning Portuguese at night school.

On Christmas Eve he arrives at his sister's house laden with presents but realises he doesn't want to spend Christmas with them; he wants to be with Aurelia. He flies out to France to track her down at the restaurant where she is working, and proceeds to propose to her in very broken Portuguese, which again is subtitled, so we are treated to the literal meaning of what he is saying.

Bill Nighy plays a has-been rock star who is vying for the Christmas number one slot against boy band Blue. He is really inappropriate in most of what he says and does, but instead of being cringeworthy it's quite sad, particularly when he prefers to spend Christmas Eve with his manager of twenty years rather than at a party at Elton John's house, after clinching the afore-mentioned top of the charts.

There is the bit where Keira Knightley realises, after watching footage that he has shot at her wedding, that the best man, her new husband's best friend, doesn't actually hate her; he has a mad crush on her.

The storyline with the newly elected prime minister, David, played by Hugh Grant, is one I particularly enjoy. He is single and falls for a member of staff, Natalie, played by Martine

McCutcheon. After an incident where the visiting American president tries to 'hit' on her, David thinks it would be better for Natalie to be moved to a different department so that it is less distracting for him. He makes out he doesn't know her name when describing her to another member of staff, who confirms her identity by saying she is chubby.

'Would we say she's chubby?' is his response, and it's the way he says it that really cracks me up!

But the bit that gets me every time is the opening of the Joni Mitchell CD Christmas gift. For those of you who don't know the movie at all, let me explain. Happily married couple Emma Thompson and Alan Rickman and their two children always open one present each on Christmas Eve. Emma Thompson's character has found a gold heart necklace in her hubbie's coat pocket and naturally assumes it is for her. She chooses to open a similar-shaped present that she has found under the Christmas tree, but on opening it discovers it isn't the necklace. Her husband had bought that for his young secretary who had been flirting with him. Emma Thompson's present is a boxed Joni Mitchell CD. What really has me blubbing is that, for once, instead of buying her the usual boring scarf for Christmas, he has put some thought into it and bought her the CD of someone she adores. It just breaks my heart.

I thought that maybe I was alone in loving this movie, however, having watched it recently and tweeted about it, I was amazed to discover that thousands of other people love it just as much as I do, and even said that the Joni Mitchell CD sequence was their favourite bit too! Great minds think alike or fools never differ!

OK, so that's at number 1 now, and here is the rest of my 'Top Ten favourite films' list:

2. ***Gone with the Wind***, as I am sure most of you know, is set in the American Deep South at the time of the war between the Unionist north and the Confederates of the south. It stars the extraordinarily beautiful British actress Vivien Leigh as Scarlett O'Hara, and the dashing American movie star Clark Gable as Rhett Butler.

Scarlett has had a very privileged upbringing in the south, but that all changes as the Yankees start to take over the huge plantations and in the process abolish slavery. I love Scarlett's strength and determination, even though she does have an unhealthy obsession with Ashley, her cousin's husband, which is really annoying. She is prepared to do whatever it takes to save Tara, her family home, even marrying her sister's intended husband, despite the fact that she doesn't love him. She is reckless and spoilt and selfish but underneath all that she has a good heart and simply will not accept that she is beaten.

I love the scene where she has her former slave, Mammie, make her a stunning hat and gown out of the green velvet curtains. She needs to look beautiful for Rhett Butler when she visits him in prison to try and borrow some money from him to save her beloved Tara. She almost has him fooled that she is still a 'lady of leisure' until he notices her rough dry hands caused by all the manual labour she has been doing. You are willing her to swallow her pride and tell Rhett how bad things really are, but it simply isn't in her nature.

I also love the scene where Mammie is wearing the red taffeta petticoat 'Mr Rhett' has bought her, even though she had vowed never to wear it. It's incredibly sad when Mammie dies as you feel that Scarlett has been abandoned.

Scarlett and Rhett do get married but after the birth of their baby daughter, Bonnie, Scarlett withdraws from her husband and refuses to have a normal marital relationship with him.

Rhett adores and spoils his daughter, but when she dies, after falling from a horse that he has bought her, there really is no reason to 'keep up appearances'.

It's tragic that she doesn't realise how much she loves Rhett

Butler until he is walking out of her life uttering the immortal line, 'Quite frankly, my dear, I don't give a damn.'

It's too late . . . or is it? After all, in Scarlett's words, 'Tomorrow is another day.'

3. *A Time To Kill*, based on a book by John Grisham, stars the amazing Matthew McConaughey as an inexperienced defence lawyer. This story, like *Gone with the Wind*, is also set in the Deep South of America, but much more recently, although still at a time of racial segregation.

A young black girl is raped and left for dead by two drunken white youths. The girl's father shoots them, fearing that they won't get the justice they deserve, and he is then put on trial for murder. It is a very complicated story with plenty of anguish and soul-searching, some violence and deceit, and until the last scene, in the courtroom, it seems very unlikely that the father will escape a death sentence.

McConaughey's closing speech is the clincher. He asks the all-white jury to close their eyes and then he retells the events of the fateful day when the little girl was raped and left for dead. As he finishes he simply says, 'Now imagine she was white.'

Every member of the jury's eyes snap open as they realise they were allowing someone's ethnicity to colour their judgement. It is a very powerful line and always makes me shiver.

4. *Big* is the story of a thirteen-year-old boy who makes a wish at a fairground to be an adult, and wakes up the next morning to find his wish has been granted.

Tom Hanks plays the 'grown up' thirteen-year-old boy brilliantly. There are some really funny moments, particularly when Hanks finds himself the love interest of someone he is working with at a toy company. He takes her on a date which ends up back at his place, a New York loft apartment complete with trampoline. He asks her to stay over and then proceeds to take the top bunk bed while she has the bottom one. She thinks she has found the perfect man, but he realises he wants to be a thirteen-year-old again.

The tear-jerker moment is after she has driven him home to his parents' house as an adult, and as he crosses the road he becomes thirteen again – I think it is the pain of her loss but also the relief for his mum that he is home safe that has me reaching for the tissues again.

Have you noticed a trend here? Most of the movies I like have me in tears at some point!

5. *The Truman Show.* The movie stars Jim Carrey, and I must be honest I am not his biggest fan, but he is brilliant in this film. He plays Truman, who was 'born' into a reality television show. He thinks it's real life, but every other character around him, including his wife and best friend, are actors playing a part. There are some very humorous moments in the early stages of the film, particularly with product placement for the benefit of the advertising revenue.

Every day starts with the line, 'Cue the sun'.

Once Truman starts to suspect that something is not quite right, the humour starts to get a little darker and you start to really feel sorry for him. I think the worst bit of the whole film is when he is sitting with his best friend Marlon, who is trying to persuade him that he doesn't want to cross the bridge to the mainland to go in search of the girl he is really in love with.

Truman has total trust in everything his best friend says to him. Marlon is trying to calm the situation and says, 'The last thing I would ever do is lie to you', which he has just been told to say, via earpiece, by the show's director, and of course everybody watching knows that he is lying through his teeth. The deception is horrible to witness.

Truman does eventually make his break for freedom in a sailing yacht and, despite the best efforts of the film company in creating a violent storm to prevent him from leaving, his boat eventually 'crashes' into the horizon and he is free.

The fickle public, who have been glued to their TV screens throughout Truman's life, simply flick channels to find something else to watch.

6. *West Side Story.* This is a modern-day version of *Romeo and Juliet* set against the backdrop of New York. The two warring gangs are the Caucasian Jets and the Puerto Rican 'Sharks'.

The sister of one of the Sharks, Maria, falls in love with one of the Jets, Tony, but they have to keep their love secret as the rival communities wouldn't approve. The musical score by Leonard Bernstein is evocative, and the choreography, by Jerome Robbins, particularly to the song 'America', is outstanding.

As a child I used to play the album and sing and dance along with all the tracks. I think my favourite song is sung by Maria and Anita after Maria's brother, who was also Anita's boyfriend, has been killed in a gang fight.

It's called 'A Boy Like That' and starts off with Anita questioning how Maria could love someone who is responsible for her own brother's death. Maria tries to make Anita realise that we don't choose who we fall in love with.

The second part of the song is 'I Have a Love' and it concludes with Anita and Maria singing the final line together, 'Your love is your life.' Cue more tears from yours truly!

7. *Angels with Dirty Faces* is a black-and-white movie starring James Cagney. It is the story of a gang of youths who commit mostly petty robberies, but when gang leader Cagney kills someone he ends up on death row.

The story centres around an Irish priest who asks Cagney to

turn 'yellow' just prior to his execution in the electric chair, so that the rest of the gang will stop idolising him and maybe return to the straight and narrow.

Cagney refuses as he wants to go to his death as a 'hero' in the eyes of his friends. As he is about to be executed he suddenly starts crying out that he doesn't want to die, and that he is afraid.

It poses the question, did he really turn coward at the end, or was he doing it to help his friends have a better life?

8. *Casino Royale* (the Daniel Craig version). I love Daniel Craig as James Bond, and this my favourite Bond movie ever.

There are so many good bits in this film it's difficult to know where to start. I love the athleticism of the chase in Madagascar, the cheekiness of the valet-parking sequence in the Bahamas and the tenderness of comforting Vesper in the shower scene in Monte Negro after the horror of being attacked by, and subsequently seeing the death of, the two Africans whose leader's money has been lost.

Bond has really fallen for Vesper and is prepared to give up his secret service life as they sail in to Venice. Unfortunately, Vesper is too embroiled with his enemies and in the end has to sacrifice her life, drowning in a lift as a Venetian renovation project sinks into the lagoon.

The sequel, *Quantum of Solace*, is about Bond trying to exact revenge on the organisation who deprived him of Vesper. I had to watch it a couple of times before I really got it, as it's quite complicated, but it also has some fantastic action sequences and the pathos of his associate, Mathis, being shot.

I went to see the latest Bond movie, *Skyfall*, within a week of its release. I really enjoyed it but, despite many people saying that it is their favourite Bond movie ever, for me it doesn't quite top *Casino Royale*.

9. *Déjà Vu.* The action starts with the blowing up and subsequent sinking of a ferry packed with people on 'Fat Tuesday', or Mardi Gras. Denzel Washington is one of the incident investigators, and after visiting the father of a young woman killed in the disaster, and also discovering that his work partner was a victim, he is determined to find the person responsible.

He finds out that a group of people working with the police department have found a way to observe what happened three days before as if it was actually happening – a kind of time warp. Washington becomes so obsessed with trying to save the girl's life and prevent the ferry sinking that he risks his own life by being transported to the past.

It is a very difficult plot to explain, but suffice to say it is gripping and action-packed right to the end.

Washington and the girl, Paula Patton, locate her vehicle, in which the bomb has been planted, on the car deck of the ferry but have a split-second decision to make. They either let the bomb explode, so the tragedy would happen just as it had in the first place, or they drive the vehicle overboard and try and escape before it detonates. They opt for the latter, but while Patton is able to escape, Denzel Washington does not and is blown up by the bomb.

The final sequence is the girl being pulled from the water alive and, as she sits shivering and wrapped in a blanket, Washington's car drives down the road. He walks over to her in his role as incident investigator.

Although she recognises him, he has no 'memory' of her, except for a split second when the Beach Boys track, 'Don't Worry Baby', plays on his car radio just as it did in her vehicle before it plunged off the ferry.

I hope I explained that sufficiently, and if not maybe I have whet your appetite to see the movie.

10. *The Sixth Sense* is the sort of film I don't normally like. It stars Bruce Willis as psychiatrist Dr Malcolm Crowe, and child actor Haley Joel Osment, whose character, Cole, 'sees dead people'. Even as I am writing this I have goosebumps, and I'm not cold! (If you haven't seen this movie and are intending to, I would hate to spoil the twist for you, so maybe just skip the rest of this chapter.)

Near the beginning of the movie, Crowe is shot and badly injured but when the action resumes, a few months later, we see him estranged from his wife, and presume that the trauma has driven them apart.

In one scene the young boy, Cole, is having his breakfast wearing a thick pair of gloves because it is so cold in the kitchen. His mum leaves the room for a couple of moments to try and fix the heating and when she comes back in all the kitchen drawers and cupboards are open. There is no way the child could have done it and anyway there was nothing wrong with the heating, it is the presence of spirits that is making it so cold. This is the final straw for the mother, who doesn't understand her son's strange behaviour, so she organises for him to get some help. Enter Crowe.

Cole is very frightened of his 'gift', particularly at night-time when the dead people trouble him the most. At first Crowe does not believe that the boy can really 'see' dead people, but once he has been convinced he suggests that Cole should find a way to communicate with the ghosts and help them finish their business on earth.

There is the ghost of a little girl who died under suspicious circumstances and who wants him to help save her sister, who is exhibiting similar symptoms. He goes to the funeral reception with Crowe and is able to reveal that her stepmother poisoned the dead girl and is doing the same to her sister. Now that her sister is safe, the dead girl can 'move on'.

Throughout the movie we keep seeing Crowe's wife on her own, and very sad.

Towards the end of the film Crowe walks into his living room where his wife has fallen asleep watching their wedding video. Something falls to the floor from her hand, and it turns out to be his wedding ring. He looks down at his finger and sees that he is not wearing it, and that prompts a flashback of him being shot in his bedroom by one of his psychiatric patients, who he now understands had the same ability to see dead people as Cole has, and he had misdiagnosed him.

In his confusion he starts to make his way upstairs and as he does so he touches his back and we see blood all over his hand. That is the moment that he realises, and on first watching I realised, that he had been fatally wounded in the shooting and that he is in fact dead. That is why his wife is so sad.

For the whole film we thought Bruce Willis as the psychiatrist was helping the boy, and it turns out it was the other way round, the boy was helping Willis to let go and 'move on' – heartbreaking!

So there are my ten favourite films at the moment, although of course this is subject to change as new films are made.

One film that won't ever feature in my top ten is another Bruce Willis film. Some of the action was shot in the bay beneath my house in Spain, which you will read about in *chapter 26*. We had noticed a yacht in the bay for a couple of days which seemed to be looking for something. I stood on our balcony and had a look through the binoculars but I couldn't really establish what was going on. It wasn't until a few days later that we discovered they had been filming for a movie called *The Cold Light of Day*.

When it was eventually released, a couple of years later, we went to see it at the cinema . . . what a disappointment!

Eleven

2011 is the year I started to
write this book.

To be honest I have tried to write a book for years. Initially it was novels and, as I mentioned in *chapter 2*, I have three part-written but put to one side accompanied by excuses, usually the quite valid one that I don't have time to write.

Then, about six years ago, I decided I would write a book about me. I was approaching my fiftieth birthday and people rather kindly kept asking if I had had 'work done' to stay looking youthful. The answer at the time was no, and still is no, although I'm not sure I'm looking quite so youthful these days. The book was broken down into four main sections: A bit about me; Skin Care; Fitness; and Healthy Eating. It's not as boring as it might sound and, if this book is a success, maybe I will go back and finish it.

It's funny, but *One Hundred Lengths of the Pool* might never have been written if it hadn't been for a rather devastating incident that happened to me in March 2011. I won't go into detail, but it acted as a kind of catalyst and made me realise that it is never a good idea to have all your eggs in one basket, even if it has always been a very reliable basket.

Instead of dwelling on the incident, I was able to put it behind me thanks in part to my favourite quote, '*That which does not kill us makes us stronger*', and also to the sage words of a couple of acquaintances. Notice I said acquaintances, and not friends.

One is the husband of a friend of mine, who kept me afloat by offering practical advice and also sending me inspirational text messages, such as '*hold her steady*'. The other is the sister of a different friend, who urged me to '*be the bigger person*'. I drew enormous strength from both of these people, who hardly knew me, and began to examine ways to develop my potential, rather than just resting on my laurels.

The seed of the idea to write this book was sown after borrowing a book from the aforementioned friend with the sister, on a trip to Canada at the end of May 2011. That book was *How to Get Rich* by Felix Dennis, and it's not the sort of book I would buy, as getting rich is not something that motivates me. However, what I did like was the style of the book. It had lots of chapters, eighty-eight to be precise, some very short and some quite lengthy.

So when I came up with the idea for this book, as I was swimming up and down my pool in Spain in early July, I knew exactly what style I would adopt, or should that be adapt? I hope you are liking it so far; if not, blame Felix Dennis.

Canada was also the birthplace of another idea I am currently working on. I have nineteen years of experience in the medium of shopping television, so why not share that experience with others? I am working with a friend, who has a background in training. It's still in the development stage but I am really looking forward to getting started as I've always loved sharing knowledge, ever since I started teaching dancing for my mum at the age of, coincidentally, eleven.

I've also set up a company and done some preliminary research for a range of clothing. My absolute priority with the brand is that it has to be 'Made in England'. It may only stay a small business but I want to do my bit to help support the dwindling rag trade in the UK and I think I've come up with a good brand name.

The fourth idea, which is very much in its infancy, is a skin-care range with a specific clientele in mind. As I say, very much a fledgling idea at the moment, but from now on I'd rather have ideas and try to progress them than sit back and expect things to fall into my lap.

If you are wondering how I have managed to work on all these new projects while still working full time at QVC, can I just ask you to cast your mind back to *chapter 1*? I was in a 'year eleven' in numerology, until my birthday in June 2012, and that is a time to try new things and move forward, but also the time for a lot of hard work.

If you are in a year eleven, good luck with all your endeavours and here's hoping something comes of all our efforts.

By the way, here's a little tip someone passed on to me the other day. If you are going to be signing any contracts, make sure you do it when the moon is waxing to help grow the subject of your contract, be it personal or business. Use the waning moon to sort things out and throw away what you no longer need.

Twelve

*Twelfth — that was the position 'The Main Event',
a group that I was part of, finished in the
1980 Song for Europe.*

Y ou might be confusing the Song for Europe with the
Eurovision Song Contest, in which case finishing twelfth
out of twenty or thirty entrants would not have been too bad.
But no, in the Song for Europe there were only twelve entries,
so we finished . . . last!

It was a shame as the song, called 'I'm Gonna Do My Best
To Please You', really wasn't that bad, particularly if you compare
it with some of the Eurovision entries the UK has put forward
over the last few years. Clearly it didn't please many of the voting
public as we finished up with the fewest points.

It had all started with an advertisement in the *Melody Maker*,
one of the main newspapers for the music industry at the time.
A songwriter was looking for two members to join an already
established band to appear on the Song for Europe.

It turned out that this band were CoCo and they had been
the UK Eurovision entrant two years previously when they had
finished eleventh. CoCo at this time was comprised of Terry
Bradford, the songwriter, Keith Hasler, Josie Andrews and Cheryl
Baker. The new band was to keep the same line-up, however Jo
was going to be a backing singer, so Terry was looking for a lead
vocalist with a powerful voice, and another backing singer.

As I have already mentioned in *chapter* 7, I can sing but I'm not a great singer. After performing my prepared song, Terry asked me to do some harmonies with him, liked what he heard, and offered me the role of backing singer. The lead role, to sing alongside Cheryl, went to a girl called Helen, who had a fabulous voice. I was delighted as it was going to be performing on live television, something I had never done before, and I'm always up for new challenges. Little did I know that years later I would do thousands of hours of live TV as a presenter.

Most of the rehearsals were at Terry's house in the East End of London but, as the date got nearer, a rehearsal room was hired and a choreographer brought in to help stage the whole performance and teach us microphone technique.

Then there were the costumes. What had seemed like a simple proposition, getting green outfits for the backing singers, turned into a bit of a nightmare. We went out shopping a couple of times but neither Jo nor I could find anything green that was suitable. That's when I suggested buying some fabric and making our costumes, which was basically me volunteering to make both outfits. They turned out OK in the end but I had to redo Jo's as the legs were too baggy for her. I think I probably overcompensated if truth be told. When I look at the clip on YouTube Jo's jumpsuit does seem a slightly odd shape on the bottom half!

The day of the show came and I was terrified. It was being broadcast from the BBC TV Theatre in Shepherd's Bush, and hosted by household name Terry Wogan.

As well as being nervous about the actual performance, I was really worried that I was going to fall off the high stiletto-heeled shoes that Cheryl had brought for me to wear. Fortunately I didn't, although when I watch the performance I think I look rather awkward moving, particularly as I was the only 'dancer' among the group. Well, we did our best to please, but it wasn't to be, and in some ways coming last is better than coming second

– at least you know you were nowhere close so you don't waste hours dreaming of the 'might have been'!

Terry kept in touch over the following few months and in fact Cheryl, Helen and I were rehearsing a song that Terry wrote called 'Harry My Honolulu Lover', a minor hit for the Nolan Sisters, when Cheryl announced that she had auditioned for a group to enter the Song for Europe again.

The band were called 'Bucks Fizz'!

Thirteen

Unlucky for some, but lucky for me in my first-ever dancing competition when I was ten years old.

It was my number in the ballet section at the Leicester heats of the 'Sunshine' dancing competition in 1967.

I was probably the youngest in the age group of eleven- to thirteen-year-olds, as it was determined by what age you would be at the final of the competition in July, by which time I would have had my eleventh birthday.

Not only was I young, I was also very inexperienced. I had only been back at dancing lessons for eighteen months following the illness and subsequent death of my maternal grandmother, Gaga at Green Street. I was studying for my grade two examination, while most of the other competitors were grade four or five.

I had already danced in one category, Modern Musical, and amazingly my routine, 'La Bella Marguerita', had won me second place. Everyone was quite surprised that the 'new kid on the block' had beaten seasoned competitors who had been doing the festivals for years, but it could have been more to do with the performance than the technique.

The ballet section was a different matter though; technique was very important. I had borrowed a pink tutu from Karen, one of the other girls, as I didn't have one of my own. I still have it, so I can only assume that money exchanged hands for it at some point. In fact, when my daughter Sophie started going to ballet class she had her photo taken in it and it's one of my favourite pictures of her. It sits on my desk at home.

I performed my dance and when all the competitors were finished we formed a semi-circle on the stage to hear the results from the adjudicator. First place went to a girl from our school called Susan who was a brilliant dancer. I don't recall who was placed second. Then the adjudicator said, 'And third place goes to number thirteen!'

I hadn't really been paying attention as I expected nothing. I was busy watching my dad, at the back of the hall, intently making a note on the programme of who was being awarded the positions. I will never forget his moment of realisation. His head shot up, then he jumped up and cried out, 'That's Ju!'

At that point I stepped forward and curtseyed and congratulated the other girls.

There were many competition wins and medals after that as you will read in *chapter 97* – yes, that many – but that moment was really special to me. It still brings tears to my eyes when I remember the surprise, but also enormous pride, in those two little words that my dad uttered.

Fourteen

I was fourteen months old when it was confirmed that
I had contracted the killer disease poliomyelitis,
commonly called polio.

I was born in West Bridgford, Nottingham, on the 10th of June
1956, at 7.15 on a beautiful, sunny Sunday morning, according
to my mum. I was actually eight days late, sadly a trait I have
continued throughout my life!

It was quite a dramatic entrance into the world, as I was born
with the umbilical cord around my neck and it was a home birth.
Fortunately the midwife was on hand to deal with things, and I
was soon nestled in my mum's arms.

Apparently it wasn't a planned pregnancy. My parents already
had two children, my sister, Lynda, aged five and a half, and my
brother, Richard, just twenty-one months old. Mum always
assures me it's the nicest accident she ever had – well, she would
say that I guess!

I don't think she was particularly looking forward to it though,
as both of my siblings had given my parents endless sleepless
nights. Even after I was born, Richard was still having trouble
sleeping through! So it was with some trepidation that my mum
gazed upon her new arrival.

She couldn't believe what a good baby I was, honestly, her
words not mine. She kept waiting for the sleepless nights, but
they just didn't come! I was a happy, smiley baby, if a little on

the 'bonnie' side. I rarely cried, apart from the time I was stung by a bee whilst in my pram in the garden.

All that changed in August 1957 when I was fourteen months old.

Shortly after the early August bank holiday I became fractious and irritable. Mum and Dad decided to take us away for a few days' holiday to a place near Barmouth, in Wales, to give my mum a bit of a break and to see if a change of scenery would brighten my mood. It didn't; in fact I got worse. Despite being quite a chubby little thing, I had been making an effort to stand, and trying to walk, but all this had stopped and I became grizzly and miserable.

As soon as we arrived home, I was taken to the doctor's, and it was his dismissive statement that probably saved my life.

'If you think it's polio, it's not,' he said. 'She's probably just teething.'

My mum had never even considered the possibility of me having contracted polio, but once the seed had been planted in her mind, she started to worry. This was 1957, and whilst a vaccine had been developed for the killer disease it hadn't filtered through to all regions of the country. None of my family had been vaccinated against it.

Over the next two days Mum watched me very carefully, and far from getting better, I was getting worse, so she called the doctor to the house. The response this time was totally different. After examining me, the doctor immediately called in a colleague for a second opinion, and within hours I was in an isolation ward in Nottingham City Hospital.

My brother was not quite three and too young to realise what was happening, but my sister, at six and a half, was hysterically crying, 'Not my little Julia.'

To confirm the initial diagnosis, the hospital had to perform a lumbar puncture, which indeed showed that I had contracted poliomyelitis, which is an inflammation of the grey matter of the spinal cord, and can cause paralysis and death. I was a very poorly little girl.

Hospitals in the late 1950s were run very differently from how they are now. There wasn't anywhere for my parents to stay to be near me, and anyway, they had my brother and sister to look after. Nor were there the communication systems we have now. You couldn't ring the ward to check how the patient was doing, you found out at visiting times and by checking the local paper, which in our case was the *Nottingham Evening Post*.

The paper published lists of the 'critically' ill, 'dangerously' ill, and 'seriously' ill, in a descending order of seriousness. Initially I was on the 'critically' ill list, and Mum and Dad checked it every night to make sure my name was still there.

Every night for three weeks my name was on that list, and then one night my dad checked and it wasn't there. He told me that he experienced a terrible moment of cold fear before he realised that I hadn't died, but instead had been moved to the 'dangerously' ill list, where I stayed for a further two weeks before being moved to the 'seriously' ill list.

It must have been an awful time for my parents, visiting the hospital on the opposite side of the city as often as they could, but only to peer at me through glass as they weren't allowed any physical contact with me. It must have been upsetting for my brother and sister, having their baby sister suddenly disappear, and it must have been pretty strange for me too, being removed from a loving, tactile environment, to one with virtually no contact. The only saving grace, from my point of view, is that I was so young I can truthfully say I have no memory of any of it.

I had gone into hospital in mid-August 1957 and was moved to an open ward in October after coming off the seriously ill list. I hadn't seen my parents for nearly two months and Mum tells me it took some time for me to realise who they were.

They had just begun to re-establish the relationship when, at the beginning of November, the ward was closed to visitors due to an outbreak of Asian Flu.

It was six weeks before my parents were allowed anywhere near me again, and when they were, they were horrified to see that I had boils all over my skin, possibly as a result of the treatment I had been having.

My mum was desperate to get me home to look after me, particularly as Christmas was approaching, so she kept asking at every visit if I could be allowed home.

'We'll have to see,' was always the very careful answer.

On Christmas Eve morning the hospital phoned to say that my parents could finally take me home.

Throughout my stay at the hospital, my brother and sister had not been allowed to visit me. It was hospital policy regarding children in those days. They were so excited that their sister was finally coming home that Mum and Dad hid them under a blanket on the back seat of the car while they went to fetch me. Minutes later I was carried out, complete with leg calliper which, on the doctor's instruction, was 'always to be worn'!

Although I was being released from hospital, it didn't mean I was well, just better than I had been. I had severely wasted muscles all down my left leg and in the left cheek of my bottom. The muscles were so badly weakened that the doctors warned my parents that I might never walk unaided.

That didn't matter to Mum and Dad that Christmas Eve; they just wanted to get me home to become part of my family again. My mum even remembers what we had for our tea that day – egg sandwiches. She recalls how I snatched at them with the look of a hungry wild animal in my eyes and stuffed them into my mouth. I guess it was a case of first-come first-served at the hospital tea table.

So I was home for Christmas, and both my parents maintained that it was the best Christmas present they have ever had.

Of course, coming out of hospital was just the beginning of a very long road to recovery which involved attending weekly physiotherapy sessions at the City Hospital, and endless hours of exercises at home. My mum was determined to make my leg the best it could be, and I do have some recollection of exercising both at home, and the sessions on the physiotherapy table at the hospital. The wasting of the muscles had also affected the length of my leg. When I did start to walk it was with a very pronounced limp, possibly also due, in part, to the weight of the calliper, sometimes referred to as a leg iron.

If you've seen the movie *Forrest Gump* you'll know what I'm talking about. I find it very difficult to watch the scene where the children are all teasing and chasing him. I had my fair, or maybe that should be unfair, share of teasing when I started school, even though by then I was no longer wearing the calliper.

Each time my mum saw the consultant at the hospital she would enquire about starting to leave the calliper off. Each time she was met with a negative response. She also asked about ballet exercises, which she had heard a different consultant was recommending, but again was told, 'No, just build up the heel of the boot.'

After discussing it with Dad they decided to take matters into their own hands. Gradually the calliper was left off for longer periods each day until eventually the only time I wore it outside of the house was on hospital visits.

As my leg got stronger I began my swimming sessions, which I will tell you more about in *chapter 25*, and I also started ballet class, *chapter 59*. I no longer wore the leg iron for support. Instead I had a pair of very sturdy leather ankle boots with the heel and sole built up to level me out. I can remember the visits to the shoe shop on Arkwright Street and my pleasure, even as a small child, every time the amount to be built up on the shoes was reduced. I progressed from boots to lace-up black Start-rite shoes and then, the first summer I was at school, I had a pair of red bar shoes. I can still remember the thrill of it, even though all the other little girls had red crepe-sole sandals.

I continued to have 'sensible' shoes throughout my childhood and by the age of eleven, Mum took the decision not to have the heel built up at all, which meant I could wear normal shoes. I have never been great with high heels though. I can manage a highish heel if it is quite broad, but I can't balance at all on skinny heels, whatever the height. I do look longingly at gorgeous shoes sometimes but I remind myself that but for my parents' patience and perseverance I might never have worn 'normal' shoes at all.

The polio has left me with a permanent weakness on my left side, which I try to keep as strong as possible through exercise. Initially it was dancing and swimming, and throughout the 1980s it was teaching numerous body-conditioning and aerobics classes, *chapter 80*.

When I started working at QVC, alongside all my other work commitments and looking after two small children, I simply didn't have the time to teach or attend exercise classes. I didn't realise that it was starting to have a detrimental effect on the way I was walking until I watched a home video of myself walking along a beach on holiday. It shocked and upset me to the point of tears to see myself walking with a very pronounced limp. I knew I had to start a regular exercise regime again to prevent further deterioration, so I bought a motorised treadmill to try and correct my walking action, and I began swimming regularly. It was also around this time that I discovered Pilates, which I write about in *chapter 100*.

I now enjoy going for walks, even though for me walking is a considered action rather than a natural one, and I'm not great on uneven surfaces. In 2007 I decided to take part in a ten-mile walk to raise money for Breast Cancer Care, as both my mother and my sister had been treated for the disease. My son Daniel, who is a qualified personal trainer, made sure that I did some training for the walk and also took the decision to accompany me, just to make sure I could finish. I'm not sure what he would have done if I had flaked out at eight miles – carried me for the last two?

I didn't have a problem with the distance, but for approximately a mile we walked on a narrow path along the edge of a field that leaned at about a forty-degree angle to the left. It felt awkward for me at the time and for weeks afterwards I had pains in my left leg and lower back. I don't regret doing the walk and helping to raise money for BCC, but another time I would have to check the planned route more carefully and keep away from fields.

As we crossed the finishing line Daniel and I were approached by the organisers and asked if we would appear in the October edition of the magazine *Woman & Home* with some of the other participants, as part of a feature on Breast Cancer Awareness month, which of course we were happy to do. They took some lovely photos of us with our medals, one of which is on display in a beautiful Butler & Wilson jewelled frame in our dining room.

I had always thought that the weakness in my left leg was the only legacy from the polio but apparently this is not necessarily so.

A few years ago, when I was working for the cable television channel featured in *chapter 17*, I was asked to do an interview with the then mayor of Merton. I had only spoken to him on the phone but, when we met in his office, I discovered he was in a wheelchair. We got on very well and after the interview we were chatting and he disclosed that he was in a wheelchair due to something called 'post-polio syndrome'. I had never heard of it, but as soon as I got home I started to investigate.

It seems that there is quite a lot of research to suggest that survivors of polio can be affected in later life by PPMA, post-poliomyelitis muscular atrophy, also known as 'the late effects of acute poliomyelitis' and 'post-polio syndrome'. One doctor also refers to it as 'things that happen to people who once had polio'. The effects tend to start thirty or more years after the acute polio infection and seem to be worse in those most impaired at the time of their acute illness and who experienced the greatest recovery of function.

Apparently, research shows that most polio survivors are A-type personalities who are prone to driving themselves to exhaustion. I must admit that I do have a tendency to 'keep going until I drop', and have lost count of the times down the years that my mum has said to me, 'Don't overdo it.'

There are a variety of symptoms to watch out for, including excessive fatigue and reduced endurance, new joint and muscle pain, breathing difficulties and progressive muscle weakness. I have experienced excessive fatigue recently but that turned out to be unrelated, as I will explain later in the book.

I know that over the years extra stress has been placed on my stronger muscles to compensate for my weakened ones. The weakened muscles themselves are often functioning at near capacity, making them more susceptible to injury. I am trying to follow the recommendations of the experts in this field by exercising three times a week. I hope that this will enable me to stay as mobile as possible for as long as possible.

Throughout my life when people have noticed my 'limp' they have asked me if I have hurt my leg. I always used to make excuses, not wanting to make the person enquiring feel awkward, but also not wanting to admit that I was less than perfect. My mum and dad had worked so hard to make me as 'normal' as possible, mostly because the acceptance of disability was much less when I was growing up and they didn't want me to be at a disadvantage.

A few years ago I made a conscious decision to answer truthfully and admit to having been a victim of polio. It does sometimes make people a little uncomfortable but for me it feels right not to hide it any more. It's not my fault I contracted polio, but neither do I have a chip on my shoulder about it . . . it is what it is.

I will be giving a donation from the profits of this book to Rotary International, who are currently spearheading a campaign called 'This Close' to eradicate poliomyelitis. The opportunity is there, if enough money can be raised, to prevent any other human being from ever suffering from the effects of this disease.

I hope my contribution, with thanks to you for buying this book, will help.

Fifteen

This was the floor of the apartment block I lived on in
Hong Kong in 1979.

For someone who doesn't have a great head for heights, this
took a bit of getting used to initially. I am also not crazy
about lifts, but living fifteen floors up I just had to get used to
that too.

The only reason I can be so specific about the floor number
I lived on – after all, we are talking over thirty years ago – is
because I found a batch of letters that my boyfriend Chris had
written to me. Nothing extraordinary about that, I hear you say,
except that Chris didn't write letters . . . ever! He was obviously
missing me, as he demonstrated the night of the typhoon.

I had flown out to Hong Kong with the dance group Dynamite,
as I will tell you more about in *chapter 95*, and May is the start
of the typhoon season. Like hurricanes, typhoons are tropical
storms that have differing levels of intensity and, like hurricanes,
they have an 'eye'. If you are not in the direct path of the eye
of the storm it's just very windy and rainy for a couple of days.
However, while I was there, Hong Kong took a direct hit.

We first found out that there was a storm headed in our
direction when the owner of the venue we were working at, the
Cabaret Club (there's an original name!), rang to say that there
was a possibility that the shows may have to be cancelled that

night. At first it wasn't too bad, just pretty windy. As the morning went on, though, the wind started howling, the rain lashed down and the building started swaying. I promise you I am not making this up. The building was actually moving!

As I discovered later, this is a good thing. All the modern buildings in Hong Kong were built this way to withstand typhoons, but at the time it was a little unnerving. We were virtual prisoners in the apartment as the lifts were out of action but as we moved into the early afternoon an eerie calm descended on us. We were in the eye of the storm.

We decided to risk the lift and travel down the fifteen floors so that we could be outside to experience this phenomenon.

It was absolutely silent, which was unheard of in Hong Kong. Not only was there no traffic noise, there was no natural noise either. Where do all the birds go in a tropical storm and how do they know it's coming?

The eye lasted an hour or two and then we were in the tail of the typhoon, which was even more ferocious. More howling and swaying, and I am talking about the wind and the building rather than the occupants of the fifteenth-floor apartment, although, as the evening wore on, we were starting to get a bit 'stir crazy'.

By the late evening the wind had died down and the lifts were working again so, as we had an unexpected night off, we decided to go clubbing. We got glammed up and headed out to our favourite nightspot on Hong Kong Island, Disco Disco.

There weren't that many people out and about and there was a little bit of damage with trees down and fallen scaffolding. Can I just mention at this point that the scaffolding in Hong Kong is made of bamboo for just this type of occasion. Bamboo is very strong but very lightweight so, if it falls from a great height, it is less likely to kill or damage anything it hits than the metal poles we use in the UK.

We had a decent night out at Disco Disco, although unsurprisingly it wasn't that busy. We arrived home at about 3 a.m. to find a note next to the phone, from one of our flatmates who hadn't gone out.

'Julia, your boyfriend called. He saw the reports of the typhoon on the news and he was worried about you. I told him you had gone clubbing'!

Thanks for that, Bob!

Sixteen

This the number of cars I have owned, part-owned or
had in my possession with the authority to drive.

It doesn't include the numerous hire cars I have driven over the
years. The easiest way to remember all the cars is to go in
chronological order, so here goes.

In 1973 when I was working as a dancer in Guernsey and
before I had learnt to drive, I had a part-share in an old, off-
white Simca who we affectionately named Bessie. There were three
dancers, Kathy, Jacqui and I, and Kathy was the only one who
could drive at the start of the summer season.

We were working at a venue called the Carlton Hotel, which
was quite a distance from the house that had been provided for
us to live in, so I guess the most cost-effective way for the owners
to get us to and from work was for us to have a vehicle. It was
a good idea, but Bessie was somewhat unreliable and often broke
down. Even when she wasn't broken she used to chuck out clouds
of blue smoke – not very environmentally friendly! I was learning
to drive that summer, as you will have read in *chapter 6*, so I did
occasionally practise in her, but I think she had finally conked
out altogether by the time I passed my test.

Next came Petal in the summer of 1974. Before you ask, I
no longer have names for my cars, although I do occasionally
call them names! I had switched Channel Islands and was doing
a summer season in Jersey at the Hotel de France. I was once

again working with Kathy but, after the experience of Bessie, she had travelled over on the ferry and taken her own car with her, a rather flash red Triumph Spitfire. Her best friend Susie was also doing the show, and so, as the Spitfire was only a two-seater, Debbie, one of the other girls, and I decided to buy a car together.

Petal was a two-tone Mini and cost us £101.

When I say two-tone you are probably imagining one colour on the body and a different colour on the roof, as was quite common in Minis at that time. Petal was a little different. She was mostly red, but the back wing and boot hatch were a sort of matte purple/pink colour. We further customised her by putting a decal of Mickey Mouse on one door and Dylan, from *The Magic Roundabout*, on the other. She was a very reliable little runner and got us through the whole summer without too much trouble. At the end of the summer we sold her back to the garage we bought her from for the princely sum of £50 . . . now that's what you call depreciation, but I think we were quite lucky to get that much!

Here is a funny coincidence. Many years later, when I was on the way home from the airport after a writing trip to Spain, a car pulled up at the traffic lights at the side of us. As it pulled away I glanced at the number plate. It was P3TAL, and guess what? It was a Mini!

Ratbag was my next car, and the first car I had sole ownership of. She also was a Mini, but the estate version – I think they called it a Mini Traveller. Once again she wasn't exactly in pristine condition. I knew when I bought her that the front bonnet was not metal but fibreglass. Instead of having a bonnet section in the middle that you propped up to check the oil, water, etc., the whole of the front, wings and all, lifted forward from two rubber clips under the windscreen. That wasn't the only issue though. I drove off after parting with my £275 and went into the nearest petrol station to fill up with fuel. I was with my mum and as we drove off the forecourt we both noticed a really strong smell of petrol. Not surprising really, as Ratbag's petrol tank was rusted away just above the halfway line, so fuel was sloshing all over the road. These days you could have taken it back for a full refund, but no such consumer protection existed in 1974! For all her faults she wasn't a bad little car and I kept her throughout the winter months before exchanging her for my first convertible in April 1975.

I had managed to audition for and get another summer season in Jersey, this time at the Watersplash in St Ouen. I decided to do what my friend Kathy had done the previous summer and take a car over with me on the ferry. Flossie was gorgeous. She was a British Racing Green Austin Healey Sprite. If you are trying to picture her, think MG Midget. They were very similar, but I always pointed out that she was a Sprite. I can still remember the number plate – MAL 276E. It didn't register at the time but if you take the numbers away you are left with MALE and there were times during our 'relationship' when I felt she would have preferred a man at the wheel!

That first summer in Jersey was brilliant, driving round in the sunshine with the roof off more times than it was on. I think the problems started when I went away on the cruise ships for six months. She stood more or less idle on my mum and dad's driveway during a British winter. It didn't help that they moved from Nottingham to the Isle of Skye while I was away, so poor old Flossie then got parked at the side of the road outside my brother's flat. He was twenty-one at the time, so do we think he took her out for an occasional spin to impress the girls?

She was still in one piece when I got back from the Caribbean and I very bravely drove from Nottingham to the Isle of Skye on my own. It's a long way, but not as far as the Isle of Skye to Barcelona, which was Flossie's next big excursion. I will tell you more about that trip in *chapter 20*, but suffice to say when I left

Barcelona, Flossie and I took the train to Bilbao, and then the ferry to Portsmouth, rather than driving up through France. I kept her for another six months after returning from Spain before selling her to a friend of mine who was a car enthusiast and already owned two Austin Healey 3000s.

The next car I bought was another soft-top, in the March of 1978. A few years previously and after selling her Lotus Elan, my mum had owned an MGB Roadster. I really liked it, so when I found one for sale, at a price I could just about afford, I didn't hesitate. She was Old English White and her name was Snowdrop. What a lovely car. She had leather seats, spoke wheels and something called overdrive, which I suppose is similar to fifth gear but really just for use on the motorway. I went everywhere in that car and I absolutely loved her – if it is possible to love a thing rather than a person. She was brilliant for trips down to the coast at Brighton and Littlehampton, and she even came in handy for transporting a carpet when we moved flats. It was November, and we had to have the roof off so it was freezing cold, but we managed it!

It broke my heart when eventually I had to sell her because I didn't have the money to repair the ageing bodywork. With the exception of one of my Mercedes CLK Cabriolets she was my favourite car . . . shhhh, don't tell the others!

Having just said that I was so broke that I had to sell Snowdrop, you will now wonder how on earth I managed to buy a brand-new car for my next set of wheels. I can't really remember the sequence of events, but I had seen an advertisement in a London paper for 'import' cars at knock-down prices. I think there was some kind of legal loophole in those days and a garage was taking advantage of it by importing left-hand drives, converting them to right-hand drives and then selling them at a reduced price from the manufacturer's UK list price. I didn't particularly want an MG Metro, but that was what was on offer and the clincher was the fact that it had red carpets! You probably think I'm joking but honestly that was the deciding factor, I loved the red carpets. I hadn't actually planned on giving this car a name; however, when the registration document arrived from the DVLA, for some reason she had been registered as a 'breakdown truck'. Correct me if you know differently but I have never seen an MG Metro breakdown truck. Obviously I had the registration document amended, but the nickname BT stuck. She was a really good little car, never a day's trouble, driving me from London to Nottingham and back on the M1 while I was doing *The Price is Right*, *chapter 34*, and generally very reliable. On the strength of this, and as she was approaching three years old, I decided that I would trade BT in for another MG Metro, this time though from a UK dealership. What a big mistake!

From the moment I took possession of my new white MG Metro, still with red carpets I might add, things started to go wrong, so much so that I refused to give her a pet name, and have never named any of my cars since! I had trouble with the paintwork – little spots of flaking paint started to appear on the bonnet and the roof within a few months of having her – so she had to go back to the dealership. They did a complete re-spray and on the day I went to collect her, a delivery van reversed into her and smashed the front in. She was back in the body shop for another couple of weeks. I also had issues getting her into gear sometimes, which had to be investigated. You're probably familiar with the phrase, 'last one off the production line on a Friday afternoon', well, I think this was definitely the case.

It was with immense relief that I traded her in for my next car, a silver Mitsubishi Spacewagon. By this time I had two young children and it had been quite awkward getting them in and out of their car seats in the back of the MG Metro as it only had two doors. The Spacewagon was a big tank of a car but extremely useful as it had two extra seats that you could put up in the back of the estate, making it a seven-seater. This came in very handy for transporting a bunch of three- and four-year-olds around to playschool, mini-gym, swimming etc.

I hadn't had the Spacewagon very long when I landed a job presenting BMW's in-house business TV programme. I had auditioned for the job and had been asked to meet up with the producer at his offices in central London. I had driven into London and parked in a multi-storey car park, which was quite unusual for me as I normally drove to a tube station, parked and took the tube in to town. Imagine my surprise when the afore-mentioned producer, upon offering me the job, handed over a set of car keys for a BMW 3 Series. This was totally unexpected and a fabulous perk, but it left me with the small problem of how to get the Spacewagon home. In the end I drove home in the Beemer, and back up to London with Chris and the children to collect my car from the multi-storey, where it had racked up quite a bill.

So there we were with three cars on the driveway, the BMW, the Spacewagon and Chris's car at the time, a Fiat Panda. Within a few months there were no cars on the driveway – let me explain!

The BMW job came to an end so I obviously had to give the car back, a great shame as it was a lovely car to drive. I have never owned a BMW but maybe that will be my next car, as I have been eyeing up the 1 Series convertible in white. About a week after the BMW had gone, I had a late-night phone call from Chris to say his Panda had been pinched from outside of the pub he had been gigging at. I ask you, who would nick a Panda? Well, someone had, so now we were down to just the one car, which we were sharing while we waited for the insurance company to pay up. Then disaster struck. On the way home from dropping the children at Montessori nursery school another driver didn't stop at a junction, and to avoid her I crashed into a wall. The car wasn't a write-off, but it was very badly damaged and as it was Japanese there was a bit of a wait involved for the necessary part to repair it. So we went from three cars to no cars in the space of a couple of weeks, particularly difficult for Chris because he was a drummer and you can't exactly carry a drum kit with you on the bus! He managed to get his hands on a dodgy old Ford Fiesta through a friend of ours to keep us mobile until the insurance paid up on the Panda and the Spacewagon was repaired.

The grey Spacewagon was a bit on the ugly side, if truth be told, but it was very handy as a people, or should that be small people, carrier. Mitsubishi had recently brought out a new model of the Spacewagon so, as I was quite busy with work, we decided to trade up to the new model. It was a lovely-looking car with deep-red metallic paintwork and silver-grey interior and it was a pleasure to drive on long distances. At first it seemed like we had made the right decision to upgrade to the new model, but have you heard of the phrase 'a bridge too far'? Well this was my 'bridge too far'. My line of work has always been very precarious but I am one of a fortunate few for whom something always 'turned up'. Well, not this time. It was July 1993 and although I was working for a cable television channel (I'll tell you about that in the next chapter) it didn't pay very well and things were starting to get tight. Something had to go. After much soul-searching and of course going through all the figures, I went back to the garage I had bought the car from just a few months before. The salesman, Les, was really kind and under-standing when I explained my predicament, and after some juggling with figures he worked out that he could take the car back from me for a couple of thousand pounds less than I had paid for it. He also threw into the bargain a Mitsubishi Galant for £2200, the exact price he had allowed in part-exchange to another customer. I think he felt sorry for me and I must confess there were a few tears involved. I think it was my pride that was hurting more than parting with the Spacewagon, after all a car is just something to get you from A to B isn't it?

So I drove away from the Mitsubishi dealership in my 'new' car, with plastic on the still wet, freshly valeted seats, feeling very sorry for myself but thankful for Les's kindness at the same time. That was the day I had the phone call to audition for QVC, as you will have read in *chapter 5*.

The Galant was quite a swish car and Chris absolutely loved it, but there were two main problems with it. Firstly it was a very high insurance group, thirteen if I remember correctly, and secondly it drank petrol. We were on an economy drive so unfortunately we knew its days were numbered as a member of our household. Well, what happened next was quite extraordinary on a number of levels. It was almost as though by recognising that I had overextended myself and been humble enough to recognise it, my luck changed virtually overnight. I went for the QVC audition and within six weeks had a new job and a brand-spanking-new Volvo.

We had to get rid of the Galant for financial reasons so I was looking for a deal against a new car. Thanks to my time with the BMW business programme, I knew that trading in against a new vehicle would give me the best possible price in part-exchange. By now it was August, and the new 'L' registration was out, so the dealerships were all very keen to reach their sales targets. I scoured the local papers and picked through all the various dealership adverts and came up with what I thought looked like the best deal. Volvo were offering £1000 off a brand-new Volvo SX and they would also consider part-exchange. We went off to the dealership, which funnily enough was located in Caterham just a couple of miles from the village we moved to a year later, and where Daniel still recollects quietly playing with the Lego while his mum was wheeler-dealing! I asked the salesman how much he could give me in part-exchange for the Galant, and after looking in his book, checking the car over and ringing a colleague he said his top price was £4000. I'm not kidding you, it was all I could do not to bite his hand off. Remember, I had only paid £2200 for the Galant, so I was going to be making a profit of £1800 and driving away in a brand-new car that was a much lower insurance group and cheaper to run. I was a nervous wreck while they were completing the paperwork. I kept thinking that they would realise they had made a mistake and retract their offer. Fortunately they didn't, so we drove away in a car that had been reduced from £11,999 to £10,999, but we had only paid £6,999 for it, thanks to the part-exchange. Maybe I missed my calling, maybe I should have been a used-car salesperson!

The Volvo had been a great buy and was solid and reliable and the first car I ever owned with heated front seats, now a requirement for me. It makes such a difference getting into a cold vehicle on a freezing morning and having instant warmth, but then I guess the Swedes know all about freezing weather conditions. I drove to and from QVC for three and a half years with never a day's trouble but in my heart of hearts, I am not a Volvo driver. As you will have read earlier in this chapter I have a bit of a penchant for sporty little numbers and I decided that my 'mumsy' days of people carriers and Volvos were over. I craved a convertible again.

It was March 1997 and I had talked it over with Chris. He would keep the Volvo, which was now paid for, and I would buy an Audi Cabriolet. It was coming up to summer so there would be loads to choose from right? Er, no, actually. I rang the nearest Audi dealership and told the salesman what I was after. He almost laughed at me as he said there was a six- to nine-month wait for a new Cabriolet and that I wouldn't be able to get one from anywhere. Well, that's sensible isn't it, summer on the doorstep and you will have to wait until winter for a new soft-top . . . I may have said something along those lines too! One quality I possess is tenacity, and I was determined I would have an Audi convertible and it would be in time to enjoy the summer weather. It was looking a bit unlikely, having rung several dealerships and being given the same story, until I rang the dealership in Horley, Surrey, near Gatwick Airport.

'What colour are you after?' the salesman asked.

'I don't really mind.'

'Manual or Automatic?' was his next question.

Same response from me.

'Hood colour?'

I felt like saying, 'Who cares!'

'We have a manual, in ming blue, sitting on the forecourt that someone ordered and can't get finance for. Would you like a test drive?'

I was there within the hour, and a couple of days later was the owner of an Audi Cabriolet in ming blue, a metallic very dark navy, with a navy hood. I have a few mottos in life and one is to persevere. My perseverance certainly paid off that summer every time we had the roof down.

I think it was Chris who suggested that I should get a new car before the Audi got to the end of its three-year MOT-free period. I was now totally hooked on soft-tops and was debating whether to get another Audi or to swap to the rather gorgeous Mercedes CLK. There was only one slight problem with the Audi: the legroom in the back was rather restricted, and as I often did the school run and the children were now twelve and thirteen, it was becoming a bit of an issue. Chris remembered that his cousin's husband was quite senior in a Mercedes dealership in Boston, Lincolnshire, so I gave him a call, fully aware that I might face a similar problem with a wait for a soft-top as it was the summer.

I spoke to cousin Phil on the phone and he asked me a few

questions like colour and engine size and said he would ring round for me. I was quite keen on a metallic lavender shade, and about thirty minutes later he rang back to say he had located a dealer who had one coming in in a few weeks' time, would I be OK to wait? What's a few weeks, I thought, so we were just placing the order when he mentioned the word 'coupe'.

'Oh no,' I said, 'I'm after the cabriolet.'

Short pause on the other end of the phone.

'Would you consider vivianite green, because if so I have one on my forecourt.'

It was a very similar scenario to the Audi. Someone else had placed the order in the autumn and hadn't been able to come up with the finance. Talk about history repeating itself. Honestly, would I have chosen vivianite green, a vibrant greeny turquoise colour? No. But everything else about the car was perfect, including the fact that it was an automatic, had heated front seats and much more legroom in the back. We went to Lincolnshire for a test drive and an appraisal on my Audi. The deal was struck and the following week Chris went back and did the changeover as I was busy working . . . probably overtime, which I needed to do a lot of to afford the new car!

I got used to the vivianite green colour eventually, after all I was sitting in it driving most of the time, not looking at it, although it did have a very long bonnet, so I could clearly see the iconic Mercedes logo standing proudly in the centre. It was a great marriage of two types of car. It had the comfort of a luxury saloon, combined with the style and speed of a sports car. Not only that but as Daniel grew taller and taller (he's now six foot four inches), it had plenty of legroom in the back.

I kept the green CLK for five years and a lot of miles before deciding to do something I had never done before. My previous two cars had been built to the specification of somebody else. Although I had been really happy with both, neither had really been intended for me. Mercedes had brought out a new style CLK, which I was lusting over. I rang cousin Phil in Lincolnshire again and ordered a new car with all the things that were important to me.

The colour was 'ice blue', a very pale metallic shade, combined with a navy hood and pale grey seats, which I would never have had when the children were younger! It was the same engine size as the previous one, 320cc, but I had the elegant walnut-trimmed interior, combined with the avant garde sports suspension. I had a CD changer and Bose sound system and, of course, heated front seats. To finish it off, and really make it special, Chris bought me a personalised number plate for my birthday, which if you screw your eyes up slightly looks like JULYA.

I went to Lincolnshire to collect my new car a couple of days before my forty-ninth birthday – Happy Birthday to me! Believe it or not, I'm not really an extravagant person. I don't have a collection of designer handbags costing a couple of thousand pounds each, or designer shoes or even many designer clothes. I'm quite happy in a pair of non-designer jeans and a T-shirt. This car was my little extravagance, and as I spent hours of my life in it, driving to and from work, usually at 'silly o'clock' in the morning, I figured I could justify it. Earlier in this chapter I said my second-favourite car was Snowdrop, my MGB Roadster; well this Merc was my dream car and I LOVED her.

I had three years' honeymoon period with my 'Ice Blue Merc' and then she started to develop little niggles. Nothing major, and nothing that couldn't be fixed, but then she let me down big time. As I've already mentioned with the reference to 'silly o'clock', I work very unsociable hours, often driving home alone at two or three in the morning. I have to have utmost confidence that my car isn't going to break down, but that is exactly what happened, fortunately not at that hour and unusually I wasn't alone!

My son Daniel sometimes used to come into QVC to demonstrate fitness equipment, as he is a qualified personal trainer, and he happened to be with me as we drove home on a freezing February night at around eight-thirty. We were on the very busy South Circular Road in Clapham, approaching some traffic lights, and the car just cut out and wouldn't start. Dan and I pushed her over to the side of the road and got out, even though it was *freezing* cold, in case someone ran into the back of us, then sat on a bench and waited for the AA to arrive. I don't remember what the problem was and it got fixed but my trust was broken. I knew I would never have total faith in her again . . . she had to go!

I had her checked over at my local village garage and then asked them to put her on the forecourt to sell, which they did within a couple of weeks to someone who lived in the village. I must admit it was a bit weird the first time I saw her on the road with someone else at the wheel, particularly as she had a new number plate.

I had kept my personalised plate for my next car, the car I drive now, an Audi TT. She has been a great little car but the pressure is on for her to keep delivering as I have already mentioned my liking of the BMW I Series.

I was always a happy, smiley baby, as this photo taken when I was 12 months old shows.

Two months later, this was on holiday in Wales, just prior to the diagnosis of my poliomyelitis – the look in my eyes is heartbreaking.

With Mum in our front garden when I was three. The building in the background is the Jesse Gray school that I attended. Notice the handbag I'm holding – I remember it was red.

This was on a family holiday in Blackpool. My sister Lynda, in the centre, is five years older than me and doesn't bear much family resemblance, but my brother Richard and I were often mistaken for twins.

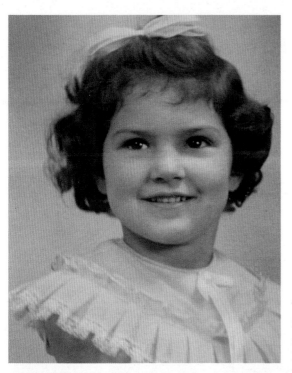

When I was five, Mum had some professional photos taken of me to enter me for the 'Miss Pears' competition – I didn't win.

This was taken before my first Speech and Drama Festival – notice the red Start-rite shoes I wore instead of sandals.

I love this picture. My dress was red satin trimmed with black lace and was for a duet I performed with my partner Kay to 'Spanish Flea'. Maybe my love for Spain started here?

I was ten when I was chosen to be the cover girl for the Be-Ro cookery book – see chapter 18.

My first day at West Bridgford Grammar School. I think that was the only day I wore my beret.

The borrowed tutu I wore to win third place in the Sunshine Festival heats in March 1967 – I still have it so I'm hoping money changed hands.

My first publicity photo, which I would send with my CV to try and get dancing auditions and work.

Chapter 16 is about my cars so here are four of them. Petal was the first car I owned for a summer season in Jersey in 1974.

Flossie was the Austin Healey Sprite that I drove through France to Spain, when I was only twenty.

My beloved Snowdrop outside my parents' cottage on the Isle of Skye.

Dad and me with BT, my MG Metro, that had red carpets and red seatbelts.

Seventeen

Cable 17 was the name of the cable television show
where I started my TV presenting career in 1990,
although when I first started, the show was called
Cable Today.

It all came about in a rather bizarre way. I was out working,
doing my first presenting job, at the 1989 Motorshow at Earls
Court, which I will tell you about in *chapter 89*. Chris was at
home looking after the children. There was a knock on the door
and a workman explained that they would be digging up the
pavement across our driveway to lay the cables for cable television, so our access would be restricted for a couple of hours.

Chris must have shown an interest as, a little later in the day,
a salesperson called and asked if we would be interested in signing
up for cable television. I think there must have been some incentive to sign up there and then as it is quite unusual for Chris
and I not to discuss things like this, because when I got home
that night he presented me with the *fait accompli!*

He also handed me the free magazine, the *Cable Guide*, and
pointed out an advert. The local TV programme were looking
for presenters for their nightly show and he had already rung
the channel and arranged for me to audition the following
week!

The audition consisted of two parts. The first was a 'piece to camera' (PTC). This is where you write a small report and deliver it directly to the camera. The second part was interviewing a 'guest'. I wrote my PTC and practised it for hours in front of a mirror so that I could watch what my face was doing in terms of expression, and also to learn to maintain eye contact with the camera. In everyday life we tend to move our eyes around a lot when we are speaking to people, which is normal, but on camera that can make you look really shifty.

After all the hours of practice I was quite happy that I had that part of my audition prepared to the best of my ability, and on the day it went off fairly smoothly, although as you can imagine I was pretty nervous. The producer of the show seemed reasonably happy with that part of my audition too and so it was on to the next stage . . . the 'guest interview'.

I hadn't been told anything about the 'guest', except his name, so it was really important for me to establish what he did and his purpose for being on the 'show' as quickly as possible.

Frazer took his seat on the sofa and I introduced him and asked him what he did.

'I'm an underwater archer,' was his response.

Talk about a curve ball! I was pretty sure there was no such thing as an 'underwater archer' but I had to play along and think of relevant questions.

What are the targets and the bows and arrows made of?

Do you use breathing apparatus or do you hold your breath?

How long has it been an established sport?

Where did it originate?

Who do you compete against?

Is it being considered as an Olympic event?

These were just a few of the questions that occurred to me on the spur of the moment.

I managed to conduct the interview in an entertaining manner and was told there and then that I had done enough to become a presenter on *Cable Today*. I would start by presenting one show a week, which would begin after the coverage of the local elections had finished.

Part of my job was to secure relevant guests for my show, although some guests were provided for me and thankfully that didn't include any more 'underwater archers'!

The main criterion was that they had to have some relevance to the five boroughs that were covered by Croydon Cable, which were Sutton, Merton, Richmond, Kingston and, of course, Croydon. This gave me plenty of scope, particularly with performers, as there were high-profile venues like the Fairfield Halls in Croydon and big theatres in both Richmond and Wimbledon, which were within the catchment area.

I knew that it was very important to make an impression with my first show and that finding the right guest was pretty crucial to the end result. How lucky was I then that the actor who played Joey in the hit BBC TV series *Bread*, Graham Bickley, just happened to shop in the same supermarket as me. I didn't actually know him, but I plucked up my courage and simply asked him if he would appear on my local television chat show. I was actually quite surprised that he said yes, but I guess all publicity is good publicity in the entertainment world. I don't think he asked how many viewers we had, which is just as well as our viewing figures in the early days were definitely in the hundreds rather than thousands.

The interview went well, but what I hadn't realised is that I had set myself a level of expectation, with regard to guests, that needed to be maintained! Out came both mine and Chris's address books as we looked for tenuous links with the area amongst any celebrities that we knew.

A friend of Chris's knew someone in the band Cutting Crew

who happened to live fairly locally, and after a bit of persuasion they agreed to do the show and let us show a clip of their massive hit 'Died in Your Arms Tonight'.

I rang Cheryl Baker, who was very busy touring with Bucks Fizz at the time, and she agreed to come on, even though it was her birthday. I think our producer spent the entire production budget for that week on a bouquet of flowers for her.

A friend of mine was married at the time to the entertainer Gary Wilmot and, after a couple of phone calls with his agent, we got him on the show too.

The importance of having big names in the early shows was to be able to list them as having appeared on the show when cold-calling agents and theatres – it gave us credibility as a promotional tool.

Cable Today already had good links with the theatres so we had a constant stream of potential guests. Robert Powell graced our sofa, as did Sacha Distel, Alistair McGowan and the composer of the *EastEnders* theme tune, Simon May.

It also had the added bonus of lots of free tickets to go and watch the shows of the guests appearing on *Cable Today*, all in the name of research, of course!

My children benefited massively from this 'fringe benefit' as they were the guinea pigs for shows like *Rod, Jane and Freddy*, *Fireman Sam* and *The Magic Roundabout*, as well as all the pantomimes at Christmas. If my children had enjoyed the performance, then there was a good chance that other children of a similar age would, even if I hadn't found it particularly entertaining.

We also used to film on location. The crew and I filmed a week-long series on Sister Sledge, who were appearing at the Fairfield Halls in concert, and Jim Davidson, who was appearing at the Wimbledon Theatre in his risqué adult pantomime *Sinderella*. We covered a charity tapathon, fronted by Lionel Blair, for which

I had to dust my tap shoes off and join in, and the Fairfield Halls Fun Day, which saw me attempting to interview Dennis the Menace and Bart Simpson.

It was the most fantastic training ground to learn all aspects of being a television presenter, whilst getting paid for it, albeit not very much. I learnt how to connect with the camera, to work with talkback via an earpiece, to read autocue without looking like you are reading, and to work to the director's count. This last discipline has proved invaluable for all the live presenting work I have done since.

Initially I had 'switched' talkback, where you don't hear the director's instructions to his cameras, you are only open to the gallery for specific instructions from the producer or director. After a while I requested to work with 'open' talkback, where you hear everything that is said in the gallery unless they 'switch' you. I found talkback surprisingly easy, listening to one thing whilst saying something else. Maybe it helped being a mum, as I was quite adept at speaking on the phone and listening to my children at the same time.

I also taught myself a really useful skill, which I used for some corporate video presentations I did, when there was a long script involved or where there was a lot of moving around, so the use of autocue was inappropriate. You recorded the entire script onto a minidisc player, and then listened to the playback through an earpiece, whilst delivering the words a split second later. Sounds pretty scary, doesn't it, and in truth it was!

In the early days, the cable shows weren't live, but we recorded them 'as live', due to time constraints, so we only stopped if there was a glaring error.

When we did eventually broadcast live, I was already working at QVC so it didn't really faze me too much, but it was like having the safety net removed!

I was quite sad to leave *Cable 17*, but after seven years I think it was the right thing to do. I had learnt so much from them, it was only fair to give someone else the opportunity I had been given to learn my trade 'on the job'!

Eighteen

One shilling and sixpence is eighteen 'old' pennies
pre-decimalisation, and that was the cost of the
Be-Ro cookery book, which I appeared on the
front cover of in 1966.

It was definitely a case of being in the right place at the right time.

I had been attending dancing classes at the Morrison School of Dancing for about a year. I had initially started attending just on a Wednesday evening after school, but Miss Morrison had wanted me to enter for my RAD Grade I examination, so had suggested that I attended an extra class on a Saturday morning.

At that time the classes were held at the Bluecoat School in Nottingham, and there was an area in the studio where parents could sit and watch a class, or stand and wait for a class to finish, along with the pupils who would be taking part in the next lesson.

One Saturday morning there was great excitement at the studio as a photographer was coming in to take some 'test shots' of some of Miss Morrison's more experienced girls who she had selected as suitable to appear on the front cover of a cookery book. Obviously I wasn't included in the line-up as I was a comparative newcomer.

As luck would have it, the photographer turned up a little

early and caught the end of the class I was in. We performed our curtsies to Miss Morrison and I trooped off with the other girls to get changed.

The girls Miss Morrison had selected were all the top achievers in the exams and dancing competitions. There was Susan, Margaret and Dinah, the apple of Miss Morrison's eye, and all were a couple of years older than me. Then there was Rosemary and Ann-Marie, a year or so younger than me, and another Susan, who was my age. As I was about to leave with Mum, Miss Morrison called over and asked Mum if we could stay just for a few minutes as the photographer had requested it.

It was a bit overwhelming for me being asked to stand next to the 'stars' of the school but, after shuffling us around a bit and taking some photos, I left with Mum, excited but not thinking too much of it.

A week or so later we had a phone call asking if I, along with a couple of the other girls from the line-up, could go to the photographer's studio for some more test shots. I don't remember too much about it, except that we were requested to wear blue, so I was able to wear my favourite dress.

Maybe that helped to relax me because, despite never having done any kind of modelling before, I was offered the job and was to be paid ten pounds for it, a lot of money in 1966.

I didn't get to wear my favourite dress for the actual shoot as it was deemed too dressy. Instead I wore a white blouse and a blue corduroy pinafore dress. I remember it seemed to take quite a long time to get the pose and the expression exactly right, but what stays in my mind more than anything else is that they had to stick the eggs to the tabletop to stop them rolling away!

I wasn't particularly popular with other girls at dancing school for a while and when the children in my class at school found out they teased me mercilessly, calling me Miss Be-Ro 1066. I had the last laugh though as with the ten pounds I opened my first bank account with the Midland Bank (now HSBC). I still bank with them 45 years later – that's loyalty for you!

There was one other occasion when I was a cover girl, this time on the front of the *TV Times*, but I'll tell you more about that in *chapter 34*.

Nineteen

This is the number of UK television commercials that I can remember doing in which I played a 'featured role'.

I say 'featured role', although that doesn't necessarily mean that it was a speaking part, just that the advertising company would have to pay either repeat fees for every time it was shown, or negotiate a 'buy-out fee'. These days I think almost all TV advertisements are done on the 'buy-out fee' basis, which is more cost-effective for the advertiser but not so lucrative for the artists involved.

In the late 1970s and early 1980s, one really high-profile commercial could financially support an actor for a whole year, so that they could then accept poorly paid or non-paid work in a theatre show and also cover periods when they were out of work or 'resting'. I was quite fortunate to be around at that time before advertisers started cutting their budgets.

Notice I am also being specific about mentioning the UK, as I used to do quite a few adverts for Spain, Germany and Italy, but to be honest I have no idea how many. What was funny about the commercials for overseas is that they invariably dubbed your voice. When we were shooting those, we were told to say anything or simply move our mouths as if we were talking. I'm sure you will have noticed adverts in the UK where they have done the same in reverse with some very strange-looking dubbing. I'm not sure why they do it as it looks terrible, but again it was probably a cost issue. I also did some for Eire, including the Harp campaign I write about in *chapter 86*.

The first commercial I featured in was for the *London Evening Standard* newspaper and I can't remember what the action was, although I do have a vague recollection of wearing a green tweed suit!

I usually enjoyed the shoot days, even though they were sometimes very long, but I was much less fond of the casting process. In fairness, I suppose an advertiser has got an image in their mind of what the characters should look like, but it is a little soul-destroying when you turn up for a casting, having spent a couple of hours getting ready and then another hour travelling, for them to give you a cursory glance before dismissing you. You have to grow a very thick skin and understand that it is not personal, you just didn't fit the brief.

You are definitely a 'type' when it comes to castings and very often it would be the same group of girls turning up for the auditions for different products. I was in my early twenties when I started with this sort of work, so usually fell into the category of 'young mum', even though I was years off having my own children. I would arrive at the offices of one of the casting directors, and there would be a room full of girls also in their early twenties with dark hair and a reasonable figure. After you had been to a few castings you would start to recognise faces, then names and the next thing you were chatting away like old friends.

I don't know why they did it, but the advertisers had a habit of selecting someone who was already featuring in other commercials. You would think they would want someone fresh so that they would only be associated with their product, but that was not the way it worked. I was the new kid on the block, but almost immediately my face fitted and I landed my first 'biggie'.

It was for the Woolwich Building Society. They had been running a campaign for quite some time using the same blonde girl, with a very 'girl next door' appeal. Her catchphrase was, 'You're welcome', and she had become something of a minor celebrity. It was a very popular campaign but perhaps someone at the advertising agency wanted to prove that they were earning their money, or the girl became pregnant, or maybe her agent asked for too much money – who knows. All I know is that they decided to have a change. They came up with a new catchphrase, and auditioned for a new 'Woolwich Girl' to deliver it. That new girl was me, and my catchphrase was, 'Can I help you?'

It was a great commercial to get so early in my career, as it was shown a lot and usually at prime time. Not only was the television campaign running, there was also a photograph of me in the window of every high-street branch, which was a little unnerving to walk past on your way to do the supermarket shopping in sloppy clothes and no make-up, particularly if someone recognised you. I was also contacted by the *Daily Mirror* newspaper as they wanted to run a story. They took some photos, and the caption read, 'New Society Girl'. At the time I was flattered, but, with the benefit of what I now know about the television industry, it was probably because there had been complaints from the general public about getting rid of the other girl.

The other great thing about being the 'face' of the Woolwich was that when the interest rate changed they had to do a reshoot with the new financial information. When my agent rang me to shoot the second commercial I had just returned from a sunshine holiday and was very tanned. That made it a little challenging for the make-up artist! They didn't always shoot a whole new advertisement; sometimes I was just asked to do a voiceover with the new rates showing on screen, and then they would edit the end of the previous commercial with me popping up to ask, 'Can I help you?'

The third, and final, commercial that we shot had a slightly different approach. They used comedienne Marti Caine, sadly no longer with us, for the main 'storyline', and I simply delivered the interest rates and my little catchphrase.

As I said earlier in this chapter, there tends to be a time when your face fits and you are flavour of the month. This was my time. I seemed to get the majority of castings that I went for, so much so that the other girls' faces would fall when I walked into the casting suite. I had experienced it myself and knew that sinking feeling.

I did commercials for all sorts of products. As well as the *Evening Standard* and the three for the Woolwich Building Society, I did two for Butlin's Holiday Camps, funnily enough filmed in Minehead where I had stayed on holiday as a child; Hovis; Total Greek Yoghurt, filmed in the early stages of pregnancy so I wanted to heave every time I had to taste the yoghurt; a children's bedtime toy called Globug; and Unibond. The Unibond adhesive advert I did was choreographed to the tune of 'You Need Hands', with a slight alteration to the main lyric . . . 'U ni bond'. Oh yes, there were some real gems, but someone **must have** had the original idea and plenty of other people must **have given** it the 'seal' of approval.

So we are already up to ten. I spent a few days in Milton Keynes filming the two adverts that launched the Vauxhall Nova car, and there were four newspaper commercials, one for the *Daily Mirror*, in which you only saw my hand with a ring on my finger and heard me say 'I do', one for the *News of the World*, in which I was reclining on a sun lounger in a bikini and had to push a waiter backwards into a swimming pool, and two for the *Sun*. One of the *Sun* commercials was related to the Weight Watchers campaign, which gets its own chapter, *88*, and the other was as a result of a frantic last-minute call from my agent.

It had been a glorious summer day, and I had spent the afternoon in the garden with my son Daniel. He was about seven or eight months old, and we had been playing in the paddling pool together so were both a dishevelled mess. The phone rang at around five and it was my agent. Could Daniel and I get to Wembley within two hours to feature in a commercial for the *Sun* newspaper?

Apparently, the baby that had been booked for the shoot wasn't co-operating, so they needed a replacement baby with its mum as soon as possible. I looked at Daniel covered in mud and grass, and thought about the drive over to Wembley, which would take at least an hour and a half at that time of day, and said, 'No problem, we'll be there.' I must have had a touch of sunstroke!

Chris was out working so I had no one to help bathe Daniel, pack his baby bag with food, nappies, bottle etc. and check the map for a route to Wembley from SE25, not to mention getting myself showered and my hair washed.

Daniel was an angel, not just getting ready and on the drive over, but with the crew when we got there, and for the shoot itself. It must have been nine o'clock by the time we were ready for action, way past Daniel's bedtime, and yet he was still smiling and happy. The action itself was very simple, reaching him up above my head and rocking him from side to side while he giggled down at me. All done in a couple of takes, what a little star.

So, if you add the two Vauxhall Nova commercials, Weight Watchers, and the four newspaper ads to our subtotal, we are now up to seventeen.

Talking of non co-operative infants, as we were with the *Sun* commercial, a similar incident had happened to me previously. I had been cast as the young mum in a Twix commercial, fetching my daughter from playschool. The little girl that had been cast as my daughter had long dark hair and a similarity of look to make it realistic. On the day of the shoot, this little girl simply would not play ball. She didn't have a lot to do, just run over to my waiting arms for a hug, and then we both bit into a Twix bar. All the cajoling and pleading from her real mum simply didn't work and by early afternoon it was clear that we were going to have to implement a plan B.

This meant using a different child, who was supposed to be one of 'my daughter's' classmates but who had exhibited a bubbly personality throughout the morning. There was a slight problem though. This child was very blonde, with blue eyes, and looked absolutely nothing like me. After weighing up the options available the producer decided to shoot the commercial as written, using the little blonde girl, after all I could have been her nanny or a friend of her mum's if anyone had ever questioned the lack of resemblance.

Because it was a food advert, and as part of the action we had to take a bite of the Twix, we were provided with spit buckets. This is to prevent you from feeling nauseous if you have to do a lot of takes to get the action right. I wish I'd eaten mine, as we did less than half a dozen takes on that sequence.

The funny footnote to this story is that when I did have my first baby, a couple of years later, he was blond and blue-eyed and didn't bear any resemblance to me at all!

So finally we reach commercial number nineteen, and possibly my favourite. I am sure a lot of you will remember the Head and Shoulders adverts with the half-head test? They washed one side of a model's hair with a non-dandruff shampoo and the other side with Head and Shoulders and *voilà*, the dandruff had gone. It was a very visual demonstration, but the manufacturers wanted the shampoo to have a wider appeal so they needed a more glamorous campaign.

I knew they had been casting for the commercial for a little while, but for some reason, maybe because my hair was very curly, I had not been asked to go along. Sometimes on a big campaign, when the clients can't decide who they want to represent their brand, they have recalls, where they bring back the favoured few and occasionally they will also bring in a new face, and that's what happened in this case. All the other girls had been seen before, but I was the new face.

After my initial five minutes with them, they asked me to wait outside while they saw the other girls. They all went in, came out and left, except one girl, Sara, who I had met at auditions before. It was a straight decision between the two of us, and I was fortunate enough to be chosen. Funnily enough, Sara is now a regular guest on QVC, and we are good friends.

My action didn't involve the half head test, they had a model for that. I am in my bathroom, about to step in to the shower, when the voiceover questions me on my choice of shampoo. I go into the shower and lather up my hair, remark about the creamy feel of the lather, then the end shot is me running my hand through my silky, shiny, blow-dried hair saying, 'It's really great!' I wonder if that rings any bells with any of you?

It was a simple-enough shoot except for one small thing. I had been asked to bring a couple of bikinis to wear for the shower shots. One had red and white stripes, the one I wore in the *Citizen Smith* episode, *chapter 31*, and the other was bright turquoise. Both of them showed through the opaque glass of the shower cubicle. There was no way I was actually going to get naked in front of the crew, I am such a prude, so they had to fiddle around with a nude-coloured bra and double-sided tape, and adjust the camera angles. They were probably quite annoyed with me, but I have my principles.

The final advert looked really good, and not just in my opinion. After it had aired, my brother rang to tell me I looked like a film star. It is one of the few times he has ever complimented me on anything to do with my work.

Twenty

I had just turned twenty when I undertook the long
drive from the Isle of Skye to Barcelona in Spain
for a dancing job.

My parents had moved from Nottingham to the Isle of Skye whilst I was away on the cruise ship SS *Doric*, sailing around the Caribbean, as I mentioned in *chapter 16*. I returned to the UK in April 1976, picked up my car from my brother's in Nottingham, and drove to my parents' house on the Isle of Skye. It's a long way, but I had no other place to call home. It was also quite a tricky location from which to try and secure my next dancing job. Auditions were out of the question because of the distance involved, and I was also a little late to try for a summer season as most of the shows had already finalised their line-up.

Mum and Dad had arranged for the *Stage* newspaper to be delivered to the newsagent's in Portree, but even that was a twenty-mile drive from their little cottage in a tiny village called Culnacnoc. It was a sweet little place with a fantastic view to the sea and the Scottish mainland beyond, but it did need a bit of modernisation in the form of a new kitchen extension, which my dad went on to build single-handedly, and redecoration throughout.

I wrote off for several jobs advertised in the back pages of the *Stage*, enclosing a CV and a full-length photo, and eventually heard back from an English choreographer who provided the dancers for a variety show at the Teatro Apollo in Barcelona. Fortunately she was happy to engage me on the strength of previous work and sent me my contract, which required me to be in Barcelona in the middle of June to rehearse for the new show, due to start at the beginning of July. The rest of the dance troupe were flying out to Spain, but I had asked if it would be OK for them to pay my ferry crossing instead of my airline ticket so that I could have Flossie, my little Austin Healey Sprite, with me. They agreed so, two days after celebrating my twentieth birthday with my parents, I started my long journey south. And it was a long journey, 1547 miles to be precise!

I had worked out that the journey would take between four and five days, and my first stop, after five hours on the road, was at my sister's in Glentrool, in south-west Scotland. From there I drove down to Parson's Green in south-west London where I had arranged to stay overnight with a friend of mine. Having left Lynda's quite early in the morning, I eventually reached Susie's in the early evening for a few hours' sleep before I needed to be on the road again to make the ferry I had booked. I was crossing from Dover to Calais and then heading towards Paris and everything went really smoothly, even the sea crossing.

Do you remember the summer of 1976? It was wall-to-wall sunshine, so as I reached the outskirts of Paris I decided to pull over and put the soft top down on my car. It wasn't the press of a button as it is these days on convertibles, and while I was in the process, a car pulled over just ahead of me with three people in it, two ladies and a man. One of the women got out of the car and came over to see if I was all right. They thought I had broken down and had seen the English registration plate so were very kindly offering help. The lady asked where I was headed and I told her Barcelona and she then asked where I was staying that night. I hadn't actually booked any accommodation, which I told her, adding that I would find a motel en route. We said goodbye and both got back into our cars to continue our respective journeys.

A couple of miles down the road I noticed their car in front of me again, and the lady in the back seat, who I had spoken to, was gesturing for me to pull over to the side of the road. I wondered if I had a puncture or something so pulled over. She got out of the car again and came over. In her broken English she said, 'We have been talking about you and wondered if you would like to stay the night at our house in the country?'

OK, as I write this now alarm bells are ringing in my head, and clearly I now realise I should have declined and just continued on my journey. However, maybe the sun had gone to my head or I was just incredibly naive and trusting, as I said 'yes'.

'Follow us,' she said, and I did.

So, I'm driving for the first time in a foreign country. I'm on my own, and it's approaching dusk. I am following a car with three people in it, who I know nothing about, down little country lanes and by the time we arrive at their house I have no idea where I am and I have very little fuel. I pull into a gravelled courtyard and the electric gates close behind me and then the man suggests we put my car in the garage, which he then locks, so that I don't need to put the roof back on in case of rain. Even to me it sounds like the early part of the plot to a horror movie!

The house was a beautifully converted farmhouse with the whole ground floor an open-plan living space, apart from the huge kitchen. They showed me around outside where they had both a swimming pool and a tennis court and extensive gardens that backed onto woodland . . . a good place to dispose of a body!

I don't remember feeling nervous with these people, even though I had put myself in a potentially dangerous position. We had dinner and talked about England and my forthcoming job in

Barcelona and then I excused myself as I was pretty exhausted. The first feelings of doubt hit me when I realised there was no lock on the bedroom door. I was tired and needed to sleep, but I knew I wouldn't close my eyes at all unless I could secure my space, so I pulled the chest of drawers across the door as a kind of barricade. Just before I dropped off to sleep one of the women knocked at the door and asked if I wanted any drinking water. I pretended to be asleep but I saw her try the door handle before saying something in French and retreating to her own room.

Breakfast felt a little awkward as clearly they knew I had barricaded myself into my room, but nothing was said. They gave me some fresh peaches from their tree before volunteering to show me the way to the nearest petrol station to refuel for the next leg of my journey.

I have no idea if I had a lucky escape or if they were just genuinely kind people but for many years I decided to keep the story to myself, rather than sharing it with my parents!

I drove for the whole of the next day, keeping to the A roads rather than the motorway, and was making such good time that I was in two minds as to whether or not to continue all the way to Barcelona. I decided against it as I wasn't keen to arrive at night and try to find the Hotel Ramblas, where I had been booked into by the theatre company. Instead I stopped at a motel in Narbonne, not far from the French–Spanish border.

The next morning I was back in my car for the last hundred miles or so before arriving in Barcelona. I don't know what I was expecting Barcelona to be like, but the size of it took me by surprise. On one of the roads into the city there were five lanes of traffic all moving in the same direction, so I got into the middle one and hoped I didn't need to turn off.

Amazingly, I found my way to the Ramblas fairly easily and without the aid of satellite navigation, which in those days had not even been thought of for use by the general public. My children both drive and use their satnavs all the time, even for quite short journeys, but I still prefer to look up my destination on a map and write out directions . . . I am so 'old school', as they would say.

When I arrived at the hotel to check in there was a note waiting for me. Apparently the new show had been postponed by a month so none of the other new dancers would be arriving for another four weeks. They had tried to contact me at my mum and dad's three days earlier but I had already left on my epic journey.

Fortunately for me, the company already had a show running at the Teatro Apollo, so they just slotted me into it with the existing company. I had to learn about ten routines over a two-day period, and then I was in the show.

I was a bit lonely at first, living in a little hotel on the Ramblas and speaking no Spanish, but thankfully I had my cassette player and Barry White for company. After a couple of weeks, Gloria, one of the girls in the show, came to my rescue. She was moving into an apartment with her boyfriend's mother – don't ask – and offered me their spare room to help with the rent. I jumped at the chance, and soon felt more settled.

When the rest of the group finally arrived in July, we rehearsed a new show, and the theatre management offered me more money to appear as a topless showgirl! I declined. I've always been well endowed up top, but I've never gone in for exposing them – even on the beach.

I had some really good times in Barcelona, including being asked to model for a magazine called *El Papus*. I had no idea at the time, but I think it was a little bit raunchy. I would pose for pictures quite scantily clad but with all the relevant bits covered up for a kind of comic book story so I had 'word bubbles' coming out of my mouth or head. I didn't speak any Spanish when I first arrived in Barcelona so I had no idea what I was supposed to be 'saying' or 'thinking', which, with the benefit of hindsight, is probably just as well! I'm quite surprised they got away with it as this was at a time when copies of the *Sun* newspaper bought in Spain had the page 3 girls' boobs covered with a coloured-in 'bra' — honestly, it's true!

Gloria and I used to head off in my car during the days, to Sitges, Castelldefels, Lloret de Mar and Tossa de Mar, and once we even went over the border into France to Perpignan.

The nightlife was brilliant too, very different from anything I had previously experienced. I particularly remember going to see a show at a club called Barcelona de Noche, where the entire cast, with the exception of one girl, were men dressed up as women, miming to the likes of Shirley Bassey. The girl started off dressed as a woman, then stripped and got redressed, on stage, as a man. It sounds weird, but it was a fabulously costumed and choreographed show.

Things started to go wrong when my car broke down. I rang my brother, who was into cars, and told him it was making a 'chuffla chuffla' sound, and there was a lot of blue smoke. He long-distance diagnosed the problem, and sent the relevant part over, which a local garage fitted for me, but after that I didn't want to risk going on long journeys, so more or less kept the car parked in a garage.

Without the car it wasn't so much fun and I started looking forward to going home, particularly as Christmas was approaching. Technically, my six-month contract finished in mid-December, but, because the new show had started a month late, the theatre management wanted me to stay until mid-January. I didn't want to be in Spain over Christmas so I made plans to leave. After the show one night I just packed my bags and left; I had fulfilled my contract.

I didn't trust the newly fixed car to drive back through France, so instead I booked Flossie and I onto the overnight train to

Bilbao, and then took the ferry to Portsmouth, as I mentioned in *chapter 16*.

Within thirty minutes of driving off the ferry, I was stopped by the police for not having a valid tax disc. I had tried to get a tax disc organised from Spain but was unable to because Flossie needed an MOT test, which I couldn't get done in Spain. It was a bit of a 'catch-22' situation so I had written to the AA to ask for their advice and they recommended getting it done as soon as possible when I got back to the UK. My brother had Flossie booked in for an MOT test the next day in Nottingham, but technically the police were within their rights and the particular officer in question was quite pedantic. I was issued with a fine but in the end the AA fought my corner for me so I didn't have to pay it.

After my stop-off in Nottingham for the MOT and to see my brother I was back on the road again, heading towards the Isle of Skye in time for Christmas.

Funny thing is, a few years ago, I had a letter at QVC from a girl called Diane, who I had danced with in that show, and we still keep in touch – it really is a small world.

Twenty One

I was twenty-one when I met my partner Chris,
although, as I discovered almost immediately, our paths
had crossed before, so maybe fate was giving us a
second chance?

I was living in Upper Norwood in south-east London at the
time, and working in pantomime at the Ashcroft Theatre in
nearby Croydon. I was quite lonely as I was living on my own,
and had just celebrated Christmas away from my family for the
first time as there was no way I could get up to the Isle of Skye
and back in the one day I had off – Christmas Day. I wasn't
alone on Christmas Day, though, as Jo, one of the other girl
dancers, had very kindly asked me to stay with her and her family
for the festivities, but it wasn't quite the same as being with your
nearest and dearest.

Unlike the pantomime at the City Varieties in Leeds, *chapter 7*,
this was a fairly short run of only six weeks. Nevertheless, we
were a very friendly cast and liked to socialise together. The
organiser was usually Gina, who had invited the entire cast to
her parents' house in Wimbledon for a party after the show on
New Year's Eve. I was terribly impressed as Michael Aspel was
also on the guest list and he was very high profile at the time.
It was a very large house, which was fortunate as several of us
needed to stay over, having no way of getting home.

Shortly after this, on the 5th of January to be precise, Gina organised another party, in part for the people who had missed out on New Year's Eve, but also as a birthday celebration for the twins who were appearing in our show. This party was at a nightclub in Streatham, which is not far from Croydon, as Gina knew one of the members of the resident band. He was living in a flat belonging to Simon, a friend of hers, who was playing one of the Ugly Sisters in the pantomime *Cinderella* elsewhere in the country. Gina thought I might be quite interested in meeting this band member as she knew I had done a couple of summer seasons in Jersey, as had this chap, so at least we would have something to talk about.

So I was introduced to Chris that night, at the Peacock Club in Streatham, because he was a casual acquaintance of a girl I was working with for eight weeks!

We hit it off immediately. I liked him because he seemed kind, had a good sense of humour and we had something in common, having both worked in Jersey. He liked me because I was wearing a low-cut, full-length red dress, one of my own creations as it happens. We both smile whenever we hear the Chris de Burgh song 'Lady in Red'.

To digress for a moment, I once met Chris de Burgh. I had gone to Anfield to watch Crystal Palace play Liverpool in the second leg of a Carling Cup semi-final. Sadly, we were beaten, but the people I had gone with were able to get us into the Players' Lounge after the game. I thought I would lessen the disappointment of losing for my son Daniel by collecting a couple of the Liverpool players' autographs. I approached Robbie Fowler at the bar, who was deep in conversation with a chap who had his back to me. I requested his autograph and he started to oblige and then said, 'Sorry love, but your pen doesn't work.'

At this point the chap with his back to me turned around and said, 'Here, borrow mine.'

I accepted the pen gratefully, and Robbie duly signed his autograph, and as he handed it back to me he said, 'Do you want his as well?'

I thought the face looked familiar, but I knew he wasn't a footballer and I was collecting signatures on my ticket for Daniel, and there wasn't a lot of room, so I said, 'No, it's OK, thanks.'

Chris de Burgh looked mildly surprised as he took his pen back, but hopefully he wasn't offended!

Anyway, back to the night I met my Chris. Maybe it was more than the plunging neckline that attracted him, as not only did he ask me for my phone number, something he assures me he had never done before, but he also suggested that perhaps I would like to pay a return visit to the club. This I duly did a couple of nights later, with Gina as my companion. She had suggested that I stay over at her parents' house again, so we went back there via Clapham Common, which was sort of on the way from Streatham to Wimbledon, and was where Chris's flat was. We only had a quick cup of coffee with Chris and his other flatmate, Vince, Simon's boyfriend, but we arranged to meet up again the following day on our way back in to work.

At this point I should mention that Vince also worked at the Peacock Club but as a waiter rather than a musician, and that Chris was living with Simon and Vince after mentioning that he was looking for somewhere to live, and Vince offered their spare room.

Gina chatted to Vince while Chris and I went for a romantic walk around the duck pond on Clapham Common in the freezing January temperatures, and I think I already knew that there was something quite special developing. With the benefit of hindsight, I think that Gina had a bit of a soft spot for Chris herself and was starting to regret playing the matchmaker.

Chris asked if I would be going to the Peacock Club again that evening after work and I said OK, as long as he would give me a lift home as I didn't have a car. Things were moving quite fast but it felt as though I had known him for years, and in fact, as I mentioned at the beginning of the chapter, I had met him three years earlier when we were both working in Jersey. Perhaps we were meant to get together then, but I had a crush on someone else so wasn't interested in getting to know Chris any better. Maybe if we had got together in Jersey that summer we wouldn't be together now, as I was only eighteen in 1974 and not ready for a long-term relationship.

I got my lift home after seeing Chris that night and also got an invitation to go to a party with him on the Sunday – talk about a whirlwind romance!

Well, the Sunday came and all day I was excited about seeing Chris again. He had arranged to pick me up at 7 p.m. so I spent a couple of hours washing and blow-drying my hair, doing my make-up, and deciding what to wear. The allotted time came and went and at first I was just a bit disappointed that he was late for our first 'proper' date. Then I started to worry that maybe he had been involved in an accident. By eight o'clock I presumed that I had read all the signs wrong and that I had been stood up, so I was feeling quite cross when the phone rang.

It was Chris. He was ringing from his flat in Clapham where he had had to return to get my phone number. It sounds so strange in this day and age when everyone has a mobile phone glued to their ear, but in 1978 there was no such thing and he couldn't even call from a phone box as he hadn't got my number with him.

So why was he late? Well, apparently, despite having dropped me at my flat two nights earlier, he couldn't find the road that I lived on. I wasn't sure that I believed him at the time but, knowing him as I do now, it was probably the truth as he is rubbish at directions – even with the help of a satnav!

At first I was a bit offhand with him and said it was too late to go to the party, but he talked me round, and when he eventually showed up thirty minutes later with a huge bar of Cadbury's Dairy Milk as an apology, I caved altogether.

I saw him a couple of times that week and then something very strange happened. He rang to tell me that Vince had picked an argument with him over our blossoming relationship and had threatened to throw him out if he didn't end it. I asked him what he wanted to do and he said he didn't want to finish with me, so I just told him to pack his things and move in with me!

When I think about it now and how I would react if my daughter Sophie did something similar, I can't imagine what I was thinking of, but, and it's a very big BUT, we are still together thirty-five years later with no wedding rings but two well-adjusted, grown-up children. Perhaps it was just meant to be.

Twenty Two

22 Roseville Street, St Helier, was my address for my second summer season in Jersey.

I had auditioned for the show at the Watersplash, which was one of the best-known venues on the island, and was pleased to be chosen as it meant I could spend another summer on lovely Jersey.

Topping the bill were Windsor Davies and Don Estelle, two well-known actors from the hit television series *It Ain't Half Hot Mum*. When they weren't recording the TV show they had formed a comedy-and-vocal double act and just prior to the season they released a track called 'Whispering Grass' – do you remember it? Also in the show were vocalists Sara and Brian, and the five girl dancers, Jo, Gwen, Irene, Linda and I.

After a couple of weeks' rehearsals in London we headed out to Jersey, the other girls by plane and I took the ferry with my beloved Flossie, as documented in *chapter 16.*

The accommodation was in a pair of semi-detached Victorian villa-type houses. Don and Windsor and their families were in number 20 and the rest of us were next door in number 22. Linda and Irene shared a room. They were both Scottish and knew each other from previously working together. Gwen and I shared a room. It was quite funny, actually, as we both had the same surname of Roberts, but in those days I used the stage name of Julia Gaye. It was my middle name and my mum and I thought it rolled off the tongue more easily than Julia Roberts . . . I'm not sure if the Hollywood actress would agree! Then Jo had a single room to herself.

The Watersplash was quite an isolated venue on the west side of the island so it was handy having my car. I used to take Gwen or Jo and the singer, Sara, would take everyone else.

Opening night was a sell-out, which was hardly surprising as Windsor and Don were romping up the charts with 'Whispering Grass'. It was all very exciting, really. When they hit the number I spot some reporters from the *Daily Mirror* came over to Jersey and took their photo with Gwen and I. It was the first time I had been photographed for a national newspaper, even though the spotlight wasn't exactly on me!

The show was built around Windsor and Don, as you would expect, but our dance routines were really good. We did the big 'feather' showgirl-type opening and finale as was expected, but we also did a funky sixties number called 'The Frug' and a cockney song-and-dance number called 'There's a Little Ditty' from the show *Oliver!* – I loved that one as I had a verse to sing on my own.

I was also vocalist Sara's understudy, for what it was worth, because no one is ever off sick in show business, are they? The show must go on, right? Well, not if you are the singer and you get laryngitis, which is exactly what happened to Sara. OK, mild panic. Although I knew the words to the songs it is a bit different when you actually have to perform them. Brian and I rehearsed solidly all day to get the duets and group numbers on for that night, and the girls had to rearrange the positioning for the dance routines as I couldn't do both. It went reasonably well and I continued to fill in for Sara until I too went down with laryngitis! The show still went on, just without a female vocalist.

My parents always tried to come and see the shows I was

doing so they booked a week's holiday in Jersey. They hadn't met the rest of the cast before coming to see the show. I had managed to get them a table at the front so that they would have a good view. We went out for the opening of the show, and when we got backstage Sara said, 'Cor, did you see that bloke in the front row? He's gorgeous.'

We were all rushing to change for our next routine but I remember thinking I hadn't spotted anyone in particular, and I would have to have a closer inspection.

After the routine we came back to the backstage area and I said to Sara, 'What is he wearing?'

'Here, I'll show you,' she said, and we peeped through the backstage curtain. 'The guy in the brown velvet jacket.'

You've guessed it. It was my dad. He was a very handsome man, but I warned Sara to keep her hands off!

Gwen and I got on well. Like me she had been to Jersey before so knew lots of people from the other shows. It made our social life very interesting on a Sunday night when we weren't working. We also used to go to the beach together sometimes although I was a bit of an early bird and Gwen often slept in.

On those days I would head down to St Brelade's Bay and sunbathe in the trampoline enclosure. I had made friends with the guy that ran the concession and if it wasn't busy he used to let me have a free 'bounce'. I was so naive that I didn't realise that having a nubile eighteen-year-old bouncing around on the 'beds', as we used to call them, was almost guaranteed to attract attention, and I didn't understand why my sessions were always cut short because a queue had formed.

I was fairly generously proportioned, but Gwen had a lovely figure. She had long slim legs, a petite bottom and a generous bust, so when we saw an advert in the local paper for the Miss Jersey competition we persuaded Gwen to enter. The two of us went bikini shopping and we bought a little brown-and-white gingham number. I bought some broderie anglaise and hand-stitched it around the top of the bra and panties to dress it up a bit.

On the day of the competition a crowd of us went down to the open-air swimming pool at Grouville to cheer her on. She came second to a local Jersey girl but, in my opinion, she should probably have won.

I also got on really well with Jo. She was older than the rest of us and the most experienced dancer. She had been in the Young Generation, one of the aspirational dance groups of the time, along with Pan's People. She admitted to twenty-eight but I think she was possibly nearer to thirty-eight. We kept in touch after the season when I went off on my Caribbean cruise and she went back to Majorca.

Actually, Jo was allowed to leave the show three weeks early as she had been offered the job in Majorca but needed to start immediately. The management were very good and said she could be released from her contract if she found a suitable replacement. Enter a fabulous dancer named Pat who had been in Jersey doing one of the touring shows. She learnt the routines in a couple of days and slotted in brilliantly. Pat changed her name to Tricia and after working in Hong Kong together, see *chapter 15*, she became and still is a firm friend.

So Jo was released to go to her job in Majorca and that is where she met her husband-to-be, a young waiter called José. He came back to the UK with Jo and they set up home in a rented flat in Clapton in the East End of London. Some years later Chris and I visited them there and we all had dinner together. José was very handsome and lovely but he didn't speak a huge amount of English. I did try out my little bit of Spanish that I had picked up in Barcelona on him but I'm not sure if I made much sense.

A few years later I was devastated to learn that Jo had fallen from the window of her flat onto some spiked railings and died. How awful. I still find it upsetting to think about.

I would be lying if I said I had a close relationship with Linda and Irene. They were fine but just kept themselves to themselves so it was very surprising to get a call from Irene, days after the season in Jersey finished, asking me if I wanted to go on her next job with her.

'What's the job?' I asked.

'A Caribbean cruise,' she replied.

Well, that was a hard decision to make . . . not!

Twenty Three

This is the number of different jobs I have done over
the years to keep a crust on the table.

Some of them were temp jobs I did when I was working for
an agency between dancing jobs and some were meant to last
longer but didn't for various reasons!

1. Dance teacher from the age of twelve
2. Chemist shop assistant (lasted two days)
3. Babysitter
4. Dressmaker for a boutique
5. Professional dancer
6. Fish and chip salesperson
7. Barmaid
8. Marks & Spencer Christmas staff
9. Cloakroom attendant in a nightclub
10. Go-go dancer
11. Driver and 'meet & greet' for a hire car company
12. Clerk at The Law Society
13. Tea lady at Granada Television's London offices
14. Sorting office at British Council on Pall Mall
15. Receptionist for Bupa and also Lambeth Council
    Environmental Health Department
16. DJ for Juliana's

17. Photographic model
18. Singer
19. Fitness teacher
20. Actress in TV commercials and corporate videos
21. Game show hostess on *The Price is Right*
22. Television presenter
23. Writer and producer of television features

It's pretty diverse, but as they say, 'variety is the spice of life'.

Twenty Four

The number 24 was the bus that transported us from West Bridgford into Nottingham from our house on Musters Road.

We lived on the bus route and if we were running a bit short on time, we could watch the bus leave the terminus at Boundary Road and still be able catch it at Malvern Road if we ran and if the bus stopped to pick up passengers at Ellesmere Road.

My dad had a car, which was provided by his work. He was a travelling salesman so was away a lot during the week, leaving my mum with the unenviable task of getting the three of us to the bus stop on time.

Mum, like most women in the 1960s, didn't drive. We used to walk to the local shops for groceries, or, if it was a big order, Mr Glenn the grocer would deliver – there's nothing new about Ocado, you know, except the method of ordering.

The bus was used for shopping trips into Nottingham city centre or for visiting my maternal grandma, who still lived just over the River Trent in the house where my mum had spent some of her youth.

Mum did learn to drive in the mid-sixties out of necessity, and to her credit, as she was forty, it only took her two attempts to pass her driving test.

Twenty Five

The first certificate I was ever awarded was for
swimming twenty-five yards.

This is slightly ironic when you consider that the inspiration
for this book was swimming a hundred lengths of the pool
at my house in Spain.

It was 1962, so I was just six years old, and I managed to
swim a length of the pool, in breast stroke, to gain my certificate.
In those days everything was in imperial measurements, so a
length of the pool was twenty-five yards, which is approximately
twenty-three metres, nearly twice the length of my pool in Spain.
That's a long way for a little girl.

I started swimming at a very early age as part of the physiotherapy to strengthen my left leg, which had been severely
weakened by polio. I think the sessions were organised by the
Infantile Paralysis Society, as I used to wear a swimming costume
with an IPF badge stitched onto it. I was also a member of the
Polio Fellowship and for years they used to invite me to their
Christmas party, which was funded by the Rotary Club, who, as
I mentioned in *chapter 14*, are still doing great work in their efforts
to eradicate polio once and for all.

My mum took me swimming, although she never actually got
in the pool with me because she can't swim. I had a swimming
teacher called Miss Knight, who was not only responsible for
teaching me to swim, but also gave me exercises to do in the

water. It was easier for me to exercise in water as it provides buoyancy, so I didn't feel so unstable, and also the water's resistance helps to work the muscles harder. Maybe that is where the idea for aqua aerobics came from?

I used to swim on a Friday morning, even after I had started infant school, if I remember correctly, and Mum and I had to travel into Nottingham by bus to get to the Victoria Baths. As the name suggests it was an old Victorian building, and it had several pools. The one I used to swim in was called the 'ladies pool'. Like a lot of pools of that era, it had the changing cubicles down the side of the pool, and there weren't any lockers, you just left your belongings in the cubicle while you swam.

I was quite nervous of the water to begin with and I do remember having to be coaxed down the corner steps of the shallow end one step at a time. Miss Knight must have had the patience of a saint. I think part of the problem was that I was so little, I couldn't stand on the bottom, even in the shallow end.

I didn't have armbands, but I did have a rubber ring, which, in those days, were actually made of rubber rather than plastic. I can still remember the distinctive smell of it. When I got a little more confident I had a rectangular float to hold on to, before finally swimming unaided.

I do have a vivid recollection of the first time Miss Knight persuaded me to jump off the side of the pool, minus any form of floatation aid, into her waiting arms. It was a trust thing. She had carefully nurtured me to the point where I would trust her not to let me drown. Isn't it funny that, even at the tender age of three or four, I was learning a life lesson. You have to decide who you can trust.

After drying off at the end of each session, Mum and I would walk back to catch the bus, stopping at a cake shop on the way.

There Mum would buy cream cakes for the family to enjoy with Saturday lunch. It was always the same line-up. Mum and Dad would have cream slices, my sister a cream doughnut, my brother a chocolate éclair and I would have an egg custard. I didn't like cream then and I can still take it or leave it now, but egg custard is one of my absolute favourites.

Once I had mastered the art of swimming, I was occasionally invited to swim in galas organised by the IPF or Polio Fellowship. I can remember one in particular where our race was two widths of the pool. There were only four of us competing, and we could swim our stroke of choice. My favourite was the breast stroke, although now I prefer back stroke, and I was reasonably quick, but my downfall was the fact that it was two widths. I have never mastered the tumble turn so that really slowed me down. I finished third and was awarded a yellow drinking mug for my efforts.

The lessons at Victoria Baths stopped fairly soon after I was awarded my certificate for swimming twenty-five yards, and I didn't really swim much until five years later, when I was in the first year at West Bridgford Grammar School.

Mum had managed to persuade the school that I shouldn't play hockey as she was worried about me being hit by a ball or a stick on my weaker leg. It was sort of true, although her real concern was more to do with protecting me for my dancing classes. Anyway, it meant that, instead of swimming and playing hockey on alternate weeks throughout the winter and spring terms, I went swimming every week. That gained me an advantage in training for the only other swimming award I attained.

Do you remember the Life Saving Award? That was the one where you had to dive into the deep end to retrieve a rubber-coated brick, swim in your pyjamas, and 'save' someone by swimming on your back whilst cupping their chin in your hands. Thankfully I've never had to use that particular skill.

Twenty Six

This is the number of my house in Spain where the
idea for this book was conceived.

I had been thinking about buying a property abroad for a very
long time and had considered various different locations. In
1995 I had thoroughly investigated buying a plot of land and
having a house built in the Dominican Republic, but in the end
we realised that it was such a long flight from the UK we would
probably only be able to visit once or twice a year, so it just
didn't seem worth it. It was another ten years before we actually
went ahead and bought somewhere.

Unlike the Dominican Republic, Spain is only a couple of
hours' flight away, so we thought we would get much more use
out of a house there and decided to examine the different areas.

On an episode of *A Place in the Sun*, the presenter Amanda
Lamb, later to sell her range of luggage on QVC, mentioned
that Jerez, in the far south of Spain, was an up-and-coming area
which was still reasonably affordable. Chris and I talked about
it and decided this was where we would begin our search.

A couple of days later, while I was at work, Chris saw a
television advert for new-build properties in 'Jerez', so he sent
away for the free DVD. It duly arrived and we sat down to watch
it, only it wasn't about Jerez, it was about a place called Javea,
hundreds of miles to the north, on the Costa Blanca. Well it
began with a 'J', was his excuse!

Javea looked really beautiful so we thought we would start our search there instead.

We contacted the company who had sent the DVD and arranged to go out for a few days and view some properties.

By this time Daniel and Sophie were seventeen and sixteen respectively, and Daniel could drive, so we were happy leaving them 'home alone', as they were both quite responsible. The funny thing is, each time we got back from a visit to Spain — and there were several while we looked for the right property — the house was immaculate. They must have thought we were stupid if they thought we didn't realise they had had a few friends round, but at least they had tidied up afterwards.

On our first excursion to Javea we fell in love with the place. It's a bit like the rocky north coast of Devon or Cornwall, but with a bit more sunshine. We didn't see any properties we liked within our budget so, when we returned a month or so later and still drew a blank, we realised that, if we wanted a significant sea view, we would have to increase our budget.

The next trip was much more productive, and we saw a property that we made an offer on. It had the type of sea view we were after but we had one or two reservations about the location with respect to winter sunshine. It was in an area called Balcon al Mar, where all the roads are named after famous composers. We loved the area, and felt it was very appropriate with Chris being a musician and a songwriter. The house, though, faced north, and we thought this might make it quite cold in the winter months, when we would be looking to escape the cold of the UK for a few days, so we reluctantly withdrew our offer before any money changed hands.

We were feeling disappointed and to kill a bit of time, before heading to the airport for our night flight home, we had a look to see what a different estate agent had on their books. There in the window was 'the one'. A really pretty house, fabulous sea views and facing south-west. There was one drawback, however. You guessed it, the price! It was way over our newly revised budget. Despite this obvious drawback, I went into the office and asked the actual location of the house. The young man behind the desk, whose name was Ricardo, said it was just two roads away from his office, and if we wanted to go and have a look at it he would take us there and then. We had forty-five minutes before we needed to leave for the airport so off we went.

The house was lovely. You entered through a wooden gate into a very private, beautifully cultivated garden, with steps leading down to a large covered porch, which the Spanish call a *naya*, and the front entrance. Inside was nicely arranged with a small but newly fitted kitchen and dining area, but it was the full-length glass doors from the lounge to the balcony, and the view beyond, which really had the wow factor. This was what I had imagined when we had first gone house-hunting in Spain. It had a master bedroom with en-suite bathroom upstairs and a bedroom downstairs leading onto the pool terrace and a small lawned area, where there was a separate self-contained annexe. It felt like home; it was love at first sight for both of us. If there was a downside to 'Ricardo's villa', it was that there was no further scope for improvement or extension. Every square metre of land had been used to full capacity.

The drive to Alicante airport alternated between excitement and despondency. We had found the right house, but the price was not right – you'll be reading more about *The Price is Right* in chapter 34.

All the way back on the plane Chris kept saying, 'You're good with money, you'll find a way,' but I think I knew that it was going to be too much of a stretch.

We had seen Ricardo's villa in early December, so it was on our minds over the whole of the festive season. If we were going to go so hugely over budget and be scrimping and saving to make the mortgage repayments, we needed to be absolutely sure that this was the right house for us. I thought the best way to do this was to make contact with a couple more estate agents and view some more properties and also to take a more leisurely look at Ricardo's, as it had been a whistle-stop tour.

Towards the end of January we headed out to Spain again. The agent I had arranged to meet in the morning failed to show up, so we just went straight to have another look at 'the house'. It was just as I had remembered it, stunning views and all, but it was a very windy day and because of the compact nature of the plot, there was nowhere to sit in the sun and be out of the wind. It was the only negative of that second visit.

After lunch we were meeting with a different agent who had sent us a photo of quite a big house that 'needed some refurbishment'! The picture looked quite good, but the view across the pool and out to sea was marred by a really huge tree that looked as though it might be on land belonging to someone else. As we drove along the road to the house, which coincidentally was located less than half a mile from Ricardo's villa, I started to feel a buzz of excitement. The views out to sea were fabulous and although it did indeed need some refurbishment, the plot was twice the size of Ricardo's and there was plenty of scope for improvement. The sun was shining onto a huge covered *naya*, the pool was a little larger and the overgrown tree turned out to be on land belonging to the villa. The other big bonus was the asking price – considerably less than Ricardo's villa, although still at the top end of our revised budget, and of course this house would need money spending on it.

We had looked at fifty or more properties and found nothing we liked and now we had found two contenders. The dilemma was whether to invest in something that had potential to grow but needed total refurbishment, or to try and finance a smaller but ready-to-live-in house that was wildly over-budget and probably overpriced. Chris really wanted us to go for the latter option, but I was leaning towards the former.

A week later we put in an offer on the bigger property, which was rejected, but the owner said he would meet us halfway between the asking price and our offer and the deal was done. Less than two months later we opened the front door to our villa and hoped that we had made the right decision. The funny thing was that I hadn't noticed the name of the villa until that day . . . 'Ma Petite Folie', which as a phrase translates to 'my little extravagance'. However, the French noun 'folie' translates to madness . . . oops!

We had asked for all the furniture to be removed from the house as it was all a bit tired, so the property was totally empty apart from the cooker. The plan was to send over furniture that was excess to requirements from our house in England so that we didn't have to buy too much new. It would also give us the opportunity to have a clear-out at home.

The children hadn't seen the house at all, so we booked flights for the Easter holidays a couple of weeks later, in early April. We arranged for the lorry loaded with our furniture to arrive in Javea at approximately the same time as us and crossed our fingers that it would, as all we had at the house were two air beds to sleep on.

We arrived at the house around lunchtime in bright sunshine and sat on the tiles of the pool deck eating our airport-bought sandwiches and enjoying the spectacular view. The children were very impressed with the house and in particular the pool.

We had just finished our picnic when the lorry arrived, so it was all hands on deck to bring everything into the house whilst it was still light. Three hours later and it looked like home from home, complete with Tiffany-style lights, which you will read more about in *chapter 29*.

Although the daytime had been sunny and warm the night was getting cool, so we lit a fire with logs we had found stacked up at the back of our swimming pool. It had been years since I had lit a fire, and it was fun showing the children how to make rolls out of newspaper to get the fire started.

There was a slight hiccup when we were trying to get hot water in the kitchen to do the washing up. Despite our best efforts, the pilot light to the over-sink boiler would not stay lit. In the end we boiled a kettle for the water and resolved to call the estate agents the next morning, as we had no idea how or where to start looking for a plumber.

We had inflated the air beds I mentioned earlier, one for Chris and I, and one for Daniel, and Sophie had a sofa bed. I had made them up with plenty of covers to keep us warm, but what I hadn't taken into consideration was that, due to the tiled floors, the air inside the air beds got very cold during the night. We solved that problem the following night by putting a quilt under as well as over us, using the principle of **a feat**herbed.

The next morning I rang the estate **agents to ask** them if they knew of a good plumber to mend the **water heater** and then we went shopping for sunbeds for the daytime and oil-filled electric radiators for the night. We also got ourselves linked up to the cable television service so that we could watch a bit of English TV in the evenings.

Shortly after arriving back from the shops a lithe young man with long dark curly hair came bounding down the front steps. He introduced himself as Felipe, the plumber, and went through to the kitchen. A few minutes later he announced in broken English that the water heater was kaput and couldn't be fixed. We were in a foreign country and we had only just met this young man and there was the possibility that he was trying to rip us off, but somehow I doubted it. There was something about Felipe that I liked from the moment I met him. Not only did he return the next day with a new water heater for us, he also brought us some adaptors free of charge so that we could plug our newly bought radiators into the villa's old-style plug sockets.

The next visitors to our villa were my mum and dad. Of course they had heard all about it from the children and were keen to see it, but I was thinking that maybe their trip would have to wait until the autumn as we were already approaching the end of April. I remember ending a telephone conversation by saying, 'Have a think about when you would like to go and see it.'

The next morning the phone rang and it was Mum.

'We were wondering if it will be too hot in the middle of May?'

To be honest I had no idea how hot it would be, but I was really touched that they were so enthusiastic about making the trip. The next question made me really laugh though: 'Will we need a passport?'

Just for clarification, my mum and dad had travelled abroad before, particularly my dad who, as I mentioned in *chapter 8*, grew up in India, but they weren't sure if you still needed a passport to travel within the EU.

I suggested they apply for their passports at the Post Office as it only cost a few pounds, and when we had it done we had our passports within a week. Sure enough, a week later they rang to say the documents had arrived so I went ahead and booked them two flights from East Midlands airport.

Chris and I had arrived the day before to make sure everything was set up for their arrival, and then we went to fetch them from Alicante airport. It was already dark when we got back to the house, but I will never forget my mum's words as she walked out onto the *naya* with the moon sparkling on the ocean beyond: 'This is paradise.'

Paradise it was not, although we knew it had huge possibilities. They put up with the dodgy old showers and lack of comfortable garden furniture, and really got into the spirit of Spain by indulging in 'foreign food', although I think it may well have been Italian rather than Spanish! It was a little warm for them in the middle of the day, but they just sat inside or had a siesta.

My dad made me laugh by keeping his vest on at all times, even when he had taken his shirt off. They helped with a little bit of gardening and also in choosing a wicker table-and-chairs set. Unfortunately the latter didn't arrive until after they had gone home, but at least they were able to make use of it the following year when they visited again. By that time we had also refitted one of the shower rooms, which made life easier for them.

My brother was the next to visit with his family. They are big fans of France normally but even they had to agree the location was fabulous.

I also managed to get my sister to visit, which was quite a big deal, as my brother-in-law, Geoff, has Parkinson's and is not great on long journeys. I lured them with the promise of going in search of the flamingos in Calpe just down the coast, as Geoff is a keen ornithologist.

I also had to promise to take my sister to Benidorm, where she was hoping to locate a Scottish band she knew that had a residency there. I'm not that familiar with Benidorm, as it is about a forty-five-minute journey away from Javea, but as we came off the motorway and its vastness became apparent, I suspected we were on a bit of a wild goose chase. I had absolutely no idea where to head, and Lynda had no address, just the name of the bar, the Shamrock.

We hadn't had dinner, so I parked the car and we walked down to a beachfront restaurant to have a bite to eat. On the way back to the car we asked a passer-by if they knew where the Shamrock pub was. You could have knocked me over with a flamingo feather when it transpired that we were two streets away – how lucky was that? Mind you, we were looking for the Shamrock pub.

What happened next is vaguely surreal. We went into the Shamrock and, sure enough, the band my sister knew were playing, but they seemed to be minus their drummer, who, we later learnt, was back in the UK on holiday.

Geoff and I went to the bar to get some drinks, my sister started jigging around on the dance floor and the next thing I knew Chris was sitting behind the drum kit. You have no idea how out of character this is. Apparently he had gone up to the band leader and asked him if he would like him to sit in for a few numbers. You can imagine what was going through the band leader's head: 'This guy has probably had a few to drink and fancies himself as a drummer – how do I get out of this?'

He played the whole set with them and was invited back any time. I was so shocked I actually took a photo on my mobile phone and sent it to the children, warning them they needed to be sitting down!

It was a really enjoyable evening, but the best moment for me came three months later when I received Lynda's Christmas family newsletter. As his highlight of the year Geoff had described the events of the evening in Benidorm.

So everyone loved the house in all its rustic charm but it certainly needed updating.

We had big plans, but, unfortunately, with big plans comes big expense, and if I had known then what I know now we might have downscaled a bit.

Whilst the plot was south-facing, great for sunshine all day long, whatever time of year, the house itself had been built angled towards the houses on the other side of the valley rather than towards the panoramic sea view. We devised a plan to build forward at an angle to change the orientation of the house so that it faced the sea. In doing that we would have to build partway over where the pool was situated, so that also meant a new swimming pool. If we were going to build a new pool we might as well make it bigger for me to really be able to swim proper lengths, and why not make it an infinity pool? You know the ones I mean, they have a side missing where the water flows over into a catchment trough to be recycled, so that when you are swimming in the pool, it almost feels like you are swimming in the sea.

And so the grand ideas went on. We engaged an architect, who said what we were proposing was entirely possible, and then we set about finding ourselves a builder.

We had three estimates for the work. The lowest and highest price quotes were both from Spanish builders, and whilst it is tempting to go with the lowest price offered I was a little concerned about communicating long distance with someone who didn't speak the same language as me. In the end we opted for the middle quote as the builder was English and had been introduced to us by Felipe, our plumber friend.

We were planning to do the work in three stages. Stage one was a side extension to create a new kitchen, and a small front extension to enlarge one of the bedrooms. Stage two was the main project, including building the new pool. Stage three was a new parking area, access steps and landscaping the garden.

By the time we had all the planning consents it was spring 2007. The finance was in place for the first stage and the diggers moved in.

Everything went to plan, and by the time the work had to stop, to comply with the rule of no noisy building work in the height of summer, we had the bare bones of a new kitchen, albeit with no work surfaces, and one habitable bedroom with a beautiful walk-in shower room.

Daniel had visited the previous summer with his school friends but he stayed away the summer of 2007. Sophie, however, decided to have a break with her friend Nicola. I warned them that the house was in a bit of a state, which was an understatement, but they still wanted to visit.

The second day of their trip I got a panicked phone call. 'Mum, there's a rat in the house!'

Fortunately, they are only tree rats and eat mainly fruit, but even so it was a bit disconcerting. It couldn't have bothered them that much though as they returned for a second visit just before the work restarted in September.

As I mentioned there had been no problem organising the finance for the first stage of the work and I presumed the next stage would be just as easy. I was wrong. The small matter of a global financial crisis had begun.

I won't go into detail, but suffice to say there were times during the following two years that I heartily wished I had never set eyes on the villa. Add to that the loss of my dad in the November of 2007 and I can honestly say I don't know how I got through it all. Well, actually, I do. My immediate family helped with the emotional side of things, and my brother was able to offer me some financial support. Nevertheless it was a very traumatic time.

We had to make regular trips over to Spain to check on the progress of the building work and to make decisions about tiles and kitchen work-tops and decor generally. Our builder had assured us that the house would be completely finished for the summer of 2008 although the garden would have to wait to be landscaped. On the strength of his assurances Daniel and six of his friends booked their flights for their holiday in the August. Two weeks prior to their trip I flew over to make sure that everything was on schedule and was a little worried to find that the kitchen had yet to be installed and that they were only just finishing tiling the pool, which would then need to be filled with water. We were also missing the glass for the balconies to the lounge and master bedroom on the upper floor, and to one of the bedrooms on the lower floor. My builder was so unsure about meeting the deadline that he suggested booking another villa for the boys to stay in for which he would meet half the cost! Fortunately his workforce put in a few hours of overtime and the house was almost ready when the lads arrived for their holiday. I say almost, as there was just one thing missing – the glass for the balconies had not arrived in time to be installed, so my builder had to improvise. So that it was not just a sheer drop to the ground from the balconies, which would have been unsafe, particularly if the lads had been enjoying the delights of the many bars on the Arenal beach, he used acrow props to create a barrier. These are normally used by builders in a vertical manner to support ceilings or where a wall has been removed before the RSJ is in place, but because of their telescopic properties they were ideal to fill the space where the glass should have been, even though they weren't very pretty to look at. It didn't bother the boys too much as apparently they sat out on the lounge balcony enjoying the view with a beer in hand on more than one occasion. More concerning were the two balconies to the bedrooms which both overhung the shallow end of the swimming pool. The lads were on strict instructions not to jump off the balconies into the pool and Daniel assured me they wouldn't and in fact told me they hadn't when he returned from his holiday. I subsequently found out from my neighbours that this was a little white lie but then I suppose 'Boys Will Be Boys' . . . there's a good title for a song, one that Chris and I wrote, actually, which you will read more about in *chapter 83*.

The house did get completely finished eventually, and is exactly how we planned it to be. It is approximately twice the size of the original house, and while it was being built it had the nickname 'Hotel Guatla', the name of the road it is on. Once it was finished we renamed it 'Casa de las Aguilas', which translates as 'Home of the Eagles'. It is stunning and I thank my lucky stars every time I sit on the balcony, or the *naya*, or swim a hundred lengths in the fabulous pool.

The top level houses three bedrooms, all with en-suite bathrooms, and a huge open-plan living, dining and kitchen area. You can see the spectacular view from each area, even when you are cooking. Two of the three bedrooms on the top floor also have amazing sea views, as does the master bathroom. You can sit on the loo and look out to sea, but it is a magic window, so at the flick of a switch it becomes opaque. How cool is that?

There are two further bedrooms downstairs, also with the incredible view, and a second open-plan lounge, dining and kitchen area, which we have used mostly as a games room.

There is a covered terrace to keep out of the midday sun, and a pool deck for the sun worshippers, and all this is set in a garden brimful of oleander, bougainvillea, palm trees, orange and lemon trees, and even an olive tree.

The house has been the setting for a wedding, and was the final holiday for a lady who died of cancer. Most recently, my niece Rachel, whose wedding I mentioned in *chapter 9*, stayed for a few days with the bump of her first baby just starting to show.

We have spent hundreds, or maybe even thousands, of happy hours at Casa de las Aguilas but there have also been times when I wondered if the house was getting its own back on me for knocking it around so much. I felt so comfortable there, and it was such a calm environment to get on with writing this book, that I occasionally went over to Spain on my own for a few days if Chris was busy working. On one of these trips I arrived on a Saturday afternoon having stopped off at the supermarket for supplies en route from the airport. I was a little surprised when the light inside the front door didn't illuminate, as it was on a sensor switch, but I presumed the bulb must have blown. I was a little more perturbed when the electric blinds, or *persianas* as the Spanish call them, didn't rise after I pressed the master switch. I tried again . . . nothing. Then I noticed that the house was completely silent, without the hum of the fridge/freezer. The light began to dawn, if you'll excuse the pun. Obviously a fuse must have blown. Fortunately I knew where the fuse box was located but unfortunately it transpired that it was not merely a tripped fuse.

Having unsuccessfully flicked the master switches in the fuse box I wondered if the area was experiencing a power cut so I went next door to my neighbours, Mike and Margaret. They had power but they were able to tell me that the area had been hit by an electrical storm a few days earlier and that a lightning bolt had struck the television aerial on the roof of my house. When we had the roof repaired we were told that we were very fortunate that the whole house hadn't gone up in smoke. As it was, I had no electric at all as all three of the huge fuses located in the street outside my house had been blown. This I discovered courtesy of my kind electrician Victor who came to answer my 'damsel in distress' call even though he was on his way to a family wedding. He was able to replace the external fuses so that I had electricity restored but he was unable to do anything about the electric *persianas* as all the individual motors had been blown in the lightning strike and he wouldn't be able to get the replacement parts until the suppliers opened on Monday morning.

So there I was in the semi-darkness, unable to look out at the beautiful view and without a television, Internet or telephone, all of which had been damaged in the strike. Fortunately the *persianas* in the kitchen were operated manually so at least I could see to clear out the ruined contents of the fridge and the freezer.

Once the electric was back on I went outside of the back of the house to access the room where the water tank was to turn on the immersion heater for hot water. I stopped dead in my tracks. Because the electric *persianas* were all stuck down I hadn't been able to see the glorious ocean view but now I could, and right in the middle of it was an oil rig. I'm not joking. I raced back inside to fetch the binoculars and on closer inspection it appeared that this oil rig was being towed, but where to? Had they discovered oil off the coast of Javea?

I had intended to do some work on my book but, after the dramas of the day, I decided to go to bed early ready to start afresh the next morning. As Scarlett would say, 'Tomorrow is another day.'

The next morning I got up in a positive frame of mind and settled myself in the kitchen, the only room with any natural light, to do some writing. I decided to tackle *chapter 75*, which I knew was going to be quite lengthy and complicated so needed to be written without the usual interruptions of answering the telephone and making meals that I have when I'm at home. The words were flowing freely and I wrote solidly for five hours with only a small break for lunch. I finished the chapter and pressed save and then gave myself a short break to hang some washing on the line and stretch my legs a bit. If the weather had been nicer, as it sometimes is in early November, I would have sat in the sunshine for a while, but it was grey and windy and anyway I didn't want to be looking at the oil rig, which was still sat in the middle of the bay. I had a wander around the garden instead, and that's when I noticed that there was a slight green tinge to my beautiful infinity pool, the inspiration for this book. Because the electric had been off for a few days the pool pumps had not been working and algae had started to grow in the water. Could anything else go wrong, I wondered?

Imagine my horror when I went back to my computer to do some more writing, clicked the file marked 'I00 lengths', where I saved all the finished chapters, and *chapter 75*, five hours of work, was nowhere to be seen. I let out a small shriek before dissolving into tears and then I rang Sophie on my English mobile phone, as she is the most computer-literate member of the family. This was not as simple as it sounds as we had a very poor mobile signal, particularly on windy days, so I had to ring from our bedroom while my computer was plugged in in the kitchen. I was only slightly hysterical as I relayed what had happened.

'Did you press save?' she asked.

'Yes,' I replied.

'Then it will be saved somewhere on your computer,' she assured me.

She then gave me instructions on how to search for the missing chapter and told me to ring her back when I had located it.

I did as instructed and, sure enough, there it was saved under 'My Documents', rather than under the book folder. Apparently I must have forgotten to open the folder when I had started writing that morning so my computer didn't know where to save it to and had assumed I would find it in 'My Documents'. Never assume anything, Mr Computer, it makes an ASS out of U and ME!

Disaster averted, I went on to write a couple more shorter chapters before getting another early night, after all there was little else to do. At least Chris was arriving the next day and potentially the blinds would be fixed so that I would no longer feel like I was living in a cave.

I got up bright and early the next morning intending to write a chapter before heading off to Alicante airport to collect Chris in the early afternoon. I needed to check that the flight was on time so I pressed the button on my mobile to switch it on so that I could text Chris . . . nothing. I tried again and still nothing. So now I had no means of communicating with the outside world. I wouldn't be able to check that Chris's flight was on time, I couldn't ring Telefonica to report that my landline and Internet weren't working, and I wouldn't be able to contact my insurance company.

All thoughts of creativity were abandoned as once again I popped round to my neighbours for help. I borrowed their phone to ring Telefonica but was unable to get through as the lines were constantly busy, probably with people reporting storm damage. Margaret was able to check that Chris's flight was on time and Mike suggested that I should visit the phone shop in person to register the problem with my landline. The electricians, Victor and Emilio, arrived laden with replacement bulbs, fuses and motors for the *persianas* and I left them to work while I headed down to the phone shop.

Two hours later I arrived back with a new Spanish mobile phone and the knowledge that the fault on my landline and Internet had been reported. Victor and Emilio had been hard at work and most of the *persianas* were now raised, allowing me to see that the oil rig had moved on. Things were looking up – even the sun was shining.

The insurance company weren't particularly helpful, refusing to believe that the house had taken a direct hit despite photographic evidence of the charred roofing felt, but at least they covered most of the cost of repairing or replacing the damaged electrical items. It transpired that one of the televisions had survived the lightning bolt; it was the satellite boxes that had not, but at least for the rest of that visit we were able to watch DVDs on the evenings we didn't go out.

In spite of that episode I have loved owning my Spanish house, so it is with a heavy heart and more than a few tears that I have just sold it. There are several reasons, but the main one is uncertainty about my future, of which you will read more later.

It was really important to me to finish writing this book in the place that had inspired it. In July 2012, before handing over to the new owners, I had a few alterations and additions to make to it, and one last chapter to write.

Daniel was with me for the first week of my final two-week holiday there, and we were joined by Sophie and her friend, Becca, for a couple of days before they all went home and Chris arrived for our last week in Casa de las Aguilas.

There was quite a lot to do in terms of making sure all the paperwork was in place for the sale and also packing up the few things we were bringing back to the UK. We had sold the house furnished, but there were some personal items we wanted to keep.

The most important of these was a painting of a Spanish dancer, entitled *Fuego Blanco* (White Fire) that I had shipped out to Spain when the building work was completed. I had bought it shortly after my dad's death in his memory. It had to come home.

Once the boxes and my painting were en route I settled down to write the final chapter of my book on the last day in my Spanish house.

I had already swum my one hundred lengths of the pool that day, but in celebration of finishing, and as a symbolic gesture, I jumped into the pool at 8 p.m. for a second and final hundred lengths of that pool.

Chris had come down to the poolside with me and he suggested that as I swam each length I should shout out the corresponding chapter in the book. It was very liberating.

When I had finished my hundred lengths, Chris made me swim one more in recognition of the chapter I have had to add, *chapter 101.*

Twenty Seven

The 27th of November 1986 was a day that quite
literally changed my life. It was the day I became
a mother.

Daniel was born exactly one week late and weighing a very
eye-watering 9lbs 1oz and from that moment I knew my
life would never be the same again.

It had been a quite straightforward pregnancy, no morning
sickness, just a little bit of heartburn towards the end as my
'bump' was very big and I was carrying him high, but nothing
that copious cups of peppermint tea couldn't deal with.

I had all the scans but neither Chris nor I wanted to know
the sex of the baby even though that meant having both boys'
and girls' names ready for the new arrival. I think a lot of people
guessed it was a boy because of the way I was carrying him, all
at the front. Even towards the end if viewed from behind I didn't
look pregnant, and then I would turn around and on occasions
there would be an audible gasp at the size of my bump.

I was very happy to be pregnant and I must have showed it
because I can remember an occasion when a car stopped at the
side of the road as Chris and I were walking to the bank. I
thought they wanted directions so went over to them but the
woman leaned out of the window and said, 'I just want to tell
you you look radiant!'

It made my day, particularly as I was about eight months pregnant and you don't get that many compliments about the way you look from complete strangers.

Before I became pregnant with Daniel, I was teaching fitness classes, which you will hear more about in *chapter 80*. I decided to keep teaching, with the approval of my doctor, for as long as I felt comfortable, and in the end continued until I was thirty-eight weeks. I'm sure it really helped the way I felt and possibly the way I looked.

We were also very busy renovating our first house, trying to get as much as possible done before our new arrival. My midwife was less enthusiastic about it, particularly after I had mentioned balancing on a ladder to paint a ceiling.

I remember ringing my mum and dad to tell them the news when I first discovered I was pregnant and they were over the moon. Chris and I had been together eight years and were very settled, and they adored him.

My brother's reaction was slightly different and he is possibly responsible for us never getting married. When I told him I was pregnant he said, 'Does that mean wedding bells?'

'No, Rich,' I said, 'that means the patter of tiny feet!'

He was very pleased for us though, as was my sister. She had five children and probably thought it was someone else's turn to provide grandchildren!

So my due date came and went, not unusual for a first pregnancy apparently, although I had got twitchy one night and asked Chris to cancel a gig he was doing several hours' drive away just in case I went into labour and he couldn't get back for the birth. I was having to do a kick chart where you sit quietly for an hour and count the baby's movements, just to make sure everything is OK. With the benefit of hindsight it was probably also a way to make me take things easy for an hour. I never have been one for sitting around doing nothing unless I'm sunbathing, and there is not much of that going on in the UK in November. Having said that it was a glorious late summer we were enjoying in 1986 and that was why Chris decided to paint the inside of his bass drum on the afternoon of the 27th.

I had made vegetarian mulligatawny soup for lunch and, for those of you who don't know, it is curry-based, which is probably what brought on the labour. I was standing by the sink washing up, while Chris got on with his painting, when my waters broke.

The painting was abandoned, we grabbed my hospital case which, miracle of miracles, I had actually packed, and headed off to the hospital. It was about 3.30 in the afternoon when we arrived at the hospital and Daniel was born at 10.40 that night. Apparently seven hours of labour is not bad for a first baby but, as you will know if you have children of your own, it wasn't exactly pleasant either!

I won't go into any gory details but at one point the lovely midwife, Scottie, suggested I stopped shouting and put all my efforts into pushing! The gas and air, mixed with the mulligatawny soup, was making me feel really sick but finally I was holding this amazing bundle in my arms.

He looked like a cherub, not a wrinkle in sight, just smooth pale skin and a light dusting of blond hair. I couldn't take my eyes off him. In fact, I didn't take my eyes off him all night, I just lay there awake staring at him. I had never felt such over-whelming love in my life and it still brings a lump to my throat when I remember the emotion I felt. When I say it changed my life for ever, I really mean it. I had my *raison d'être* – my reason to be.

We were allowed to go home earlier than usual because Daniel quickly regained the couple of ounces of weight he lost after his birth. In 1986 you were supposed to stay in hospital for up to five days with a first baby, but we managed to escape after three.

I'm not a fan of hospitals, most likely a subconscious throwback to my early days and the amount of time I spent there.

I will always remember Daniel's first bath time at home in front of the fire. His tummy button was oozing and I started to panic that something was wrong and that his insides were about to fall out. A quick phone call to the ward sister soon eased my mind, but she was probably thinking that I shouldn't have been in such a hurry to go home!

Daniel was a really good baby generally, although, like most newborns, he didn't sleep all through the night at first. He had a rocking cradle that we put at my side of the bed so that when he woke in the middle of the night for his feed I could pick him up without disturbing Chris too much. That said, Chris was usually the one to do the nappy change before we put Daniel back in his cradle.

If he wouldn't settle I would stick a foot out of bed and rock the cradle until he dropped off. On the odd occasions where he simply wouldn't settle I would stand and rock him singing 'When the Boat Comes In'. I have no idea why it was that song, but it usually did the trick.

Miraculously, from about six weeks, just as you are getting to the point where you think you can't take any more sleepless nights, Daniel started to sleep through and that was it, no more broken nights apart from the odd one when he was teething.

Twenty Eight

This is the number of pounds I lost on my last and
hopefully final diet.

I say 'final diet' because, having lost so much weight, I will
endeavour not to allow myself to put on more than a few
pounds over my ideal weight ever again. That means I won't
have to 'go on a diet', as such, just cut down for a few days to
get back to where I strayed from.

I am not a big fan of diets as over the years I have tried most
of them, with varying degrees of success. When I was at school
I did the milk and banana diet, and the cheese and orange diet.
Both were very boring and, although I lost weight on them, the
minute I started eating normally again the weight went straight
back on.

When I was a professional dancer I was always doing some
crazy diet or other as I was a 'curvy' girl and most dancers aren't,
so it was always a struggle to keep to a reasonable weight.

The worst job for me, in terms of weight worries, was when
I was a dancer on the SS *Doric* for six months. Cruise ships are
notorious for feeding their passengers at every opportunity and,
unfortunately, I took every opportunity offered initially, before
realising that I had put on over half a stone and could barely fit
into any of my costumes! Breakfast was followed by mid-morning
coffee, then lunch followed by afternoon tea, then dinner, not
forgetting the midnight buffet. That was just the food; add to

that the calorific Caribbean cocktails and it was a wonder it was only half a stone!

I think I developed a better relationship with food after the children were born, probably because I made sure I cooked them healthy meals from when they were very young. I wanted them to enjoy the taste of things that were nutritious, rather than just full of sugar and salt, and we didn't have sugary fizzy drinks in the house until they were nine or ten years old.

It also helped that I had landed a Weight Watchers commercial nine months after giving birth to Sophie, *chapter 88*, which taught me some good habits and helped me drop the baby weight I had gained.

Even so, I still had weight fluctuations down the years, often associated with emotions, and that was definitely the case with my most recent weight gain.

My dad died quite suddenly in 2007, *chapter 87*, and, although I initially lost weight, as you would expect, I also seemed to lose all sense of 'the meaning of life'. I don't particularly remember comfort eating, but I guess I must have done because, before I knew it, I was weighing in at over 11 stone. I hadn't been that heavy since my second pregnancy and although I really hated it, and felt uncomfortable in my clothes, I lacked the will to do anything about it.

I had more or less stopped any kind of exercise programme too which is most unusual for me.

In 2009, QVC started to sell a weight-loss meal programme called Diet Chef. They wanted volunteers to have 'before' shots done, go on the diet and then have 'after' shots done to show the results. Much as I really wanted to do it, I wasn't sure that I could lose weight – after all, I was fifty-three and everyone knows how hard it is to shift excess weight once you've turned fifty.

I wasn't one of the first group of volunteers but, when I saw the great results the test group were having, I decided to give it a go, although without the 'before' shots.

In part, this was because I didn't want to put any pressure on myself by telling everyone I was doing it, and I also didn't want to start until I felt ready.

January 2010 came and went, as did February, and then, on the 1st of March, weighing 11st 6lbs, I finally felt ready to start Diet Chef and restart my exercise routine of Pilates, swimming and walking on the treadmill.

Within three weeks I had lost half a stone and people were starting to ask me how I was doing it. That gave me a real incentive to keep going, and I was also feeling so much better too. I stuck to Diet Chef rigidly for the first month, then started to introduce some family meals that I had cooked, alternating with Diet Chef dinners, for another month, by which time I had lost well over a stone.

Using the good habits I had learnt, and enforcing portion control, I just kept on getting lighter and lighter, even though I was increasing muscle mass because of my exercise schedule three or four days a week. My target initially had been to get down to 10 stone and back comfortably into size 12 clothes, but when I reached 10 stone I knew there was still a little more to lose so I just revised my target.

The day I fitted comfortably back into a pair of size 10 jeans that I hadn't been able to wear for five years (thank goodness bootleg were back in fashion) I knew that I had lost enough weight. I stood on the scales and, to my amazement, I weighed 9st 6lbs. I had lost exactly 2 stone and it had taken me about six months to do it. That was in September 2010 and although I have gained a few pounds as I write this, I am still within half a stone of my ideal weight.

I don't want to lose any more weight as my face starts to look very gaunt if I get too thin, and I don't want to put any weight on as I'm not sure my skin will have the elasticity to shrink back again as it did, thankfully, this time.

So, although I'm no goody two shoes, particularly where chocolate and ice cream are concerned, my mantra now is moderation and if I have had a bit of a naughty week I just spend a bit longer on the treadmill or in the pool.

Twenty Nine

This is the number of Tiffany-style lights I have!

I know this sounds rather excessive, and I must admit when I counted them all up I was quite surprised myself, but it's true!

For those of you who don't watch QVC you may not be familiar with these lights. They are reproductions of the beautiful cut-glass lights first designed by Louis Comfort Tiffany around the same time as Edison invented the electric light. The idea was based on the way sunlight streams through a stained-glass church window but the beauty is you don't have to rely on natural sunlight, which is just as well in the UK.

I fell in love with these copies the moment I saw them and have collected them ever since. It's a shame they aren't the real thing, as with a collection of twenty-nine originals I could retire in 'comfort' (just a little joke) for the rest of my life.

I have three standard lamps, one in the conservatory, one in the family room and one in the lounge. There are two more lamps in the lounge, three more in the family room, one in the hall and one in my office, so we are up to ten and we haven't gone upstairs yet!

There are three in my bedroom, two bedside and a feature lamp, two in the guest bedroom, one on the landing and two in Sophie's room. If Sophie had her way I'm not sure she would choose them, but they needed a 'home', and Sophie needed bedside lamps. So we have now accounted for eighteen.

Three lamps didn't get unpacked when we moved last year as there was nowhere to put them, so now we are up to twenty-one. So where are the other eight?

Believe it or not, I sent some out to Spain when we shipped some furniture over, and I brought them back with the few possessions we kept after selling the house, so they are boxed up awaiting a new home.

In Spain we had three in our bedroom, two in another bedroom and two in the lounge. There was also an art deco-style uplighter but sadly that got broken in transit. So am I cheating by counting that one?

Not at all. The twenty-ninth lamp is a really cute Santa, complete with his sack of toys, so he is stored away with all the other Christmas decorations for all but four weeks of the year.

So there you have it, twenty-nine Tiffany-style lights . . . until another one takes my fancy!

Thirty

Chris and I celebrated the thirtieth anniversary of our
living together in Barbados, a place we both love.

In the early years of our relationship, nobody really recognised
Chris's and my anniversary except ourselves. After all, there was
no big ceremony, no family knees-up, just Chris arriving on my
doorstep with all his worldly possessions exactly two weeks after
we met!

It was always a bit of a grey area. Should we celebrate the
anniversary on the 5th of January, the day we met and, coincidentally my sister's birthday, or should we celebrate on the 19th
of January, the day we started living together?

It was my mum in the end who made the decision for us. I
hadn't exactly told them how quickly Chris and I started living
together but once they had met him, and the longer we were
together, more of the truth started to come out. There were no
anniversary cards in the first few years because I think both Mum
and Dad secretly hoped that Chris and I would get married, but,
after eight years together and once I had told them I was expecting
our first baby, I think they realised that wedding bells were
unlikely. That was when my mum asked if we wanted to mark
the 5th or the 19th as our special day, and I think we decided
the 19th was probably more relevant.

Since then Mum has sent us a card and a little gift each year.

On our tenth anniversary she had a cake made for us and sent a beautiful bouquet of flowers. After that we started to make a bit more of an effort too.

For our twentieth I organised a couple of nights away at a luxury hotel in Gloucestershire, courtesy of a friend of mine who worked for the hotel group in question. On that occasion we took the children with us, but when we were deliberating where to go for our 25th – or should that be Silver Anniversary – we decided that it should just be the two of us.

A friend of mine lives in the north-east of Majorca and she helped me to find a very nice hotel for a mini-break of five days. The weather wasn't particularly hot, but most of the time it was sunny and in truth it was lovely to get away on our own, as up to that point we had always taken the children everywhere with us.

By the time we were celebrating our thirtieth anniversary, both of the children were at university so there was never a question of them coming with us.

It was a particularly difficult time for me as we had lost my lovely dad less than two months previously and I must say that I did experience a certain amount of guilt at the thought of leaving my mum. We had talked about visiting Barbados for our anniversary before my dad died, as we had been before on a family holiday with the children and we both really wanted to go back just as a couple. I was unsure what to do, but Chris realised that I was in a state of shock and grief and decided that I really needed to get away. I think it was the right decision.

We booked a hotel called the Crystal Cove on the recommendation of another friend of mine who used to work for Virgin Atlantic. (Reading this chapter back, I realise I have a lot of very helpful friends!) It was quite a last-minute booking and the hotel was very full. We checked in and were taken to our room and I must admit to feeling a bit disappointed.

The room was located on the stairs that led from the pool area to the reception and for some reason it felt a bit cave-like, not to mention the noise of people constantly walking past the door. I didn't say anything to Chris, and we unpacked and went to dinner at one of the outdoor restaurants.

The next morning we had breakfast and while I was putting my sun cream on Chris disappeared. When he came back he had a big grin on his face.

'We're changing rooms after lunch,' he announced. 'It's a bit more expensive but I think it's worth it.'

To say I was surprised is an understatement. It was so out of character for Chris to make a fuss about anything, let alone anything as major as actually complaining about a room and asking to be moved. But he wanted everything to be as good as it could be in difficult circumstances.

We went to the beach for a couple of hours before returning to our 'cave' to repack our suitcases. Off we went to the new room. I couldn't believe it. It was right on the beach with a fabulous view of the sea and the sunset, as we were on the west coast. Talk about a stroke of luck that we had been able to move into one of the best-located rooms in the hotel. Or was it just luck? On more than one occasion on that holiday, and many times since, I felt like my dad was watching over me.

We did have a very good time. The hotel was located on quite a private strip of beach with a cliff at one end of it so there were fewer people walking past as there was nowhere to go. Most days we stayed on that beach but we also took a water taxi to a different beach, another surprise move by Chris, who hates boats because he can't swim.

We hired a car for a couple of days and drove up to the north of the island, and then across to the breathtaking Atlantic side to a place called Bathsheba where all the surfers congregate. It was raining but that didn't spoil things for us. We sat in the car and ate our packed lunch like you would do at an English seaside resort in the height of summer! On the second day we had the car we went to Bottom Bay in the south, which we had discovered when we had visited previously with the children. The whole holiday felt like I had escaped from my life and the reality of recent events.

On the last evening, as we were waiting in the reception area for our taxi to the airport, a wedding party were also waiting for transport to their reception. The bride started talking to us as she had recognised me off QVC . . . it really is a small world, isn't it!

It is our thirty-fifth anniversary in 2013 so perhaps Chris is planning something. It will need to be pretty special to top Barbados.

Thirty One

The Christmas special of *Citizen Smith*, entitled
'Buon Natale', was broadcast on the
31st of December 1980.

I know this because I have the *Radio Times* magazine with the listing in it, and I kept this particular copy because I was in this Christmas episode.

I don't actually remember how I got cast for the role of 'girl on beach', as I don't recall going for an audition, but it was probably because of my Mediterranean look and olive skin tone. The funny thing is, when I visit Spain or Italy on holiday, the local people speak to me in their language and are always surprised if I don't respond. I speak a little Spanish and even less Italian, but it is the speed at which they speak that catches me out.

What I do remember is travelling by train, not to the exotic Mediterranean location portrayed in the programme, but to the rather less warm but nevertheless beautiful north Wales coast.

The actual location was Portmeirion, the Italian-style village where the 1960s cult TV show *The Prisoner* starring Patrick McGoohan was filmed. You may well remember the famous line, 'I am not a number, I am a free man', and you may also remember the huge 'bubble' chasing him along the beach. Well it was on that very beach that my action took place.

If you were a follower of *Citizen Smith*, you will know that it featured two main characters, Wolfie, played by Robert Lindsay, and Ken, played by Mike Grady, and most of the action was set in Tooting. However this was the Christmas special and it saw the two stars on holiday in Italy.

As I mentioned earlier, I had been cast as 'girl on beach'. I had been asked to take along a selection of my own bikinis for them to choose from, but before you start imagining that this was the middle of summer, so bikini weather, it was actually late spring, and definitely not bikini weather. Also, because it was not the height of summer, and long before I ever started taking winter sun holidays, I had no suntan, so they had to apply tan body make-up all over me.

My action started with me lying on my front on the beach sunbathing with my bikini top undone. Wolfie deliberately flicks ice cream on my back to startle me and make me get up minus top. I was such a prude that I had the make-up girls stick triangles of tissue over my nipples because I didn't want people looking. To be honest, I'm not sure I was the right girl for the job as I've never been overly confident about my body, and I've never even sunbathed topless in the privacy of my own back garden!

Anyway, I then shot Wolfie a glare, before marching off down the beach for a swim. Urged on by Wolfie, Ken decides to take a swim to try and impress me. The next piece of action you see is me carrying Ken out of the water after he has got into difficulties swimming, and depositing him unceremoniously on the beach.

Three things to mention here. The Irish sea is very, very cold for swimming in in late spring. After each take the 'tan' body make-up had to be re-applied so that it didn't look streaky. And Ken was very heavy!

And that was it for my part. It was just a few minutes at the beginning of the episode but it was very exciting for me as it was the first time my name appeared in a cast list, albeit right near the bottom. I wasn't the last name listed though; that privilege was afforded to 'man on bicycle'.

It is not even my real name that appears in the *Radio Times*. At the time I was still working as Julia Gaye, my 'stage name', as explained in *chapter 22*. I didn't start using my real name, Julia Roberts, until I worked on *The Price is Right* some three years later, just prior to the release of *Steel Magnolias*, the movie that catapulted the 'other' Julia Roberts to megastardom. My timing has always been a bit off!

Incidentally, if my description of the 'action' in 'Buon Natale' has whet your appetite to see it, you can find it on YouTube, under 'Julia Roberts from QVC UK in a very early role'. At last count it had around 300,000 views.

Thirty Two

This is the number of rows, including casting on and casting off, in the snood I knitted for my son in Winter 2010.

In case you don't know, a snood is a neck warmer, a sort of cross between a scarf and a hood.

I had unearthed my knitting bag to teach my daughter how to knit, a skill I had learnt at the age of seven by watching my maternal grandmother. The problem with learning to knit by watching someone else is that I don't do it properly. It's a mixture of left-handed and right-handed knitting. I put the needle into the work with the right hand, but then carry the wool around the needle with the left. It's very odd but over the years it has delivered some great results.

I knitted a Guernsey for my dad, an Aran cardigan for my partner Chris and all sorts of outfits for myself from jumpers with snowflakes on to a matching skirt and top, which took me months, and when I'd finished it I didn't think it suited me, so hardly wore it!

I also designed and made a *Price is Right* jumper when I was working on the show, which you will be hearing about in *chapter 34*. It was in royal blue mohair with *The Price is Right* logo on the front, which Chris helped me create using graph paper. I only ever wore it to rehearsals, so when I received a letter from a viewer asking for something personal to be auctioned for charity, it seemed the perfect thing. I hope it raised a few pounds for the charity concerned.

Even before Daniel was born I made him his first outfit. It was a cardigan and trouser set with matching hat, mittens and bootees in pale green and pale blue. I tried to keep the colour unisex as I didn't know if I was expecting a boy or a girl. I also knitted a baby blanket to match and the whole ensemble is stored away safely for the next generation . . . maybe!

One of the first things I knitted for Sophie was a pink-and-white striped dress with a Peter Pan collar. She had her photo taken in it when she wore it to our friends' wedding at just six weeks old and it is probably my favourite baby picture of her.

I was constantly making them something new to wear and as they got older I had a great time creating 'My Little Pony' and 'Fireman Sam' sweaters and also 'Teenage Mutant Hero Turtles' – Sophie was Donatello and Daniel was Raphael.

So while I was teaching Sophie the rudiments of knitting – she is left-handed so took to my method quite readily – I also decided to knit a little hat and jacket for the newborn baby of a friend of hers.

Daniel watched the speed at which my knitting grew, and asked me if I would make him a snood as they were the in thing, particularly amongst footballers.

He found a pattern for me on the Internet, I bought the wool and the needles, and a day later he had his snood ready to wear for his football coaching session.

What I wasn't expecting was for him to come home brandishing a ten-pound note and saying, 'I've got you an order for a snood.'

I had to nip that in the bud pretty quickly, although I did fulfil the order he had already taken! Come to think of it, I bought the wool and put in the labour and yet he kept the money . . . ?!

Thirty Three

I was thirty-three when I caught the chicken pox.

Daniel had just turned three and we had held a small party for some of his friends from playgroup to celebrate. A couple of days later one of the mums rang me to tell me her son had broken out in spots and that the doctor had confirmed chicken pox.

For a few days I kept an eye on Daniel and Sophie, waiting for any sign of a temperature or irritable behaviour and I thought we were going to be lucky, but about ten days after the party Daniel started to show signs of being unwell. The good news was that Sophie, who was just coming up to two, was perfectly OK; the bad news is that I was also feeling unwell.

I hadn't succumbed to chicken pox as a child, although I had both measles and German measles or, to give it its proper title, rubella. I think I may even have had the mumps, but I had avoided chicken pox until 1989. It is not a very pleasant illness at any age, particularly when the spots are itching like crazy and you know you mustn't scratch them, but as an adult it takes on a whole new dimension.

My fever was much more intense than Daniel's, with my temperature soaring to 106. One moment I felt like I was on fire, and the next I was shivering uncontrollably and simply couldn't get warm no matter how many clothes I was wearing.

To make matters worse it was two weeks before Christmas

so it was Chris's busiest time of year for work, with all the company Christmas parties wanting live music. We weren't in a financial position for Chris not to work, so I was on my own most days, trying to look after a very poorly little boy and take care of, and keep amused, a not-quite two-year-old Sophie. There were times when Sophie, at her tender age, actually turned into our 'carer'. Both Daniel and I had a raging thirst and, on more than one occasion, 'nurse Sophie' went to fetch us little cartons of juice from the fridge.

Then there were the spots. Initially they were terribly itchy, and no amount of calamine lotion seemed to help. Mine were so bad that I actually had Chris take a photo of me just so that I would remember how awful they were. My face was terribly swollen but I kept my hands off them as I was afraid if they scarred that I might never work in television again. Fortunately for me, Chris knew a girl singer who recommended vitamin E oil to help prevent scarring and, with the exception of one spot in the centre of my forehead, this seemed to do the trick.

Daniel and I were over the worst of it by Christmas Day with just a few spots still needing to heal, but on Boxing Day Sophie started with the fever. Her birthday is exactly two weeks after Christmas so it was a race against time to get her well for her birthday, but we just about managed it, although she does look a little nonplussed in some of her birthday photographs.

Thirty Four

This is the number of episodes of the game show,
The Price is Right, that I featured on as a
hostess over the first two series.

I'm not really sure how I became a hostess on a game show,
it just sort of happened. Let's face it: I'm not archetypal
hostess material. I'm not tall, blonde or leggy, all of which
seemed to be the main attributes of other game show hostesses
at the time.

My agent had told me, when she suggested that I should
audition, that the show's producers were looking for actresses
rather than 'dolly birds' as they wanted interaction between the
show's host and the girls. The audition was in the West End of
London, although the show itself was to be filmed at Central
Studios in Nottingham, my home town. They were looking for
four girls, and although looks were important, the priority was
personality.

The first thing the show's producer said to me when I went
in for my audition was, 'You look exactly like my first wife.'

How do you respond to that? It's a bonus in one way, as
obviously I had a look that had appealed to him when he met
his first wife, but on the other hand, if they were divorced, maybe
he would associate certain of her less likeable personality traits
with me! The funny thing was, it transpired that she had origi-
nated from West Bridgford in Nottingham, my exact place of

birth. Who knows, maybe we were distantly related? Whatever similarities I had with Bill's first wife, it worked in my favour as I was subsequently offered the job.

Incidentally, you are probably familiar with the producer of the show. His name is William G. Stewart and he went on to host a show called *Fifteen to One* on Channel 4.

One other thing I remember from the audition was getting a lift back to Clapham North tube station, where I had parked my car, with one of the other auditionees. Her name was Debbie, and I'm not sure if she was offered the job or not, but I have a suspicion that she would have declined anyway as she had just been offered a job as a magician's assistant. The magician in question was Paul Daniels and of course Debbie (McGee) later became his wife. How different her life might have been if she had taken *The Price is Right* job instead!

A few weeks later I headed up the MI to Nottingham to shoot a pilot for the show. Well, strictly speaking, that should be two pilots. Although the producer had decided on his hostesses, the final decision was yet to be made on the show's host.

There were two contenders and they were chalk and cheese. Leslie Crowther, who went on to host the show, was mature, suave and debonair. By contrast, the other pilot we recorded was with cheeky cockney chappy Joe Brown. They were both really good in their differing ways but Leslie edged it, quite possibly because he seemed to have a better memory, and there was a lot to remember in that show!

It was very exciting to be in at the start of a whole new era for the game show. In the early 1980s most shows of this type were pretty similar. You answered general knowledge questions and you won prizes. Even *3-2-1*, with its cryptic clues in the final round, relied on general knowledge in the first couple of rounds.

There were no general knowledge questions in *The Price is Right*, it was purely about guessing the cost of everyday items. The person with the nearest guess to the actual price, without going higher than the price, won the item and moved on to the next round. It was a simple concept, but massively popular in America.

Part of the reason for that popularity was the prizes, but that had almost been the stumbling block in bringing it to the UK. There had been a limit on the value of 'star' prizes on game shows, usually a family car or a holiday on shows like *Sale of the Century* and *3-2-1*. That limit was lifted, and I think the value of our first 'Showcase Showdown' was not far off £20,000 – unheard of in the UK – which led to a lot of publicity surrounding the show.

I mentioned that there were four hostesses for that first series. We were all very different in looks and probably personality too. Marie-Elise was tall and slim with a deep husky voice and was ever so slightly bonkers . . . in the nicest possible way. I remember going to a party with her, hosted by a very important bigwig at Central Television. We hadn't been there long, so she hadn't had much to drink, when I spied her dipping her hand in the bowl of potpourri used to fragrance the room, and eating it. She explained afterwards that she thought it was the spicy nibbles that you have in Indian restaurants, but surely she must have noticed the rather odd taste! Years later she appeared on QVC as a model for Zandra Rhodes fashion.

Then there was Jacqui. She was even shorter than me and very, very slender. She was in a girl band at the time and going out with a musician, so we had a certain amount in common. She split with her musician, though, and ended up marrying a *Coronation Street* actor.

Obviously there was me, and the final girl to make up the quartet was Denise, who became, and still is, one of my best friends. Denise is a year younger than me, but she seemed so worldly wise, whereas in certain ways I was incredibly naive. I was very envious of her ability to be 'one of the boys' whilst looking every inch a glamour girl. I can always remember on the first day of rehearsals Denise wore the brightest coloured orange top you have ever seen. It was the depths of winter but the colour from her top bounced a warming glow onto her face so, instead of looking pallid, like the rest of us, she looked healthy and radiant. I have always remembered the tip and do it myself on days when I look tired and pale. Denise also still uses the same trick as she illustrated by wearing a fluorescent coral sweater when we met up for lunch recently.

Initially we rehearsed at the Albert Hall Institute in Nottingham prior to the studio rehearsals and the start of the show recordings. It was an exciting time for me as I hadn't been involved in a television series before, and had only seen the inside of a television studio when I had worked as an 'extra'.

Everything was going to plan beautifully until the ACTT Union brought its members out on strike. I don't know why they were striking, and there was maybe some justification in it, but for us it was very demoralising. We would turn up at the studio, have our hair and make-up done and get into costume, only to be told that there would be no recording that day.

It wasn't just *The Price is Right* that was affected, it was all shows that were recording at that time, one of which was *Shine on Harvey Moon*. It was vaguely surreal to be sat in make-up with the cast of a show that you normally only admired from the sofa in your front room. We were staying in the same hotel too, so occasionally we would find ourselves in the bar together late at night. Normally I was quite shy but after a couple of crème de menthe on the rocks (whose idea was that?) I seem to remember telling some pretty awful jokes in a very loud manner, probably egged on by the other girls!

I also felt very sorry for the studio audiences who would arrive full of excitement and leave totally deflated.

This went on for a number of weeks, and at one point it looked like the show would be cancelled as the air dates were already booked and if *The Price is Right* couldn't be recorded, the prime time Saturday evening slots would have to be filled with something else. I presume the TV companies and the union reached an agreement, as eventually the first series did get recorded, though if I remember rightly we were a few shows light of the contracted number.

After all the delays it was fantastic to finally get into the studio with the live audience and witness their delight, not just at winning but also at taking part. None of the contestants were selected prior to coming to the studios so, as they stood in line waiting to take their seats, they were gently quizzed by the researchers looking for people they thought would be entertaining. When you saw the look of complete surprise on the contestants' faces when Leslie called their names to 'COME ON DOWN', it was totally genuine and not hammed up for the cameras.

Our outfits for the show were interesting. As I mentioned, the producer was trying to move away from the stereotypical game-show hostess so, instead of a figure-hugging evening dress, we wore suits! Several people commented that we looked more like air stewardesses than hostesses but maybe that was the look they were trying to achieve.

We did have slightly more revealing costumes though when we demonstrated some of the prizes. I seemed to spend quite a lot of time in white shorts, even though I was very self-conscious about the size of my legs and bottom. Looking back at the photographs I have no idea what I was worrying about; I certainly wish I looked like that now.

On one occasion, Denise and I were sporting the white shorts ensemble to show off a speedboat, which was part of the star prize at the end of the show. It had been stored outside and it had been raining so a big puddle had collected at the end where I was sitting when they elevated the front of the boat to make it look good on camera. Denise was positioned in the front of the boat. What neither of us realised was that we had been placed to balance the boat on its stand so, after I caught sight of the shot on a backstage monitor, I beckoned her over to have a look and the whole boat tipped up. We both got drenched and had to be rescued by the backstage crew. We weren't very popular for a while after that!

After all the hassle and delays we were usually very well behaved in the studio and no one played any pranks until the rehearsal for the last show. One of the prizes was a quite expensive Portmeirion dinner service. It was set up on a table which was on a revolving platform that had to be manually operated. Everyone was in on the joke except the producer, Bill. As Leslie called for the prize to be revealed the platform shuddered a bit and then stopped abruptly accompanied by a very loud smashing sound. Bill raced across the studio floor with steam coming out of his ears and a torrent of abuse from his mouth, only to find the props guys in hysterics behind the set, surrounded not by shattered Portmeirion but oddments from the canteen that they had dropped in a 'crash box'. Bill did see the funny side of it . . . eventually!

There was a lot of publicity associated with the show, including being photographed with Leslie Crowther for the front page of the *TV Times* magazine. Like the *Radio Times* with the *Citizen Smith* mention in it, I still have a copy of the magazine. When I was going through all my memorabilia for this book I opened it up and the main story inside was about skating duo Torville and Dean, also from Nottingham.

We attended various promotional events including a day at

the Nottingham races. I had never been to the races before and was keen to place my first-ever bet. I selected my horse because it looked pretty with a sheepskin noseband. To my surprise it won; however, it was clearly beginner's luck as nothing else I had a flutter on was placed. I was photographed that day with boxer Herol Graham, known as 'Bomber Graham', for the *Nottingham Evening Post*.

On the night the first show was broadcast, Bill had invited all the girls to his house so that we could watch it all together. His eldest son from his first marriage was there and Bill's first words when I arrived were, 'Doesn't she look like your mum?'

He never let that particular chestnut rest!

The show aired to the biggest ever ITV Saturday night audience, although I am sure it will have been topped since, of around 25 million people!

I enjoyed the little bit of limelight that came with the territory. You know the sort of thing, being recognised in the supermarket and the bank, and being asked to judge talent contests and dog shows. It was fun, but I have never wanted to be so famous that you can't do the everyday normal things.

The Price is Right was a huge success, and a second series was commissioned, which we were all asked to do again. I was very grateful for this as I had just put down a deposit on our first house, *chapter 46*.

I only did two series of the show but during that time I grew very fond of Leslie Crowther, particularly his quirky laugh, and so it was a tremendous shock to learn of his car accident and subsequent death a few years later.

Just as a footnote to this chapter and in case you think all the prizes on *The Price is Right* were fantastic, I thought I would share this with you.

My brother saw an advert in the small ads section of the

Nottingham Evening Post. I can't remember what it was for or how much the people were asking, but the small print read 'unwanted Price is Right prize'.

There's no pleasing some folk!

Thirty Five

I have read almost every book written by
Mary Higgins Clark, and a few of the ones she has
written in conjunction with her daughter,
Carol Higgins Clark.

She is American and the first book I read of hers was back in
1976. As you can see, I am a very loyal fan and I have now
converted both my mum and my sister too. I wait with anticipation for her next book as soon as I have finished the one I am
reading. I have just read her latest one entitled *I'll Walk Alone*,
bringing my total to thirty-five, and I've been reading her books
for thirty-five years, so one a year! I know it's a lot of books to
read from one author, but I really enjoy her style of writing,
keeping you in suspense until the very last moment, a real 'page
turner', as book critics would say!

Where Are the Children was the title of the first book I read
of hers in 1976. I was working in a theatre show in Barcelona
and picked it up off a book stand on Las Ramblas, a beautiful
leafy avenue that leads down to the sea. I started reading the
book in bed after the show one night and was so gripped
by the story that I simply couldn't put it down. I'm not
joking. I read all night and into the morning, finally going to
sleep when I had finished the book. I'm not going to tell you
the story, just in case this inspires you to read it, but suffice

to say, particularly if you have children, which I didn't at the time, you won't be able to rest until you know the outcome.

I love reading and always have done, even as a child. Don't laugh, but my mum once found me in the small space between the settee and the wall in our lounge reading . . . wait for it . . . *The Complete Works of Shakespeare*. I was nine or ten years old at the time.

I didn't only read high-brow literature though; I was a huge fan of Enid Blyton, particularly her Famous Five series. I was so hooked, I even wrote to her asking where Kirrin Island was so that I could go and visit it. I had a lovely letter back telling me that there wasn't a real place called Kirrin Island, but that it was inspired by an island off the Dorset coast. I've often wondered where. I was also sent a badge of some description. I think maybe I had inadvertently joined the Famous Five fan club. Although I loved all the main characters, including Timmy the dog, I had a fascination with a gypsy girl called Jo who appeared in a few of the books. Maybe that harks back to my ancestry, but that's a story for another day!

Do you remember the 'mickey take' series that Dawn French and co. did? I was determined not to like it. How dare they poke fun at my childhood heroes! Of course, it was brilliant, as is most stuff Dawn French does. She even had a 'pop' at QVC in the early days with the 'Emeraldique' necklace. What is the saying? Imitation is the sincerest form of flattery, which in itself is funny when talking about imitation gemstones!

There is still a lot of diversity in my reading material, although I'm sorry to admit it's all popular authors rather than the classics. I don't have a lot of time to read but when I am away on holiday I can get through a couple of books a week. I usually choose something intense like John Grisham, and something lightweight like Adele Parks.

I do remember one holiday lying on the beach in floods of tears – I was reading an Anita Shreve, which Chris has now banned for holiday reading!

Thirty Six

I do thirty-six minutes on my treadmill in one session,
and if you are thinking it is a bit of a random number,
why not do thirty-five or forty, there is a reason.

It equates to 3.5 kilometres and burning 280 calories, although the latter is only a generalisation, of course. You may also be thinking that 3.5 kilometres is not very far to travel in a thirty-six-minute session but that is only walking, I don't run. Actually, I should correct that statement to say that I can't run for any prolonged length of time, like running on a treadmill or going out for a jog.

It all stems back to the imbalance created by my polio. The muscles on the left side of my body from the waist down were quite badly wasted while I was so sick and so my left leg is shorter and weaker than my right. When I stopped wearing the leg iron, I had to have special boots which were built up on the left side to balance my hips and shoulders, which I told you about in *chapter 14*. Gradually the amount of the rise was decreased until I just started wearing regular shoes, but there is still a slight difference in the length of my legs.

When I try to run I have further to fall on the left side and also less support from the muscles, which makes it very uncomfortable for my back. Rather than risk injury I stick to walking, but it is still very effective.

I first started my treadmill sessions after watching a video of myself walking along the beach on a family holiday. I had really been enjoying recounting all the fun we had in the Bahamas, but when that sequence came on my delight turned to shock. I had thought I was able to hide my imbalance quite effectively but in the video I was walking with a very pronounced limp.

Never one to accept that things can't be improved upon, I decided to buy a treadmill and train myself to walk better. The reason I decided to invest in a treadmill rather than just going out for walks, although I now love to do that too, was that it is a totally even surface so I could pay attention to keeping my hips and shoulders as level as possible by watching myself in a mirror. At first it was a real strain but, as I have never found the action of walking as natural as most people do, I concentrated even harder until I had retrained my body to be more in alignment.

Like my exercise session in the pool that I outline in *chapter 39*, I have a routine that I more or less stick to, although I did increase my minutes from thirty to thirty-six at the beginning of the year. I hope I won't need to do that every year or eventually I'll never be off the thing!

I had to buy a new treadmill last year as the old one, which we had had for about ten years, survived our house move but didn't survive Daniel running on it. Well, let's face it, the poor thing must have got the shock of its life, someone actually running on it! The old machine was very straightforward but this new one is a bit more 'gadgety'. It's taken a while but I have just about mastered it.

The first 400 metres is a warm-up, gradually picking up the pace, and then after that I vary height and speed, staying in the fat-burning or aerobic zone, with an occasional dip into endurance. The last 400 metres I am gradually slowing down. I also wear wrist weights to help tone my arms while walking, but nothing too heavy; they are only 1lb each, as I just want shape, not bulk.

It is surprising how much a brisk walk can make you sweat!

Thirty Seven

This is the number of letters in my favourite quote
from German philosopher Friedrich Nietzsche:
'Das, was uns nicht umbringt macht uns stärker.'

As you will know from reading *chapter 8*, my German is not
brilliant. Fortunately, courtesy of translations down the years,
I can offer it to you in English, which, coincidentally, also has
thirty-seven letters:

'That which does not kill us makes us stronger.'

I believe this quote with every fibre of my being. When the dark
and desperate times strike, if you survive it, you emerge having
learnt another of life's lessons. In other words: 'If I can deal with
that I can deal with anything.'

The quote itself is often misquoted. In fact, it wasn't until
I started researching this book that I realised that my Hotmail
profile message, 'that which does not kill you makes you
stronger', was incorrect, although it amounts to the same
message.

I'm not the only one to misquote it, although it's not always
unintentional, as a form of it has been used by many lyricists in
songs. The most recent of these is the Kelly Clarkson song
'Stronger', which has been a bit of an anthem for me since it
was released.

Friedrich Nietzsche has a whole list of brilliant quotes attributed to him, and if you have access to the internet you should check them out.

My second favourite quote of his is: 'Become who you are.'

Thirty Eight

There are thirty-eight league games in a
Premiership football season.

Unfortunately my team, Crystal Palace, have not been in the Premiership since 2005. I have nothing else to say on this subject at this time except:

COME ON YOU EAGLES!!!!!!!!!!!!!!

Thirty Nine

It takes me approximately thirty-nine minutes to swim
one hundred lengths of my pool, although it does
fluctuate depending on how energetic I am feeling.

It is also not quite as impressive as it sounds because, as I
mentioned in the introduction to this book, my pool is only
twelve metres long, so a length comprises between eight and
eleven strokes.

I have a routine, which I keep basically the same as it seems
to work quite well. I start off with a sort of warm-up of twenty
lengths' breast stroke, then for the next ten lengths I swim one
length back stroke and one length breast stroke at a fairly relaxed
pace. Then the hard work starts!

I stay with one length backstroke and one length breast stroke
for the next sixty lengths but every third length is a power length,
i.e., I swim as fast as I can. I do sometimes vary this to do two
power lengths one after the other and then two more relaxed
lengths, but that is usually when I am doing a shorter swim of
sixty or seventy lengths.

The final ten lengths are sort of cooling down. I do eight
lengths on my front holding a noodle out in front of me doing
front crawl legs. When I say noodle, I am not talking about the
edible variety as that wouldn't give me much buoyancy; I mean
the long tubular floats. The next length is breast stroke, arms
only without any movement in the legs, and the final length is

'Hugging a tree' in Barbados, long before I was a vegetarian. This was taken on my first trip to Barbados when I was a dancer on the *SS Doric* in 1976.

Outside the flat in Upper Norwood in 1978. It was my first Christmas with Chris and not only did I make the cake, I also crocheted the hat.

Me and fellow dancer Karen at the Stork Room in London's West End in 1979. I was also working in pantomime at the same time with . . .

Barbara Windsor
and Norman
Vaughan.

The view over Hong Kong from Victoria Peak in May 1979. As you can see, my hair went crazy in the humidity.

Chris and me on board the *SS Canberra* when he was doing a month-long gig as a musician. I was sea sick in the Bay of Biscay, even though I'd spent six months on a cruise ship previously.

JOOLS & THE FOOLS

Jools and the Fools, the band I fronted in 1983. The legs on my left belong to Chris, and those on my right to bass guitarist Paul.

Me with Leslie Crowther in the bar at Central Studios when we were filming *The Price is Right* together.

With my friend Tricia in my first house on Ross Road. Tricia is holding Dylan and I have Charlie.

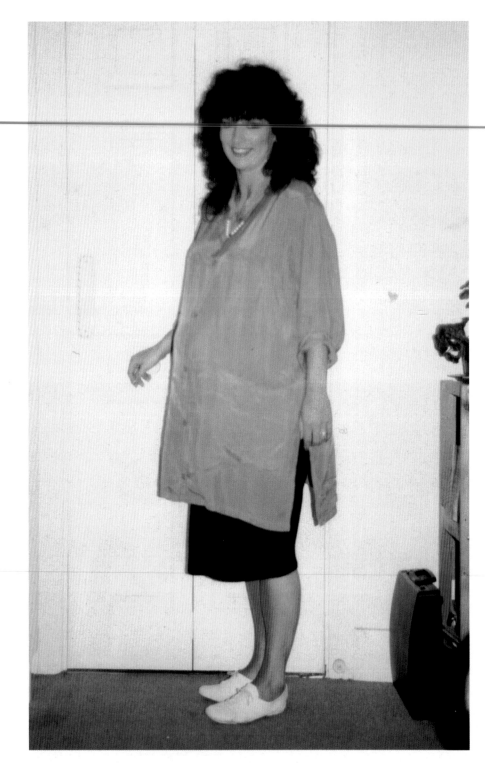

This was taken two weeks before I gave birth to Daniel. I'm standing ¾ profile so I don't look that big but I was huge!

on my back doing breast stroke legs and wafting my arms around a bit. And that's it: one hundred lengths of the pool.

You can probably now see why I need to have things associated with each length as it is easy to lose count, but also quite boring, even though when I am doing backstroke I am usually fortunate enough to be staring up at a glorious blue sky!

I just read this chapter back and couldn't help but notice the number of times I wrote length or lengths . . . TWENTY!

Well actually twenty-two now that I added those last two lengths . . . now it's twenty-three – I think I had better stop there!

Forty

This was the number of lucky dip prizes I had in the
box at the Pink Party I organised in the
summer of 2011.

I had intended to have a birthday party in June but I was a little late organising it, so as I had promised two of my work colleagues a party, I decided to have a Pink Party to raise money for Breast Cancer Care and Macmillan Nurses.

Breast Cancer Care is QVC's main charity and every October they dedicate three hours of airtime to raising money with the support of many of the brands who supply products for nothing, and of course the viewers, who actually buy the products. It's a really good concept and they have raised millions of pounds since they started the event.

Needless to say my little 'do' was not on this scale but I did want to support the charities as both my mum and my sister have had breast cancer and earlier in the year one of my friends at QVC had been diagnosed with this awful disease, not to mention one of our lovely models.

So the theme for the evening was **PINK!**

Everyone had to wear something pink, we had pink cava, rosé wine and pink soft drinks, pink cupcakes and wafers and sweeties, like 'Percy Pigs' and 'pink shrimps', and I made Eton Mess, which had a slight pinky tinge due to the strawberries and the 'drop' of port! I drew the line at pink sandwich fillings, although

I did make a pink cream cheese dip, coloured pink with tomato ketchup . . . sounds vile but it was actually really nice! I had pink balloons everywhere, pink flowers and even a pink Yankee candle burning, giving off the aroma of fresh-cut roses.

As well as the pink theme, I also wanted to have a kind of children's party feeling with games like 'pin the tail on the donkey' and 'pass the parcel'! Can you imagine trying to get a bunch of adults out into the garden to throw a parcel around? To their credit all the guests joined in bar two . . . I know who you are!

I had spent the previous couple of weeks looking for inexpensive 'pass the parcel' and 'lucky dip' prizes with a pink theme. I bought pink pens, notebooks, drink bottles, bars of chocolate, cuddly toys and even a pink memory stick. I constructed the 'pass the parcel' with little prizes in some of the layers, and wrapped all the 'lucky dip' prizes in pink tissue paper. The latter were then put into a pink-paper-covered cardboard box along with a load of polystyrene S's which were just about the only non-pink thing on the night. Everyone was happy to pay £2 to have a dip – some were luckier than others but I guess the clue is in the name.

We also had a tombola stall with some lovely prizes and, of course, the raffle, which raised the majority of the money.

Some of our lovely QVC guests had donated prizes for the raffle, notably a gorgeous Butler & Wilson crystal heart necklace and a really adorable Charlie Bear, but the main hook was the offer of a four-night stay at my villa in Spain.

Just before we started the draw I did a little speech to thank everyone for coming and also for their generosity in taking part in all the little fundraisers.

I also introduced my landlord to the gathering saying, 'So have fun but don't trash the house!'

I had invited my landlord to the party as a thank you for

giving me permission to hold it, and because he was a really nice chap. In return he bought plenty of raffle tickets for his friends and family.

Daniel, my son, was in charge of drawing the tickets out of the bag for the ten prizes that were up for grabs. The first pick, for the tenth prize, went to a fellow presenter from QVC. Next pick went to my landlord. Next pick went to my landlord! He was embarrassed so asked for it to be drawn again. Kind of him, and that prize went to a work colleague. Next pick went to my landlord! This time I said he had to keep the prize. Next pick, a work colleague and next pick . . . you guessed it, my landlord again!

What happened next was very funny. One of the guys to whom I had promised a party cried out, 'Trash the house!'

There was a momentary pause before everyone burst out laughing, including – thankfully – my landlord.

Would you believe that out of the ten prizes on offer he won five either personally or with the tickets he had bought for friends, and that didn't include the prize he put back!

He didn't win the 'Star Prize' though; that went to a girl at work who hadn't had a holiday since she had been made redundant two years previously. Although disappointed for themselves, I think everyone was really pleased it had gone to someone who really needed a bit of luck. As for my landlord, I think he was just regretting not having done the lottery that night!

After the raffle we started on the karaoke. I had intended to present a pink toilet roll to the worst singer of the night but we were all having so much fun delivering terrible renditions of pop and rock songs, including of course 'So What' by Pink, performed very badly by yours truly, that I simply forgot.

I also forgot to get everyone involved in a game of 'pin the tail on the donkey', which was a real shame for my friend Denise's boyfriend Steve. He had spent half of his evening working out a technique so that he could position the donkey's tail perfectly whilst blindfolded . . . oops!

We wound things up around midnight and one of my lasting images will always be of my mate Dickie exiting the premises with a full bottle of wine in the back pocket of his jeans, which were already slung very low, revealing his pink underpants! Fortunately it wasn't the one that my partner Chris had tried to open earlier in the evening using a corkscrew, despite the fact that it was a screw-top bottle, much to the amusement of the aforementioned Dickie.

We raised over £1100 and a good time was had by all . . . at least that's what they told me!

Forty One

This is the number of countries I have been fortunate
to visit, either through work or on holiday.

I love travelling and there are so many more places I would like
to visit, the prime one being India, where my Dad grew up.

I figured alphabetical order is the best way of recounting them
to you:

1. **Antigua** in the Caribbean, when I was working on the cruise
ship the SS *Doric*. It is famed for having a different beach for
every day of the year – my type of island!

2. **Aruba.** Also visited while I was on the SS *Doric*. It is one of
the Netherland Antilles islands in the Caribbean and famous for
its divi-divi trees.

3. **Austria** with my parents when I was fifteen, which I will tell
you more about in *chapter 71*.

4. **Bahamas.** I've been to Paradise Island three times. The first was
as a port of call when I was on the cruise ship in 1976. It was
very different then, with just a few hotels, and was totally unspoilt.
That was before they opened the road bridge from Providence
Island to Paradise Island so we had to catch a small ferry and then

walk through the woods to get to the best beaches. It was years before Atlantis was even a twinkle in the developer's eye.

Both of the other occasions I visited, I stayed at Atlantis. The first time was for work when we broadcast a series of live shows back to the UK for QVC, and the second was as a result of the first, both of which you will read more about in *chapter 84*.

5. Barbados. Again I've been three times. The first time was on the cruise ship when I was lucky enough to visit the original Sandy Lane Hotel before they pulled it down and rebuilt it.

The second was a family holiday in 2002 when we stayed at the Almond Beach Club, just along the beach from Sandy Lane. We had actually been booked into the Almond Beach Village, which was further up the west coast of Barbados, but when we arrived there after our very long flight from the UK, we were told there was no accommodation available. After an hour in the manager's office we agreed to stay at the Almond Beach Club, despite the fact that it was supposed to be over-eighteens only and Daniel and Sophie were both under eighteen at the time. It was actually much better for us as there were no young children running around and we were given a bottle of champagne as an apology.

The third time was in 2008 when Chris and I went on our own to celebrate our thirtieth anniversary of being together, which I went into more detail about in *chapter 30*.

6. Belgium. I went there to rehearse for a job on a Greek cruise ship. Unfortunately I fell on the stairs of the apartment building we were staying in and injured my leg, so I wasn't able to go on the ship.

7. Bermuda was a port of call on the SS *Doric* and somewhere I would love to revisit on holiday one day.

8. Canada. I went there on an unexpected trip in 2011, which was part business and part pleasure. I finally got to see Niagara Falls which was on my 'to do before I die' list. Absolutely breath-taking. We also visited a winery where they explained how they make 'ice wine'. It has to do with picking the grapes while they are frozen, and produces a very sweet wine, which was not to my taste. Whilst we were looking around the gift shop a lady came up to me and said, 'You're a long way from home.'

She was a QVC viewer who was on holiday from her home in Scotland, as I discovered whilst we had our photo taken together.

9. China. We crossed into China on three occasions when we went on a buying trip to Hong Kong with QVC in 2005.

10. Curaçao. Another of the Netherland Antilles islands visited courtesy of the SS *Doric*.

11. Dominican Republic, also on the SS *Doric*. Sadly we didn't visit any of the beach resorts, only the capital, Santo Domingo.

12. Dubai in transit on the way to and from the Maldives the second time we went.

13. Eire. I have been on two separate occasions, both to film television commercials for Irish lager. You will read more about the second trip in *chapter 86*.

14. France – several times. The first time was when I travelled through by train en route to rehearsals in Rapallo, Italy, for the cruise ship that has had so many mentions in this chapter.

The second was also in transit, driving to Barcelona for my job at the Teatro Apollo, which I told you about in *chapter 20*.

The third time was for a modelling job in Paris. It sounds glamorous but wasn't, as we travelled by minibus and it was the depths of winter, although I'm not complaining as I was able to go up the Eiffel Tower.

And I have holidayed twice at the French retreat of my friend and fellow QVC presenter Julian Ballantyne, near Carcassone. The first time was as a family and one of the highlights was watching an amazing thunderstorm over the nearby Pyrenees mountain range. The second time I took Daniel and Sophie, who each took a friend. Steve was one of Daniel's friends from his football club and Sophie took her best friend from school, Becca. Sophie had lost touch with Becca until Christmas 2011, much to my dismay, as she is a lovely girl. Coincidentally the QVC Christmas party and the party of the recruiting company, where Becca works, were both held at the same venue, and although they didn't see each other on the night it prompted them to get back in touch. Sophie now works with Becca in recruiting, and we enjoyed a couple of days' holiday together at my house in Spain last summer just prior to selling it. Steve wasn't with us but we did play the card game Cheat in his honour!

15. Germany. The first time was with my parents when we flew into Munich airport before travelling to our holiday destination in Austria.

I have also shot a television commercial in Düsseldorf and filmed at the Munich Oktoberfest for QVC on two occasions. My favourite piece of footage was at the end of the piece where I was sat with a group of Bayern Munich football fans. The Bayern Munich kit that season was almost identical to that of my team, Crystal Palace, whose nickname is the 'Eagles'. I managed to persuade the fans to raise their beer glasses in a toast and say, 'Eagles!'

I don't think they knew what they were doing, but it made my day.

16. Gibraltar – that was a day trip when we were holidaying in Puerto Banus, Spain, and it was the day we discovered that Daniel really doesn't like heights. We were driving up the rock of Gibraltar to see the notorious apes. When we reached the viewing point he refused to get out of the car. He has since amazed us by climbing the Montgo mountain in Javea at a height of over 750 metres. I know that's not exactly Mount Everest but to someone who doesn't like heights I'm sure it felt like it! That is what you call facing your fears head on.

17. Greece, well Skiathos actually, when we holidayed there with the children in 1997. It's the only time I have taken the children out of school for a holiday, but we hadn't been able to go anywhere during the summer break as Sophie had broken her arm, so we went in early October instead. We did do a bit of learning there – counting from one to ten in Greek, which I mentioned in *chapter 8*.

I always remember waiting at the airport for the flight home. Skiathos is renowned for having a fairly short runway, so the pilot has to gauge the approach perfectly. The plane that we were going to be travelling back to the UK on was coming in to land but at the last minute pulled out of the landing and circled before coming in for a second attempt. The passengers were slightly unnerved by this but what happened next certainly put us all at our ease. As we were climbing the aircraft steps onto the plane, we glanced up at the cockpit. The pilot had propped up a book for everyone to see on which he had mocked up the title, 'How to Fly a Plane' – very amusing.

18. Grenada – once again a Caribbean port of call on the SS *Doric*. It is sometimes referred to as 'Spice Island', and it was there that I discovered what real nutmeg looks like, rather than the ready-grated variety that I used to sprinkle on the top of home-made egg custard.

19. Haiti – the cruise ship again.

20. Hong Kong. I've been twice and love it. The first time was as a singer/dancer in 1979 and the second was on a trip with our QVC buyers. There is a little about both trips in *chapters 15* and *95.*

21. Ibiza. We booked a 'cheapy' last-minute family holiday one October half-term as the weather in the UK had been terrible.

22. Italy. The first time was to Rapallo for the rehearsals for the cruise ship, when I also visited Genoa and Milan.

The second was a brief port of call at Naples when I was on the SS *Canberra* with Chris, when he was working.

The third was to film in Marostica, near Verona, for QVC, and on that visit we also managed a trip to Venice, which I would love to revisit.

I have also presented live-broadcast *Vicenza Gold* shows for QVC twice, once with Dale Franklin and once with Alison Keenan, and I have been out to the area on two other occasions to visit the Vicenza Jewellery Fair.

23. Lanzarote. This was our first family holiday abroad when the children were five and six. We stayed in a resort called Playa Blanca.

24. Majorca. I've been twice. The first time I took the children away for a week's holiday to give their dad a break from them.

The second time Chris and I stayed in a place called Ratjada, in the north-east of the island, near where my childhood friend from dancing school now lives with her Spanish husband. Chris and I were celebrating twenty-five years of being 'an item'!

25. Maldives. Again I've been twice, both times on family holidays, which you can read about in *chapter 85.*

26. Malta. Twice again!! The first time as a port of call on the SS *Canberra* cruise. The second time was another holiday for just the children and I. We didn't hire a car on that holiday, as I had been advised against it, so we travelled everywhere by bus. They were old UK buses, which were charming if a little bumpy. It was on that holiday that the children were taught to dive by an elderly gentleman that we nicknamed 'The Major', as he bore a striking resemblance to the character from the TV series *Fawlty Towers.*

27. Martinique. A French island in the Caribbean, which was another port of call for the SS *Doric.*

28. Menorca. Back to twice! Both were family holidays. The first time we stayed in a resort called Cala'n Bosch in a small self-catering complex owned by a relative of one of the original QVC Presenters, Suzanne Evert.

The second time we stayed in a hotel in Cala'n Porter, recommended to us by QVC fans Dorothy and Jim, who lived close by. We spent some time with them, and I was very sad to learn a few years later that Dorothy had passed away. Jim still sends us Christmas cards though.

29. Philippines. My friend Tricia and I tagged a few days' holiday in the Philippines on to the end of our dancing job in Hong Kong, as we had no idea if we would ever visit that part of the globe again. We enjoyed it, but both of us were quite shocked by the poverty outside of the resort hotels.

30. Portugal. Three or four times, depending whether you count landing in Faro before driving over the border into southern Spain for a holiday.

The first time was as a stop on the SS *Canberra*. The ship moored in Lisbon but, rather than exploring the culture of the capital city, Chris and I decided to get the train up the coast to the resort town of Estoril. I really am a beach bum!

The first time we stayed on holiday it was in a dreadful apartment in the heart of Albufeira, opposite a nightclub that didn't close until 5 or 6 a.m. – not ideal when you have two small children. Both the children were ill that holiday – I think the sanitation in the apartment block left a lot to be desired!

The second time was totally different as we stayed in a luxury apartment on a golf complex in Quinta de Lago. We nearly didn't get there though, as British Airways **had** overbooked the plane so we were told only two of us **could fly**. When it was explained that the other two would be put on the next flight a couple of hours later, and that we would get £250 compensation for the inconvenience, we reluctantly agreed to travel separately. Daniel and I had to rush through Gatwick airport dragging our case behind us in order to make it on to the flight.

You know the look we all give people when they are the last on board and have delayed take-off? Well, that day we were on the receiving end of those looks, even though it wasn't our fault!

31. Sardinia. This was a family holiday, and here's a tip. Don't go to Sardinia in August. Firstly it is very, very hot, and our 'family-run' hotel only had air conditioning in the restaurant. Fortunately we had taken two portable fans, so we had one for each bedroom. Every night, after their bath, Chris would wet the children's towels with ice-cold water and lay the towels over them to cool them down. It was a lovely little hotel, but could definitely have been improved with air con.

August is also the month when Italians take their summer holiday and it seemed as though they had all descended on Sardinia! One beach, Costa Smeralda, that we drove for an hour and a half to visit as it had been recommended by someone Chris was talking to on the plane, actually didn't have a square inch to sit down on . . . I'm not exaggerating! We had to lay our towels out on the rocks and even then we could only sit rather than lie down! We had wanted to see it as apparently the sea was bright green. We were not disappointed in that, just the lack of space to enjoy it. Even the town beach in Alghero, where our hotel was, was packed to the rafters. One day we got to the beach early and spread out our towels to sit down. An hour or so later two people arrived and sat down almost on top of us. I thought it was rather odd that they had sat so close to us until the extended family began to arrive. There were about twenty of them in total and they were virtually sitting on our towels. Lovely place, but if we ever went back I would avoid August!

32. Singapore. I only had an overnight stop there, again on the tail end of the Hong Kong dancing job, but we did enjoy after-noon tea at the famous Raffles Hotel. I also had my palm read there and apparently I was going to own seven houses and have four children . . . or was that seven children and four houses, one of which was going to be in Australia? Either way, it was inac-curate on both counts!

33. Spain – It is impossible to remember all the times I have been to Spain since we bought the house in Javea.

My first trip was the dancing job in Barcelona that I told you about in *chapter 20*. During that six-month stay I also visited

Zaragoza and a small town called Manresa, as well as the coastal resorts of Sitges, Tossa de Mar and Castelldefels.

Chris and I had a port of call in Vigo in the north-west of Spain when we were on the SS *Canberra*.

I had a three-day break on my own at the Four Seasons Hotel near Marbella.

We had a family holiday in Puerto Banus one October half-term. It was beautiful weather the day we arrived, and we were staying in a lovely little town house on a golf course. It started to rain the next morning and continued for much of the rest of our stay. The highlight of that trip was walking out along the breakwater and admiring all the luxury yachts in the harbour. There were so many stray cats that we rechristened it the 'cat walk'.

I also took the children on holiday to Spain twice on my own. The first time was to a hotel called the Aloha Gardens. It had a huge swimming pool that the children took full advantage of and we also played tennis quite a bit. It was a challenge with just the three of us, as Sophie always had to play with either Daniel or me – she wasn't accomplished enough to play on her own. That meant that the person playing alone was always at a disadvantage, so if that person was Daniel I used to let him win, although I'm sure he would dispute that!

The second time I took them to Spain on holiday they were a bit older, and we had a great time. We actually flew into Faro in Portugal and then crossed over into Spain on a coach transfer, which took around forty-five minutes.

We were staying on the Isla Canela, which was a very flat and quite marshy area in the far south of Spain. We had called at several hotels, dropping people off, before arriving at our hotel. As we pulled up outside, there was a gathering of people that looked like journalists, and a film crew. For a moment I did wonder if word had got out that 'Julia Roberts' was booked into the hotel, and that they had thought it was the Hollywood actress!

As we signed in I asked the receptionist who the welcoming party was for, and she said the Spanish under-19 football team were staying at the hotel as a training camp base in preparation for the European tournament in Norway. Daniel couldn't believe it when I told him, and was even more thrilled when it transpired that their goalie was staying in the room next to ours!

We didn't see a lot of them as they were training every day, but we did share the lift with them a few times. One of their star players was a local lad named José Antonio Reyes, who at the time played for Seville. Any Arsenal fans will recognise the name, as the following season he signed for the Gunners. Daniel really wanted his autograph but was too shy to ask. Sophie didn't share his timidity and for months afterwards had his signature pinned up on her wall, even though she had no idea who he was!

Also in the Spanish under-19 side at the time were Chelsea and former Liverpool striker Fernando Torres, and Barcelona midfielder Andrés Iniesta.

The team were allowed to come down to the hotel swimming pool after their morning training session and prior to lunch, presumably to cool off as it must have been very hot for them training in the sweltering heat of the Spanish summer. On one of these occasions a young girl of about eight or nine was bothering Torres while he sat poolside by repeatedly hitting him with her snorkelling mask. He was probably very tempted to whack her back, but, to his credit, after tolerating it for a while he jumped in the pool to escape.

After their lunch all the players were supposed to have a rest period in their rooms. I say 'supposed to' have a rest period, as the goalkeeper in the room next to ours had no rest at all. He spent the entire time on his mobile phone, which we could clearly hear from the shade of our balcony as we ate our picnic lunch each day. Fortunately for him none of us was very fluent in Spanish!

They had another training session in the early evening before trooping into a roped-off section of the dining room for dinner. The excitement of having the footballers around really made the children's holiday, especially as they went on to win the European tournament they were training for.

It was only a couple of years after that holiday that Chris and I began our search for a Spanish property that I told you about in *chapter 26.*

34. St Kitts, in the Caribbean, another stop on the cruise ship SS *Doric.* Back in 1976 it was very undeveloped, and maybe it has stayed that way, as it has black sands rather than the golden variety enjoyed by many of its more commercialised neighbours.

35. St Lucia. Again a port of call on one of the Caribbean cruises on the SS *Doric.*

36. St Maarten. And yet another Caribbean stop-off. I tried water skiing for the second time, having failed miserably to master the art whilst I was working in Jersey. I failed miserably again, and haven't tried since!

37. St Thomas. An American Caribbean island that was a regular stop-off on most of our two-week cruises on the SS *Doric.*

38. Trinidad. Just the once as a port of call, and sadly it didn't coincide with carnival time!

39. Tunisia. This was a family holiday in Skanes, although for some reason we had been booked onto flights arriving in Tunis, the capital, several hours' drive away. The most memorable thing about that holiday was a local trying to swap his headgear for

Daniel's baseball cap, and Sophie nearly being carried off by the horse she was riding on the beach.

40. United States. I have visited America lots of times, most often for work through QVC, as it is an American company.

The first time I went was back in 1975 when we joined ship in New York for our season of cruising on the SS *Doric*. That was in the November, and in the January of 1976 our base changed to Port Everglades in Fort Lauderdale, Florida, to avoid the choppy Atlantic waters in the winter months.

I didn't return to the States for eighteen years until I visited the QVC America studios in Westchester, Philadelphia. That was the trip where we also managed to squeeze in a visit to the gambling metropolis that is Atlantic City.

A couple of years later I revisited Westchester, and also spent a few days in the Black Hills of South Dakota, learning about a range of jewellery QVC were selling at the time.

We had a family holiday in Florida in the year 2000 which was perfect timing, as the children were thirteen and twelve at the time so old enough to enjoy all that the theme parks had to offer. It was a two-week 'vacation', and the second week was spent on the Gulf Coast island of Captiva, which we all thoroughly enjoyed.

I also had the good fortune to spend a few days in Tucson, Arizona, to visit a gem fair and present a live-broadcast three-hour show for QVC.

And then there is Los Angeles. I have visited the city twice. The first time was ten years ago and I had flown out with the beauty expert from QVC, Alison Young, to host a couple of live shows.

The second visit to LA was in February 2011 and I was there in the week running up to the Oscars to report on the celebrity preparations for the red carpet event. It culminated in the QVC

Red Carpet Party where I had access to interview the likes of the Kardashians, Helena Bonham Carter, Donald Trump and of course former QVC favourite Joan Rivers. I also interviewed actress Melissa Leo, who went on to win Best Supporting Actress for her role in *The Fighter*. She looked very different from her role in the film when she was on the red carpet, I can tell you! I also got a little star struck at coming within touching distance of eventual Oscar winner Colin Firth in the foyer of the Beverly Hills Four Seasons hotel.

41. Venezuela. We visited Caracas, the capital, once as a port of call on the good ship SS *Doric*.

So there you have it. I have been very fortunate to visit so many places for work, and hopefully there will be plenty more.

As for holidays, when I retire I fully intend to take a world cruise and really rack the numbers up!

Forty Two

I have forty-two grammes of granola for breakfast
most mornings in the summer, and yes, I do weigh it
every single day.

The reason for this is simple. As I explained in *chapter 28*, the last diet I went on is the last diet I ever want to go on, so I keep an eye on the quantity of food I am eating.

Being a vegetarian I have a generally healthy diet with lots of fruit and vegetables and as long as I restrict myself to no more than two slices of bread a day I don't have to worry too much about what I eat, just how much of it I eat.

When I first came off Diet Chef I did a little test. I put what I thought was a reasonable amount of granola into a breakfast bowl, then I weighed it. I was horrified to discover that there was nearly double the amount of cereal in my bowl than you get in the Diet Chef sachets. I was occasionally a little peckish by mid-morning when I was on Diet Chef, so I adjusted it to a level that would see me through to lunch without a snack, and that amount for me is forty-two grammes.

By starting my day as I mean to go on I have been able to eat enough to satisfy my hunger but not too much to make me put on weight. If you are trying to drop a few pounds this little tip may help you too.

Forty Three

Forty-three is the number of pounds I put on during
my second pregnancy, which is just over three stone.

I think it was partly due to my body having had only four
months to recover after the birth of my first baby, but it was
also due in part to the food cravings I had.

With Daniel I had loved anything bitter and acidy, like Granny
Smith apples, tomatoes and vinegar. With Sophie I just wanted
to eat sweet sugary stuff, things that I would not normally eat,
so no wonder I piled on the weight.

Sophie was not a planned pregnancy. I hadn't really restarted
my menstrual cycle after Daniel was born, and I was still breast-
feeding him, so I considered that I was relatively safe
– WRONG!

Whilst doing some heavy-duty gardening, carrying bricks to
build a garden wall to be precise, I started to bleed, and presumed
it must be my period. When the bleeding stopped that evening
and didn't restart, I had a feeling that I was pregnant again, which
a pregnancy test confirmed.

I had had such an easy time with Daniel, apart from the
heartburn, that I just carried on as normal, which meant teaching
ten fitness classes a week. During one of my classes, I suddenly
got terrible stomach cramps, and after visiting the loo was
convinced that I had had a miscarriage. Fortunately for me, Dr

Marion, an obstetrician, was in the class, and she advised me to go straight home to bed, and call the doctor the next morning, which I did.

The doctor duly arrived, and on hearing the amount of blood I had lost, and after examining me, also thought that I had suffered a miscarriage. However, just to be sure, she wanted to do a pregnancy test, and the results revealed I was still pregnant.

To this day, I don't know for certain if I had been carrying twins and miscarried one, which apparently is more common than you might imagine. I am just so thankful that Sophie survived. Funny thing is, she is a natural left-hander, and I once watched a TV programme which suggested that all natural left-handers were originally a twin pregnancy.

I did continue teaching the fitness classes but I didn't get so actively involved until I had passed twenty-four weeks, and she would have been viable. Again I taught up to thirty-eight weeks with Sophie, but it was more of a struggle, as I had put on so much weight.

She was due three days after Christmas, but Christmas came and went, as did New Year, and still no sign. Then one day I was out shopping, and the contractions started very gently. I nipped into the bank, and the cashier said, 'Haven't you had that baby yet?'

'No,' I replied, 'but I'm in labour right now.'

That drew some anxious glances from the other customers in the bank.

I had planned to have Sophie at home with my midwife present but unfortunately, when Chris rang to tell her I was in labour, she said she would be unable to deliver me at home as she had the flu.

The contractions continued for the rest of the day and evening and by 2 a.m. they had started to get stronger so we headed for the hospital. I was examined on arrival and the midwife said I had a long way to go, so hooked me up to a machine to measure my contractions. When she came back to check on me she told me I was not in labour, and to go home. Having had a baby just thirteen months previously, I knew what contractions felt like and insisted that I was most definitely in labour.

At eight in the morning they decided to move me from the delivery room onto a ward and told Chris to go home. I had just arrived on the ward and Chris was about to leave, when I was sick. Mild panic ensued. They examined me again and I was eight centimetres dilated, which apparently meant I was fairly imminent. They wheeled me back to the delivery room and began the preparations for Sophie's arrival.

There was a trainee midwife, Isabel, attending to me at this point and she was lovely but, with me just about to give birth, the hatchet-faced senior midwife told Isabel to go and have her coffee break. My pleading for her to stay made no difference, even though Isabel wanted to stay.

Sophie was born while Isabel was on her coffee break, but she had been so kind to me when everyone else was not, that I gave Sophie the middle name of Isabel. She weighed in at a fairly hefty 9lbs 5oz, beating her brother's weight by 4oz, which I'm sure she is delighted by as they have always had a healthy rivalry in all sorts of different areas.

The senior midwife had ruined the whole experience for me, so much so that, initially, I did not want to hold Sophie. Fortunately her dad was on hand to hold her and encourage me to do the same.

We were deposited in a ward and Chris went home to share the good news and get a little bit of sleep. I tried to do the same but Sophie was crying a lot, and every time I fed her she was sick. Eventually they took her away to have her stomach pumped as they thought she must have swallowed some meconium during the birth. She was a little better after that and managed to keep her milk down, although she was still crying a lot, probably due to the rather unpleasant experience she had just been through. Fortunately she soon put on enough weight to allow us both to go home to a welcome party of my mum and dad and her big brother Daniel.

As I mentioned in *chapter 27*, Daniel was a really good baby, but unfortunately history didn't repeat itself, although Sophie had nothing on my brother who, as I mentioned in *chapter 14*, was still disturbing my parents' sleep after I was born, twenty-one months his junior!

She was quite a happy baby during the day but at night-time she really didn't want to sleep. Some things never change as she is still a bit of a night owl! The six-week point, which is when her brother started to sleep through, came and went, but by twelve weeks we had the breakthrough and she started to go from about 10 p.m. to 6 a.m.

Unfortunately, when she started teething, the broken nights started all over again. I had read somewhere about checking to make sure everything looked all right and then simply leaving them to cry. It may seem cruel, but apparently if there is nothing really wrong apart from wanting a bit of attention, they soon go back to sleep and eventually stop waking up. The problem was, I couldn't go back to sleep if I could hear her crying, and I was also concerned that she would set her brother off, so I would keep getting up to her.

After about a week or so of her waking with no real issue, we took the decision to move her cot downstairs to the dining room where she wouldn't disturb people if she cried. It still woke me. I was probably listening out for her, just as you do when your children are older and come in late from a night out, but once I had checked to see all was OK, I could then get off to sleep even if she was still crying.

It did the trick within a week and she didn't seem to suffer any ill effects.

Even with two very young children to run round after, I was finding it very difficult to shift the forty-three pounds I had put on during the pregnancy.

Fortunately the Weight Watchers commercial, which you will read about in *chapter 88*, came along at just the right time!

Forty Four

This was the row I sat on in the aeroplane back from
New York after I had finished my six-month job as a
dancer cruising around the Caribbean on the *SS Doric*,
which you will read about in *chapter 75*.

You are probably wondering how I remember the seat row
with such clarity. Well, I used to keep a diary from 1974
through to 1981, and as well as writing in it every day, I also
used to stick interesting objects into it. There are cards that came
with flowers, the odd photo, receipts, even a feather from a feather
boa and my boarding pass from the flight back to the UK from
New York.

The date was the 27th of March 1976 and I was in seat 9,
row 44, and guess what? I was in a smoking zone! Not that I
smoked, I've never really smoked apart from the occasional one
to see what it was like, it's just that I had forgotten they used
to allow smoking on planes.

How times have changed, haven't they, when you consider you
can't smoke indoors in a public place at all now! Personally it's
OK with me as I have a very highly developed sense of smell
and I used to hate going into pubs and restaurants and then have
my hair and clothes reek of cigarette smoke. I'm sure not all of
you would agree, but I do hope it has encouraged a lot of people
to quit as we all know it can 'seriously damage your health', or
so it says on the packets!

The other exciting thing about this flight was that it was on a jumbo jet, a fact I had written on to my boarding pass with an exclamation mark after it, so I was obviously very impressed.

We had flown out to New York from Milan on a much smaller aircraft. I think the jumbos, or should I say Boeing 747s, had only been flying since the early 1970s and probably only on certain routes, so it was quite a big deal for a nineteen-year-old.

I have flown on jumbo jets many times since that flight in 1976 but there is one flight that will always remain special.

It was a flight back from Nassau in the Bahamas where I had been presenting some on-location shows for QVC. I know, tough job but someone had to do it.

I was on my own, and had been booked to fly business class. It was a very full plane, as confirmed by the pilot when he welcomed us on board. 'Good evening ladies and gentlemen and welcome on board this busy flight back to London Heathrow. There isn't a spare seat on the plane.'

Really? I looked at the spare seat next to me and wondered if my travelling companion was the invisible man.

The cabin doors closed, we buckled up and took off and still no occupant to the seat adjacent to mine.

The announcement was made: 'Cabin crew, you are released.' (Is it just me, or does that make you giggle too? Released from what exactly?)

Anyway, moments later, a man in uniform slid into the seat next to mine. This was slightly disconcerting as it looked like a pilot's uniform. If this was the pilot, who was flying the plane?

It turned out that this was indeed one of the three pilots on board, and that the seat next to mine had been allocated as the sleep seat.

I wasn't going to talk to him at all as I didn't want to be responsible for him making a mistake out of tiredness because he'd been kept awake by some woman nattering. However, he started a conversation as we ate our dinner and we somehow got onto talking about football. Oh dear. If there's one subject I can really talk about it's the 'beautiful game' and we were still chatting three hours later at the end of his rest period.

He was replaced by the co-pilot for his 'rest', and in due course by the pilot, and then shortly before landing the original officer came back and asked me if I would like to go and have a look at the cockpit. You have probably noticed that I have carefully avoided using names because I'm not entirely sure that passengers were allowed onto the flight deck, even in those days. It was such a fantastic view from 'up front', which of course I commented on, to which the pilot asked, 'Well, would you like to sit up front for the landing?'

I'm pretty certain that is not allowed in any airlines rule book, but how could I pass up such an opportunity?

I went back to my seat to get my hand luggage and received some very quizzical looks from the other passengers, and some frosty glares from the stewardesses. Back on the flight deck I had to be strapped in to the spare seat with a sort of harness just as we started our descent.

Talk about a bird's-eye view. I can truly say it's an experience I will never forget.

Forty Five

It seems a bit weird that I am going to have to explain
this sentence for younger readers, but forty-five is the
number of revolutions per minute of a single record.

Before downloads and compact discs, or CDs as they are better
known, and even cassettes, we all listened to our music on
records. When they were first invented they rotated at 78rpm,
but it changed to 45rpm for singles and 33rpm for LPs, or long
plays, to give them their full title.

The relevance of this in my life is that for a while, in the late
1970s, I was a club DJ at various venues in London for a company
called Juliana's.

I had spent the summer of 1977 on Guernsey in the Channel
Islands. I hadn't been working in a summer show, just working
at whatever came up, initially for a hire car company and later
as a go-go dancer, as documented in *chapter 23*. I had kept taking
the *Stage* newspaper, scanning the adverts for potential jobs, and
it became clear to me that I needed to live in London to be able
to get to auditions easily. The problem was that I needed somewhere to live and a job that would earn me enough money to
pay London rent.

The offer of a flat came up, as you will read about in *chapter
67*, and at about the same time I saw an advert to train to be a
DJ for Juliana's. I wrote to them with a brief CV and enclosed

a photo, and a week or so later they wrote back giving me an interview date for late September.

Juliana's was based in Kensington, which is where I had to go for my initial interview. They decided I had possibilities and agreed to take me on for a week's training. I guess they were an agency, really, providing predominantly girl DJs for clubs and cruise liners. The beauty was that you didn't need to have your own extensive record collection or equipment, you just turned up at the venue and used what was there.

I enjoyed the training and found it quite easy, probably because of my dancing and singing background. At the end of the training they organised a test night. Mine was at a hotel in Kensington called the Tara. I was very nervous and totally out of my comfort zone, but I knew I needed to impress for them to give me some work.

Well, I must have done all right – although in truth I don't remember – because a few days later they offered me my first paid gig.

Initially I was just cover for the regular DJs when they wanted a night off. I always made myself available even at short notice and pretty soon I was the first call when anyone needed covering. I worked at Le Perroquet off Knightsbridge, the Intercontinental on Park Lane, Wedgies on the King's Road and had a fairly regular slot at an Italian club called Mario and Franco's off Grosvenor Square.

I have already mentioned that I needed to earn enough money to pay my London rent, and in case you are thinking that DJing was a highly paid job, it wasn't. I also had to work during the day to make ends meet. I had enrolled at a college in central London to learn shorthand and typing, but after just three days I couldn't bear to go back, so I had to take unskilled temp jobs, which unfortunately weren't as well paid. The beauty of the temp jobs was that I could take time off to go to auditions, which was my reason for being in London in the first place.

One such audition was for the pantomime *Aladdin*, being staged at the Ashcroft Theatre in Croydon, my local town. I was really pleased when I got the job as I didn't have a car at the time and it was only a fifteen-minute bus ride away. I continued DJing right through rehearsals but obviously had to stop when the show opened, apart from an occasional Sunday evening. Where on earth did I get all that energy from?

One of the Sunday evenings that I did was at an Italian restaurant called Cinecitta on Marylebone Lane. They really liked me and wanted me to take the gig full time as their regular girl was leaving. Unfortunately I couldn't because of the pantomime, so they used a series of girls until my eight-week show run had finished and then offered me the residency.

By this time I had met my partner Chris, who worked late nights as a musician, so the situation suited me, apart from still not having my own transport. Taxis were proving to be very expensive but were the only option for getting home on my own in the early hours of the morning. I had to make a decision to either leave Cinecitta or buy a car. I didn't want to leave the restaurant as the people were so lovely to work for, so I bought my beloved Snowdrop with a bit of help from Mum and Dad.

Cinecitta was a very easy gig. I would get to work around 8.30 p.m. to start playing music at 9 p.m. I would usually start with a long-play 45 – 'Breezin' by George Benson was a favourite – so that I could plan a bit of a playlist. I had grown quite adept at mixing between tracks and loved to play around with the speed of the turntables so that there would be no obvious change in tempo from one track to the next. These days it's all done digitally but back then I literally played it by ear!

Cinecitta was one of the few venues I worked at that liked you to talk on the microphone for birthday announcements and to get people up and dancing. Maybe that was why I liked it so much; I've always enjoyed communicating with my audience. People could come up and request songs which I would try and fit in, but the bane of my life was 'Dancing Queen' by Abba, which was quite a plodding tempo and almost always cleared the dance floor!

I was also expected to include a few Italian tracks for the Italian clientele. I was playing 'Ti Amo' by Umberto Tozzi back in 1978 long before it became a UK hit in the early 1980s. Another favourite of mine was a song called 'Solo', which unfortunately did not enjoy the same UK success.

After the smoochy tunes heading towards our finish at 1 a.m. I would play the 'Blue Danube' waltz to signify the end of the evening and clear the dance floor. It usually worked, but sometimes we would have couples waltzing around crazily until the last note!

I stayed at Cinecitta for the whole summer and autumn of 1978 before going back into pantomime at the Ashcroft in Croydon for a second year. I did return to Cinecitta for a couple of months in early 1979 but, when I was offered a job singing and dancing in Hong Kong in the April, it was an offer I couldn't refuse!

Forty Six

£46,000 was the asking price for the first house Chris
and I bought in 1985.

We had been renting a flat at the top of a Victorian house for the previous five years and decided that we should think about getting onto the property ladder.

We had a little money saved courtesy of two series of *The Price is Right*, and Chris was working with a high-profile comedian at the time. Some friends of ours had recently bought a maisonette, so we thought we would follow suit and start looking. As soon as I saw the picture in the estate agent's window, I knew it was the house for us.

The property was only a couple of miles from where we were living and was semi-detached, but not in the manner you might be imagining. Most semi-detached houses are a matching pair, but, as you've probably realised by now, I like to be different. This was a former coach house built onto the side of a big four-storey Victorian house, and the previous owners had called it, quite appropriately, *La Casita*, which, if you know Spanish, translates as 'the little house'.

Although the name was fitting we decided to change it to 'The Coach House' in recognition of its former use.

It had two bedrooms and a bathroom upstairs, and downstairs was a lounge, a tiny kitchen and a dining room, which had been recently converted from a garage by the builder who was selling it. The builder had also very thoughtfully covered every wall in woodchip paper and painted it magnolia! The real bonus was that it had off-street parking and a back garden with a great view over the surrounding area.

It was love at first sight for me and I was all for putting in an offer for the full asking price immediately. I don't know what Kirsty and Phil off *Location, Location, Location* would have had to say about that. Fortunately we had a mortgage broker who had a lot more experience than the pair of us. He recommended waiting a couple of days and then putting in a lower offer. I remember him asking us, 'How much do you want this house?'

'We really, really want it,' was our reply.

In the end we offered just a thousand pounds less than the asking price, and our offer was accepted immediately. Maybe we could have got it for a better price but we didn't want to lose it.

It was pretty scary after we had paid over the deposit, wondering if we had done the right thing, but I think you always feel that way when you are spending such a huge amount of money, and the majority of it is not yours!

My brother helped us to move house. He runs a transport business in Nottingham so he came down in one of his vans with one of his drivers. The two of them and Chris carried our belongings down two flights of stairs and loaded them onto the van. The worst thing to move was the old electric cooker, which technically wasn't ours but wasn't on the inventory for the flat either so we claimed ownership of it. After the lads had struggled down the stairs with it we all realised why the previous tenant hadn't bothered to take it!

Everything got deposited at our new house, including our cats Dylan and Charlie, and then my brother headed back to Nottingham, leaving Chris and I with a lot of sorting out to do.

I will always remember that first night in our first house. We fetched a Chinese takeaway, which we washed down with a bottle of champagne, and then decided to run a bath to wash away the grime of moving. The kitchen was located directly underneath the bathroom and I was in there washing the dishes when water started leaking through the strip light. It turned out that the builders had cut the waste pipe for the bath too short so the joint hadn't sealed properly, but we didn't know that at the time!

Once we had unpacked all our belongings and settled in to the house we started to think about all the things we were going to change over the following months and years.

We started with the garden, which both front and back was a bit of a mess. The front garden had been concreted, badly, to provide parking for three cars. It then sloped towards the front of the house where the builder had created a brick-framed planting area which was filled with builder's rubble. It took a skip and then a delivery of topsoil before we could even consider planting anything.

The back garden was more or less the sloping hillside, complete with brambles and weeds to shoulder height or above. Fortunately for us, both sets of parents were keen gardeners and Chris's dad had been a bricklayer by profession, whilst my dad was a very able handyman. With Chris and I as willing labourers we transformed the hillside into a proper garden on three levels.

Nearest the house we levelled out an area which would later become a patio. Chris and his dad built steps through the centre of the rockery we had created down to the next level, which was to be laid to lawn. Then we had a sloped area, also to be grass-seeded, ending at the rustic, beyond which was the vegetable plot. It sounds as though it was a really big garden but in fact it was long at 150 feet, but only 20 feet wide. By London standards it was a pretty generous outside space, as I discovered in later years when I was the one doing most of the gardening!

Once we had the desired layout we took our time with the planting, in part due to time constraints, but a lack of funds also played its part. We had used all the money I had saved from *The Price is Right* as a deposit for the house and to buy some fairly basic furniture. We were managing to make the mortgage payments but when my niece told me that a friend of hers was coming down from Scotland to study at the London College of Fashion, we decided to take her in as a lodger to help make ends meet.

We hadn't really paid any attention to the inside of the house during the summer months, as we were trying to get the garden sorted, but, with Trisha arriving in September, I bought fabric to make some curtains for her room and a Japanese-style paper lampshade to try and make it more homely. She was a really good lodger, clean and tidy and quiet, but I have to say I really didn't like sharing our new home with anyone else, so, when I discovered I was pregnant in the March of the following year, we helped her to find somewhere else to live.

During the time Trisha had been living with us we had been making plans for alterations to the house, which we couldn't really start until she left as it would have been unfair to expect her to pay rent whilst living in a building site. With the discovery that I was expecting our first baby we had to go into overdrive to get the main building works done as quickly as possible.

We needed to change the layout upstairs, as you had to go through one or other of the bedrooms to get to the bathroom. Our bedroom was ridiculously large, so we chopped three feet off it to create a corridor leading to the bathroom and, while we were at it, made a small en-suite shower room with hand basin. We also reduced the size of the other bedroom to create a third small bedroom, which became Daniel's room when he was a few months old.

We decided to knock out the old concrete stairs as the weight of them was causing some movement to the house. I remember discussing this with our builder Vernon one morning before Chris and I went out to the supermarket. I was about seven months pregnant at the time, so imagine my horror when we returned to find that Vernon had already knocked the old staircase out, and that the only access to the only toilet in the house was up a very precarious-looking ladder! Thankfully I had very friendly neighbours.

The downstairs was also in need of a makeover but, apart from chipping the plaster off the chimney breast to reveal the 'old London stocks' brickwork and the addition of a roof and doors to the passageway at the side of the house to create an entrance hall and utility room, everything else had to wait until after Daniel had been born.

Daniel arrived in late November and we continued with our renovations the following March, this time knocking a hole through the wall between the lounge and the dining room to create double doors, and also creating a larger opening from the dining room to the minuscule kitchen to create an open-plan feel. Everybody does this sort of thing now, but this was the mid-eighties and it did cause a few raised eyebrows. We also knocked out the old sash window in the lounge to install French doors to the garden and to let in a bit more light.

When I think back I do feel a little sorry for Daniel, who spent the first year or so of his life living amongst rubble. We have some great photos of him before his first birthday 'helping' his dad with bricklaying, trowel in hand, and at the top of a stepladder 'assisting' me with the painting. Daniel was only four months old when I fell pregnant again, so then the pressure really was on to get everything finished before Sophie was born. One toddler sitting in a playpen in a building site is just about OK but two could have been disastrous.

The hard work was all worth it as we ended up with a lovely family home in which to raise our young family.

I have many fond memories of our first house. It was where I was living when I got the *Beadle's About* job and my presenting job with the local cable television station, which led on to QVC and Sky Sports.

It was less than a hundred yards from a large, tree-filled park where we spent hundreds of happy hours pushing swings, teaching the children to ride their bikes and playing tennis. The children both had their 'first day at school' photos taken outside the front door in their red and grey uniforms, although ultimately the local school was my reason for moving.

The infant school had been fantastic, but I was less impressed with the potential junior school when Daniel was due to move on. Maybe it was the smell of the toilets that seemed to permeate the entire building that I was not keen on, but after going for a look round, which happened to coincide with meeting up with an old friend at Wimbledon Theatre, who told us about the amazing village school her son went to in a village called Woldingham, we put the house on the market.

That was the first week of July, and less than ten weeks later we moved into our new home.

Forty Seven

There were forty-seven pupils in my class at
Jesse Gray Primary School, West Bridgford,
in the summer term of 1965.

How do I know this? Well fairly recently my mum was doing a bit of sorting out and she came across some old school reports of mine, one of which was this particular term when I was in 2S. The 2 symbolised the second year of junior school, now called Year 4, and the S was my teacher, Mr Syson.

I know I was only a little girl, I had just turned nine, but Mr Syson was a very 'mature' teacher. I reckon he must have been approaching retirement, but that did not stop him from being an energetic, enthusiastic and engaging teacher; in fact, I would go as far as to say he was the best teacher I ever encountered. He had a fantastic knack of making every subject interesting. I think I learnt more about history in his lessons than I did in the whole of my GCE course, and it wasn't actually a separate curriculum subject.

What amazes me, though, is that one teacher, without the help of classroom assistants, had total control of forty-seven children aged eight and nine, and managed to make lessons interesting and get results out of his pupils. Everyone moans about class sizes these days but I bet there are very few schools in the UK that have anything approaching that number per class.

His summary at the bottom of the report stated that I was

good at all subjects, but that I myself preferred English. He also said I was good at PE, which reminded me that he invented a game we used to play. It was called 'stool ball' and was a bit like cricket, except instead of stumps there was a stand at each end with a white, square board on it at shoulder height, and instead of a cricket bat it was played with a rounders bat. The principle was the same – making runs until you were bowled out by the ball hitting the white square, or you were caught out or run out. I wonder if he patented it?

Apparently my position in class that term was fourth, not bad out of forty-seven, but on none of my school reports was I ever top of the class, which I think I was probably striving for.

Still, I did my best and that's all you can ask for, really.

Forty Eight

In 1848, Johann Strauss senior wrote the
Radetzky March.

It was dedicated to the Austrian Field Marshall Joseph Radetzky von Radetz.

What has this to do with me, I hear you ask? Well, when I was a little girl, the Radetzky March was a call to action.

I am not sure who used to instigate this, either my mum or my dad I would imagine, but upon hearing the opening bars blasting out from the radiogram, we would stop whatever we were doing and 'assemble' in the lounge. Once gathered we would start our 'march' around the house.

My dad would lead the way, followed by mum, then Lynda, Richard, me and, bringing up the rear, Paddy, our dog!

If anyone had ever seen us they would probably have thought we were all bonkers, and maybe that wouldn't have been far from the truth, but that spontaneous march around the house, through the bedrooms and bathroom, and even occasionally out of the kitchen door to the garden and back in through the French doors to the lounge, somehow united us as a family.

We would all be la la'ing at the tops of our voices and Paddy would join in by barking, madly wagging his little stump of a tail. Goodness knows what the neighbours thought, but honestly, I don't really care.

Paddy was a wire fox terrier and he was the most loving and

patient pet a family could ever wish to own. If you are not familiar with the breed, they are a medium-sized dog with a curly coat of white with black-and-tan markings. Paddy was a lovely example of the breed, with the black 'saddle' markings across his back and tan ears and crown of the head. He could probably have been a show dog but for his stump of a tail.

I'm not sure if they still do it, but in those days the breeders used to dock the tails of the wire fox terrier, and whoever had done Paddy's had been a little over enthusiastic. The result was a stump, but we did used to let the fur on it grow as long as possible in order to disguise it for him.

I admit we used to tease him a bit – OK, a lot. He knew the words for walk and lead, so we used to say words that rhymed to get him all excited in anticipation of his outing round the block. He would run to the hook his lead was hanging from, jumping up at it and barking, and then run back and stand in front of us, stump wagging frantically.

We also used to have him balance on his bottom, front legs raised, to 'beg' for treats. This must have been quite tricky for him without the aid of a proper tail to act as a stabiliser, but he never snatched his titbit, he always accepted graciously.

It was a devastating blow to all of us when Paddy had a stroke and had to be put to sleep two days before Christmas 1969.

If there is a 'doggy heaven', I am certain Paddy is there.

Forty Nine

On the 8th of May 1993 Crystal Palace were relegated
from the Premier League having amassed a total of
forty-nine points.

It remains the highest number of points achieved that led to
relegation from the top flight of English football. That said,
it was the only Premiership season where twenty-two clubs
contested the league title instead of the twenty that there have
been ever since, so there were forty-two games from which to
accrue points rather than thirty-eight.

However, it was also the only season where four clubs
went down instead of three, and yes, we were fourth from
bottom.

What made it worse was that it had really seemed like we were
going to survive the drop. We won a game against West Ham
against all the odds and at that point the other teams in the
relegation dogfight only had a mathematical chance of surviving.
It was Oldham who wouldn't accept their fate and went on a
winning run.

They had needed to win all their remaining fixtures and to
hope that we would lose all of ours. Sadly, we obliged, and the
3–1 defeat to Arsenal at Highbury on the final day of the season
lost us our Premier League status.

We did bounce straight back the following season, as you
will read about in *chapter 94*, but at the time it was a bitter blow

and led to the resignation of our much-loved manager Steve Coppell.

It may be good to hold records, but this is one that I think all Palace fans would gladly have lived without.

Fifty

Some people approach turning fifty with dread,
but I decided to have a party to celebrate.

The date, the 10th of June, coincided with England's opening game of the 2006 World Cup and fortunately it turned out to be a double celebration, never a certainty when our national football team play, as England beat Paraguay 1–0.

Rather than hiring a hall, which I felt would be a bit impersonal, the venue was our house. My partner Chris had spent the previous fortnight secretly gathering together photographs from my childhood and earlier life and photocopying them. He and the children had spent the evening before decorating the walls with them while I was out at work.

The downstairs layout of our house was ideal for hosting a party for the fifty or so people who had been invited. The children's games room had a small bar in it so became the main party area, leading out to the garden in one direction, and to my small home gym in the other.

The gym had a wooden floor, perfect for dancing, and mirrors all down one side, which fortunately made it seem bigger than it was. All the gym equipment had been packed away at one end of the room, in front of which the DJ had set up all his gear. The DJ was Sophie's boyfriend at the time, Rick, and, as she had given him 'insider information' on all the music I liked, I knew we were in for a good night musically.

It was a lovely sunny day, so we set up tables and chairs in the garden to enable people to collect food from the spread we had laid out in the dining room and enjoy it al fresco. I must confess I was also thinking it would be much easier to clear up afterwards, and not such a drama if anything got spilt or dropped.

My friend from QVC, Ali Keenan, had stayed over the night before to help with the food preparations. It's a good job she did, as we were still threading mini-mozzarella balls, cherry tomatoes and basil leaves onto long cocktail sticks when the first guest arrived.

She had also baked me a beautiful birthday cake, decorated with real frosted roses. It looked very classy, and tasted pretty good too. It was actually one of three birthday cakes I had that year.

Normally I make my own chocolate birthday cake but had decided that with all the other goodies on offer I wouldn't bother, although I was hoping the family might buy me one. As it turned out they didn't need to. As well as Ali's cake, I had a huge pink confection, courtesy of QVC, and an amazing 'ladybird' cake from Simon Wilson of Butler & Wilson. If you are wondering why the latter was in the style of a ladybird, all is revealed in *chapter 74*.

When I had first mentioned having the party at home, Chris's main concern was where people would park their cars. Our house was on the main road through Woldingham village, and although roadside parking is allowed, Chris was worried that cars could potentially get damaged after darkness fell as there was no street lighting. We came up with the idea of having people park in the station car park at the bottom of the hill and then chauffeuring them to the front door. A friend of mine, David, volunteered his driver for the evening, so everyone arrived in style and were met at the front door by Daniel or Sophie offering Buck's Fizz.

Sometimes as the host or hostess of a party you don't really have chance to enjoy it yourself, but I can honestly say I had a fabulous evening. My highlight was probably dancing and singing along to one of my favourite songs, 'Unwritten' by Natasha Bedingfield.

It's a great tune but it is the words that I really relate to, particularly this line: 'Feel the rain on your skin, No one else can feel it for you' . . . so true!

Fifty One

Number 51 was the colour code for the
coral-coloured maternity top I modelled in the
1987 Mothercare catalogue when I was pregnant
with Daniel.

I hadn't really thought about doing any maternity modelling, particularly after the stress of the Harp commercial I had filmed in Dublin early on in my pregnancy, which you will read about in *chapter 86*.

It was late September 1986, so I was seven months pregnant, when my agent, who unsurprisingly I hadn't heard from in a couple of months, rang.

Apparently, one of the girls who had been engaged to appear in the aforementioned Mothercare catalogue had gone into early labour, and they were desperately trying to replace her at very short notice. Let me clarify that sentence. They needed someone the next day as the shoot had already started and couldn't be postponed as the other models were pregnant, and getting bigger by the day.

Generally speaking Mothercare liked their models to be twenty-eight to thirty weeks pregnant. I was already thirty-two weeks, but they didn't really have many other options so I was hired.

There were three days of shooting for me. The first day was studio-based and was the easiest in terms of practicality as there were no issues nipping to the loo when required, which, as you will know if you have ever been pregnant, can be very frequent in the third trimester.

We had a day on location outside the Albert Hall, which must have been quite surreal for any passers-by, watching four fairly heavily pregnant women pile out of a minibus to have their photograph taken with one man.

The other location was at a beautiful house in Sevenoaks, Kent. I remember thinking at the time that I wished I really did live there. It was a glorious sunny day which was just as well as, in addition to the interior shots, there were some exterior scenes that involved sitting on the grass.

It was a very welcome and unexpected pay cheque, particularly after the debacle of my former agent declaring himself bankrupt and owing me my hard-earned wages from the Harp commercial.

How is this for a coincidence? One of the other 'mum to be' models was a girl called Ruby Hammer, who later went on to create the make-up brand Ruby and Millie. Her husband at the time was George Hammer, who was responsible for bringing the Aveda haircare and lifestyle brand to QVC.

Although QVC no longer sell the range I still have my hair cut and coloured at their flagship Aveda Concept Salon in the West End of London.

Fifty Two

I will always remember pulling up outside 52 Harold Road, taking one look at the building and saying to my partner Chris, 'We can't live there.'

It was a big Victorian detached property in need of a lot of TLC. We were there to look at Flat 9 with a view to moving in as we needed to vacate the flat we were sub-letting from a friend of mine. She was moving to Hove and giving up her tenancy so we had to find somewhere else to live.

We had decided it might be quite nice to rent an unfurnished property so that we could surround ourselves with our own things rather than someone else's, but there were two issues. Firstly, it was proving very difficult to find an unfurnished property at all, let alone one we could afford, and secondly, we didn't have any 'things' to surround ourselves with, i.e. we had no furniture . . . at all!

When the agent had described Flat 9 as being a bright, self-contained, one-bedroom, top-floor flat, it had sounded like just what we were looking for. The reality was something else.

The house was divided into eleven flats over three floors. The ground floor comprised four bedsits sharing bathroom facilities. The first floor was meant to be four bedsits, but, in actuality, three of the rooms were used by one tenant and her husband, and the fourth was a bedsit. The top floor was two bedsits, which used the bathroom facilities on the floor below, and the flat we had come to see.

It was very different from what we had been used to for the previous two years, but time was running out and although we had initially declined the flat, a week later, when we had found nothing else close to our budget, we had to return to the agent and say we would take it.

Moving day arrived and, despite not having any furniture to take to the new flat, it still took us several journeys in my old MGB Roadster, the last one of which required us to take the soft top off – bear in mind this was late November – so that we could move the carpet that my friend had kindly said we could have!

To take stock, we had the aforementioned carpet, an old electric cooker that had been left by the previous tenant, a 1950s kitchen cupboard with glass doors and two lilos, which we slept on for the first month we lived in our new flat. We had no heating and there was no double glazing; in fact it was not unusual for us to find the water in the loo iced over, not to mention Jack Frost patterns on the inside of the windows.

The very first thing we bought was a Calor gas heater, swiftly followed by a second-hand fridge. We paid five pounds for that fridge, and, after thoroughly cleaning it, sanding it down to get rid of the rust and spray-painting it, it looked as good as new. We kept it for years, even taking it to our first house five years later. That is probably the best five pounds I have ever spent!

We started sprucing the place up immediately. We lined the walls with something called 'warmafoam', so that they wouldn't feel so cold to the touch, then we papered over it. We concentrated on the kitchen, bedroom and shower room to start with as we were both working, so time was quite limited. I'm not sure who thought it was a good idea to paint the shower room in bright blue gloss paint but it had to go! And whoever heard of a toilet and shower but no hand basin? We had to brush our teeth and wash in the kitchen sink!

I had started rehearsals for pantomime at the Palace Theatre in Watford, about thirty-five miles away, so my days were really long with all the travelling that that entailed. I came home from rehearsals one day, just before Christmas, to find that Chris had sawn the front off the top of the kitchen cupboard to make me a 'Welsh dresser' because I had said I liked them.

The lilos were gradually starting to deflate, section by section, so we treated ourselves to an early Christmas present. No, we couldn't afford a bed, but we did buy two square pouffes that could unfold into foam mattresses to sleep on, a vast improvement on the almost airless lilos. We kept those pouffes for thirty years and they came in so handy for when the children had their friends for sleepovers. We only parted company with them a couple of years ago when we moved from The Downs Cottage and, like so many other things that I had been hoarding, they ended up in a skip.

By Christmas we had just about finished decorating the three rooms, but we still had precious little furniture. We ate our Christmas lunch from the top of a Farfisa piano/organ that I had covered with a lace tablecloth for the occasion and watched television on Chris's black-and-white, twelve-inch-screen portable.

Once my pantomime season finished at the end of January we had a little more time to make a start on the lounge.

It was a good-sized room with a big bay window that let in lots of light. We painted the walls pale green and bought a chocolate-brown carpet and then we bought our first piece of furniture, a wooden rocking chair from MFI. This was swiftly followed by a wooden table and chairs, also from MFI, and then, luxury of luxuries, Chris's mum and dad gave us an old bed. We were then able to move the pouffes into the lounge to sit on.

Gradually, with a lot of hard work and very little cash, we had started to create our first 'home'.

It was while we were living there that we adopted, or should I say were adopted, by our first cat, Dylan, whose story I told you in *chapter 4*. He already knew the house well as he had been abandoned by his previous owners. About a month after we had taken ownership of him, both Chris and I started itching like mad. You guessed it. Not only had we taken Dylan in, but all his fleas too. We had never had a cat before, so it didn't occur to us that he might be infested. Not the greatest of starts for Dylan, but he made up for it with all the love he gave us over twenty years.

Dylan, at approximately two years old, was quite a docile cat, preferring to sit quietly with us rather than run around, but all that changed when Charlie arrived on the scene. Initially Charlie was so tiny that he didn't do much running around, but as he grew larger so did his appetite for playing and Dylan joined in.

I should explain that our living room was three steps up from the level that the kitchen and bedroom were on. Their favourite game was to race from the living room through the kitchen to the bedroom, thundering down the steps in one go! I have no idea how two comparatively small cats can make such a racket but they obviously did, as our neighbour downstairs would bang on her ceiling with a broom to register her disapproval.

We did have a communal garden that Dylan was allowed out in, as he was used to going out, but we kept Charlie as a house cat until he was six months old and we moved to our first house with its own garden. We weren't being cruel, we were just concerned for his safety as there had been a couple of incidents with cats being knocked down on the road outside our flat.

On one occasion we were sitting in our living room quite late at night and there was a squeal of brakes followed by a thud. We looked out of our top-floor window and could see a cat lying in the road motionless. Chris went running down the stairs to try and get to the cat before another vehicle came along. I had followed him down and recognised the cat, who was in a very bad way, as belonging to our neighbour. I rang their doorbell but there was no reply so, after scribbling a short note and posting it through their door, we carefully lifted the cat onto a blanket and drove it to the PDSA in Wimbledon. It had broken its pelvis, but thanks to our quick actions and the medical care it received, it survived.

Dylan and Charlie weren't the only animals who stayed at our flat. When we first moved in we had a problem with mice that I left Chris to deal with, and I really don't want to know how he dealt with it.

And then, for one night only, we had a bat in residence! We had gone to bed one night and were disturbed by a fluttering sound coming from the front room. We thought it was a bird, so Chris went to investigate. He came back a few minutes later to explain that it wasn't a bird, it was a bat. It must have flown in through the open window. We did try to encourage the bat back out of the open window using a tennis racket, and I should explain that we weren't hitting it, just trying to usher it, but it didn't want to know. In the end we decided it would probably be easier to deal with in daylight when the bat would be less active.

It was with great trepidation that we opened our bedroom door the next morning to look for our 'guest'. At first we couldn't see it anywhere, but then we noticed it hanging upside down in the folds of the curtain near the open window. Very carefully, I unhooked the curtain, folded it over and pushed it out of the window. It must have looked a little strange to passers-by seeing a curtain 'flying' out of a top-floor window not unlike a parachute!

When we went to gather up the curtain the bat had gone, so

I'm hoping it managed to fly away, although I guess it must have been pretty startled to have been woken from its daytime slumber.

The flat was far from luxurious, but we made it comfortable and it was our home for over five years, until we had managed to save up enough of a deposit for our first house.

Fifty Three

Appearances can be deceptive, and that is definitely
the case with my skin. I am very fortunate that, despite
my age, I still have quite plump firm skin that people
often remark on. I put it down to good genes and
good skin care. The skin on my face is usually well
behaved but that was not the case in October 2009,
when I was fifty-three years old.

I have always had issues with my skin. As a very small child I
had problems with eczema. I used to get a terrible rash behind
my knees, on the inside of my thighs and in the bend of my
elbows. Although it was confined to these areas I can still
remember scratching it to the point of bleeding because it was
so itchy. My mum used to put Anthisan cream on it and
occasionally made me wear gloves if my scratching got too
violent.

Like a lot of children I eventually grew out of it and my skin
was fairly well behaved even during adolescence. It wasn't until
after I had the chicken pox as an adult, which I wrote about in
chapter 33, that my skin became troublesome again.

I had started my job at QVC in October 1993 and by the
time we moved into The Downs Cottage in September 1994 my
eczema had reared its ugly head in the form of severely thickened
skin on the palm of my left hand. I have no definitive answers
as to why it flared up but it could well have been the stress of

working at QVC, Sky Sports and my cable programme, combined with bringing up two small children and moving house!

Whatever caused it, it was a nightmare to live with. It seemed to follow a cycle. The skin on my palm would itch, I would scratch it, then the skin would get really thick. Once it had got really thick it would crack along the natural lines of the palm, often bleeding or 'weeping', and at this stage I could peel it off, revealing red raw skin underneath similar to a third-degree burn. It was very painful and I was terrified that it would become infected.

Obviously I saw my doctor about it and he gave me a cream called Fucibet, which was a combined steroid and anti-bacterial concoction, to try and keep it under control. It was bad enough having to cope with it in everyday life, but the worst thing was trying to hide it 'on air' at QVC, particularly during close-ups in jewellery shows. I became a past master at angling my hand in such away that the raw flesh was only visible to me and not to the viewers at home.

This went on in varying degrees for years, about twelve years actually, during which time I saw different skin specialists, some of whom took scrapings of the offending palm, but no one came up with a cure. I was told time and again that this was just something I was going to have to live with. And that did seem to be the case until my skin really threw a wobbler in the autumn of 2009.

As well as the problem with my left hand, I would sometimes get patches of eczema behind my left ear, another joy to hide, particularly when selling earrings, and raised irritated patches along my hair line after I had my hair colour done. All of this was unpleasant but manageable until my skin had a major reaction to something and the red raised patches started to spread.

At first I had a few on my chest and neck, which I managed to cover with make-up, then my skin simply erupted. I had itchy red patches everywhere — my limbs, my abdomen, but worst of all my face. It was very distressing. At the time I was self-employed so if I couldn't work, I wouldn't get paid. The more stressed I got the worse my skin became.

I went to see my doctor, whose first course of action was to do a full blood count to make sure that my skin was not just acting as an indicator to an underlying health problem. The blood tests were all completely normal, so he then referred me to a dermatological nurse. She prescribed some medicated lotions and bathing products to try and calm the flare-up. They did offer some mild relief, particularly during the day, but at night I couldn't sleep because I was so itchy that I just wanted to rip my skin off. Chris would put a cream that had menthol in it all over my arms, legs and abdomen to cool the itch and then I would begin to shiver uncontrollably. He would then make me a cup of chamomile tea to warm me up and calm me down. Honestly, sometimes I think I live with a saint.

Christmas was just a couple of weeks away, with all the added stress that brings, so Chris suggested we should book some flights to Spain for just after New Year to see if a bit of relaxation and sunshine would help.

To be honest I was dubious even as we booked the flights for the 2nd of January, and when Chris was ill in bed all New Year's Day — not due to alcohol I might add, as at this time he didn't drink at all — we should have just cancelled rather than change the booking. Chris was insistent though as he knew from past experience that I could truly relax in Spain, so we managed to change our booking to the following day.

By this time the red raised skin was almost covering my entire face and neck, and I was embarrassed to be seen out in public. I remember getting on the early morning easyJet flight to Alicante on the 3rd of January feeling tearful and pulling my hair around my face to hide it.

It was meant to be a five-day break but almost immediately I knew we had made a mistake as, far from helping my skin, the warm January Spanish sun just made it itchier. I couldn't sleep at all and spent most of the night sitting watching television, to try and take my mind off my skin, and crying. The next morning I begged Chris to take me home.

At this time we had no Internet at the Spanish house, so we had to ring the children and ask them to get us on the first available flight home, regardless of the cost. Fortunately they managed to book us on a flight for that evening. I also rang a work colleague who had told me of a Harley Street consultant dermatologist who had helped her husband with a skin disorder. I asked her to book me the first available appointment as a matter of urgency.

The flight home was as bad as the flight out to Spain had been the previous morning, but it was an enormous relief to get back to the UK, particularly as I knew I had an appointment with the skin expert booked for the following evening. It couldn't come soon enough, as far as I was concerned, as I was almost at the end of my tether.

I couldn't face travelling on public transport, so Chris drove me up to the West End of London, and he then waited outside the clinic while Sophie took me in. We had to wait quite a while to be seen, as obviously I had been squeezed onto the consultant's list at the last minute.

When I did finally go through for my appointment I was totally taken aback by his complete lack of a bedside manner. He asked me a few questions, gave me a cursory examination, and came to the conclusion that it was a flare-up of my eczema caused, in his opinion, by a reaction to a beauty product. He then prescribed a cream, which he told me potentially had certain side effects, one of which was a rash. As my skin was already so reactive, I asked him if he thought I would be OK to use it, to which his response was, and I apologise in advance for his language, 'You can use it, or you can piss on it, your choice!'

I know he had squeezed me onto his list that evening, for which I was very grateful, but I was truly shocked by his behaviour, particularly as he could see I was already in a very distressed state.

We filled the prescription at a supermarket late-night pharmacy counter and went home to start the treatment.

The next morning I rang my doctor to let him know what had happened with the consultant, and he immediately arranged for me to have an appointment for a second opinion, with a skin specialist that he knew, for the Saturday morning.

It was like chalk and cheese. This doctor was so kind and considerate and took a much longer look at my skin. His opinion was that it was psoriasis and that it was too enflamed for a cream alone to calm down. He put me on a course of steroid tablets called Prednisilone, and prescribed steroid creams in different strengths for the various affected parts of my body. He wrote me a long list of instructions of what to use where and when, and also gave me his email address in case I needed further help over the weekend. He also took a look at my hand and said that, in his opinion, it was palmopsoriasis and that he thought the steroid tablets would help.

His attitude towards me could not have been more different and I came out of that hospital feeling that he actually cared about me and confident that his diagnosis was correct. He didn't think that it was a reaction to a particular beauty product, more a build up over time, and probably exacerbated by stress.

I had to book some time off work, but fortunately I had plenty of holiday days still available to me that year so I took them rather than sick leave, for which I would not have been paid. The doctor also told me that I should try and avoid any beauty products, including shampoo and conditioner, and only use the medicated products he had prescribed.

I hated taking the steroid tablets, particularly as they made my tongue numb and made me feel drowsy, but even within a few days things started to calm down a little. The most dramatic effect was on the palm of my left hand, which healed completely within a month of starting the steroid tablets, and which has never been affected since – touch wood!

After a couple of weeks my skin had improved to the extent that I was able to go back to work, but there were still many nights where I couldn't sleep because of the itchiness, and days where I was so upset by the look of my skin that I would break down and sob uncontrollably. These crying fits would last for twenty minutes or so, and then I would change into my fitness clothes and go in the gym for an hour or more. I think it was a way of punishing my body for misbehaving.

There were occasions when I really didn't feel that I could face going in to work because I didn't want to be 'on show', but my family always managed to reassure me that I looked OK on screen.

Going back to work had brought its own challenges. Because I had no idea what had ultimately triggered this massive flare-up I was advised to keep my skin-care routine as simple as possible. Obviously I had to wear make-up for work but I had to keep it to the bare minimum and I also needed something to remove it with.

I asked my friend and QVC beauty expert Alison Young for her advice and she ordered me a selection of basic oils to use as my face cleanser and moisturiser, and even as a pre-treatment for my hair, as I still couldn't risk using a conditioner. Wheatgerm oil seemed to work best on my hair, and avocado oil on my skin, and of course I was still using the steroid creams as prescribed. This went on for three months before Ali decided that we could gradually start to introduce beauty products one at a time.

If anyone has ever doubted the efficacy of anti-ageing products, try leaving them out of your skin-care regime for a few months and I would be amazed if you didn't notice the difference to your skin – I know I did!

It was about nine months before I was able to use most of the products I had previously enjoyed, but there were a couple of ingredients that had flagged up as irritant when I had my skin patch testing done in the June of 2010, which meant I could no longer use some things that I used to.

I wanted to try and avoid a recurrence of this massive flare-up so, although I know that psoriasis is something you have for life and have to just learn to manage, I arranged to have some patch testing done to see if we could identify particular ingredients that might be a trigger. I was asked to take along all the beauty products I had previously been able to use, from which they would take samples and then stick them onto my torso for three days to see if any would cause a reaction – I don't think they were expecting the eighty or so products I took along with me for testing – and they also needed to test known skin irritants.

Each patch was able to hold ten samples, so I had to have twelve patches attached to me. I had eight on my back, in two rows, and another four across my midriff section. It was June and it was very hot, and I had to keep them on for three days, and I wasn't allowed to take a shower. It was a horribly uncomfortable three days, particularly as some of the patches were indeed causing an itchy reaction, but I stuck with it, if you'll excuse the pun, as I hoped that we might be able to identify substances that I was allergic to.

Three days later I went back to the clinic to have the patches removed and to have the results assessed. I had had mild reactions to quite a few products but was told that it was probably because my skin was in a sensitised state. However, there were quite severe reactions to about a dozen of the patches, some of which were products I had quite happily used for years prior to my flare-up.

I still sometimes have a reaction on my hairline when I have my hair colour done, which unfortunately for me is once a month as my hair grows so quickly, but it disappears within a couple of days, usually.

I haven't had to use any steroid creams for about a year now but I have them on standby just in case.

Fifty Four

This is the number of shrubs and trees we planted when creating, from scratch, the garden at my old house, The Downs Cottage.

You will read more about the house renovations and extension we carried out in *chapter 96*, but when we had finished all the building work, we were left with a building site for a garden. I would describe myself as an able gardener but certainly no expert, although I have been gardening for a long time.

My first experience was when I was four or five years old. My sister, brother and I all had our own allocated 'patch' in the back garden of our home in West Bridgford. It was a big garden with a rockery near the house, two areas of lawn for us to play on, and the flower and vegetable garden down at the bottom. This bottom section of the garden, which also housed our swing and seesaw, was where our individual flowerbeds were.

We each took great pride in our gardens, digging them over, choosing and planting seeds, and then weeding and watering through the summer. It is something I regret not doing with my own children as it taught us to have responsibility to nurture something we had planted. I can remember the excitement I felt as I rushed up the garden to tell Mum and Dad that the seeds had pushed through the soil with their first green shoots. I grew cornflowers, candytuft, night-scented stocks and nasturtiums, but probably varied it with other choices from year to year.

I think my dad was the inspiration for us as he spent hours and hours every weekend tending to his flowers and vegetables, and mowing the lawn. Dad used to grow potatoes, carrots, peas and runner beans, and also care for his soft fruit canes and his apple, pear and plum trees. The latter was a Victoria plum tree and most years would produce bumper crops. Not only did we eat them fresh, absolutely the best plums I have ever eaten, but my dad used to make plum jam and I think he used to bottle some too, along with the Williams pears.

He also grew flowers, mostly lots of different varieties of roses and his trademark sweet peas. Whenever I smell the distinctive pungent aroma of sweet peas it instantly transports me back to my childhood as our house was full of vases of the cut flowers throughout the summer.

I hadn't really shown a great deal of interest in gardening throughout my teens and twenties, probably because I hadn't had a home and garden of my own, but when we bought our first house on Ross Road, *chapter 46*, my interest was rekindled out of necessity. Because of the shape of our garden there, it ended up being almost a carbon copy of my garden growing up, albeit a narrower version. The Downs Cottage, however, was a totally different kettle of fish.

Although we had ideas on the layout, it was not straightforward. It wasn't a particularly big garden and, because the house was built into a hillside, it was on different levels and included a roof terrace.

We had created the lower level that you walked out into from the conservatory by closing off the original vehicular access with a low wall and fence at one end, and big wooden gates at the other. There was still room to park a car on the block paving behind the gates if we needed to, but for the most part that area housed the rotary washing line.

The whole driveway had been a covered in tarmac and I'm

not too sure why we didn't dig it all up before attempting to lay a lawn but we didn't, and that was probably why the lawn was never really lush, as the turf had been laid over just a few inches of soil. I know grass has a shallow-spreading root habit, but I'm not sure we gave it a fighting chance!

There was a small gravelled area between the conservatory and the retaining red-brick garden wall that included a fountain and a table with two chairs, and was a sheltered spot to catch the sun over a morning cup of coffee. We had dug into the wall and the hillside to create some sweeping steps up to the next level, where we had made a patio area for the dining table and chairs and also the children's playhouse.

That playhouse was a labour of love in itself. Chris and I had to clear and flatten the area, before laying slabs for it to stand on. We then constructed it, I varnished it and Chris roofed it. We were so pleased with ourselves when it was finished. The children were delighted and played in it non-stop for about twelve months, after which it became mostly an additional storage shed! In their defence, they were both a bit too big for it really by the time it was finished.

There was also another small area of lawn on the upper level leading to a few more steps up to the roof garden. I say roof garden, as it was built on top of the games room, but it was really a kind of terrace for the master bedroom.

So, as you can probably tell, it was a complicated layout and it was important to maximise the amount of space available to us with some clever planting. Enter Richard Jackson, QVC's gardening expert.

Richard was brilliant. Chris had done a couple of sketches of the layout in advance, and I had filled him in on the direction the garden faced and whether the areas had full sun, partial sun or shade. We walked round the garden/building site and marked down what Richard thought would work well in each location.

He suggested **honeysuckle** and **jasmine** for fragrance in areas where we would be sitting or have nearby windows open. We had **pyracantha** to disguise the height of the retaining wall and **box** in planters either side of the sweeping steps. There were three arches in the garden. The first, a wooden arch, had spring-flowering **clematis** to scramble over it. Two climbing **roses** met in the middle of the wrought-iron arch, and adjacent to the arch framing the entrance to the roof garden we planted a fragrant **wisteria**. I always felt that we would sell the house the year that the wisteria had climbed over the arch and along the railings of the roof garden, a distance of about twenty feet. We did.

There were so many other clever suggestions, like **ceonothus** for its bright purple flowers and fragrant pink **peonies**, not to mention **choisya**, **cistus**, **lilac** and a variety of different shades and styles of **roses**. The one thing Richard didn't recommend was the **flowering cherry tree**. We had a weeping cherry at our previous house that my mum and dad had bought us.

It was sort of a tradition in our family as the one we had in our front garden when I was a child very possibly saved our lives. That sounds a bit dramatic but it was probably true. The tree was positioned in the corner of our front garden next to the drive and the road.

Each May it was a riot of frothy pink blossoms until one year it looked very sorry for itself. It looked like it was dying. Mum was outside examining it when she thought she could smell gas. She called the gas board and sure enough the main pipe, which ran beneath the pavement outside our house, had a massive fracture in it and was leaking. Who knows what might have happened if a passer-by had lit up a cigarette in the vicinity. The poor old cherry tree didn't survive, but, thanks to it, we all did.

So, once again, Mum and Dad said they would like to treat us to a cherry tree. We went off to the garden centre and selected the specimen we most liked the look of and took it home to plant. What followed was a comedy moment. Chris was outside with the tree, and Mum, Dad and I were inside the conservatory directing him, courtesy of hand signals, as the conservatory was double glazed. We wanted it to be in the prime position for us to be able to see it whether sitting at the table, on the sofas or even viewing it from the lounge. I guess you had to be there, but for some reason it brings to mind Eric Sykes' *The Plank!*

The most enduring memories of my dad, particularly in his latter years, are of him pottering around that beautiful garden he had helped create wearing his cricket hat in the summer to keep his head cool, and a chunky sweater in the winter. He always had to be dragged indoors and told, 'You've done enough now!'

I was sad in a lot of respects to leave The Downs Cottage after it had been our home for sixteen years, but the real wrench was leaving the garden, although we didn't leave entirely empty-handed. Everything that was in a planter moved with us and helped decorate the new garden.

Fifty Five

Johnson's pH 5.5 was probably the biggest voiceover
campaign that I did.

It was a TV commercial and I was the voice you heard. It is an area of the entertainment field that I always wanted to get more involved in but it never really happened, maybe because I didn't devote enough time and energy to it.

Before I moved into presenting, when I was still appearing in lots of television commercials, I had to go along to a voiceover studio and post-synch a line I had spoken in a Guinness advert. I'm not sure of the reason – maybe the inflection had not been what the client wanted, or maybe there had been a technical error – whatever, I had to go and re-record the line.

Post-synchronisation is where you watch the lips of the person you are going to speak the line for and try to match your words with their lip movements exactly. This is quite tricky when you are dubbing someone else, but actually quite easy when you are dubbing yourself. It didn't take me long to get a perfect lip synch and the sound engineer was impressed and asked me if I had a voice showreel. At the time I didn't, so I set about putting one together, with the help of some friends who did a lot of voiceover work, and then sat back and waited for work to drop into my lap. Unsurprisingly it didn't, apart from odd bits and pieces, so I decided I needed a proper voiceover agent.

That is easier said than done. Most of the agents like to

represent well-known actors with really distinctive voices or people who are brilliant at doing a variety of accents. I was neither of the aforementioned so I was very fortunate to be given a chance with a well-known agency, Talking Heads . . . great name don't you think?

They did manage to get me some work, including the Johnson's pH 5.5 campaign, but I was already working at QVC four days a week, still presenting my *Cable 17* show twice a week and doing features for Sky Sports. I was a very busy girl and the children were still only seven and eight, so I needed to be there for them as much as possible. There just wasn't time to develop my fledgling career.

I stayed with Talking Heads for a couple of years and then moved to the Excellent Voice Company, which is run by Jon Briggs, who was the other 'first face on QVC' when it launched in 1993. They are a very successful voice agency, with Jon himself heading up the team of 'voices'. He has been the voice on the television show *The Weakest Link* for a number of years and recently got the plum job of the UK voice of the iPhone! Unfortunately, Excellent thought my talent lay as an 'in vision' presenter, so my voiceover career kind of fizzled out.

Who knows, now that the children are grown-up and I may soon have to start thinking about not having my face on TV, particularly with the advent of high definition TV, perhaps I could resurrect my voiceover work . . . I'm sure I've still got my showreel somewhere?

Fifty Six

1956 was the year I was born, so I thought I would
dedicate this chapter to a few of the world events that
happened that year.

It was an Olympic year and the Winter Olympics opened on
January the 26th in Cortina d'Amepezzo in Italy. I'm no good
at winter sports like skiing and ice skating; in fact I can barely
stand up on slippery surfaces, let alone move on them. Thank
goodness for the WinterTrax shoe grips that we sell at QVC – at
least I can now venture out of the house when it's snowed!

In February the film version of the Rogers and Hammerstein
show *Carousel* was released. The show has relevance for me as it
was the first Nottingham Operatic Society show that I watched
in which both my parents appeared. For some reason the main
thing I remember was my mum's curly hairpiece flying off as she
was twirled around in a dance routine! That and the song 'My
Boy Bill', sung by the male lead. Even at the tender age of five
it reduced me to tears with its final line, which referred to money
to support his unborn child: 'I'll go out and make it, or steal it,
or fake it, or die.' The show also included 'You'll Never Walk
Alone', which Liverpool Football Club have adopted as their
anthem.

February was also the month that Marilyn Monroe legally
changed her name from Norma Jean Mortenson prior to marrying
playwright Arthur Miller in late June. I've always been fascinated

by Marilyn Monroe since discovering that her birthday was the 2nd of June, the date I was due. I was eight days late and ended up sharing my birthday with another tragic Hollywood star, one Frances Gumm, otherwise known as Judy Garland.

In March both Morocco and Tunisia declared independence from France. I haven't visited Morocco, but we did have a family holiday in Tunisia once.

April saw the fairy-tale marriage of Hollywood actress Grace Kelly to Prince Rainier of Monaco and also the retirement of the 'real' Rocky Marciano without him ever losing a professional fight. I'm not a fan of boxing, which wasn't very helpful when I was asked to do a piece on ladies boxing for Sky Sports featuring Jane Couch, 'The Fleetwood Assassin', which I talk about in *chapter 94*.

The very first Eurovision Song Contest was broadcast from Lugano in Switzerland on the 24th of May. Who would have thought that twenty-four years later I was very close to appearing in the 1980 contest with the group 'The Main Event'? Well, perhaps not that close, as you will have read about in *chapter 12*.

On the day that I was born the Summer Olympic Games opened in Stockholm, Sweden, with the equestrian events. The weird thing was that the rest of the Olympic Games of 1956 were held in Melbourne, Australia, in November – hardly a close neighbour!

Eight days after I was born the last foreign troops left Egypt, an event that was to lead to the news story of the year, the Suez Crisis.

June also saw the release of another Rogers and Hammerstein musical on film, *The King and I*, starring Yul Brynner and Deborah Kerr. Once again this has relevance for me as I was one of the Siamese children in the aforementioned Nottingham Operatic Society's version of the show in 1963, which I will tell you more about in *chapter 59*.

In September the hard disc drive was invented by IBM. It's ironic that the computer was 'born' the same year as me when I am a self-confessed technophobe!

In October the Hungarian Revolution broke out but was crushed less than a fortnight later, on the 4th of November.

November also saw the release of Roger Vadim's film *And God Created Woman*, which propelled Brigitte Bardot into the public spotlight as a 'sex kitten'.

I thought you might also be interested in some famous births in the same year as mine.

January was a busy month with Mel Gibson, actresses Imelda Staunton and Geena Davis, current (at least as I write this) Fulham manager Martin Jol, and musicians Paul Young and Johnny Rotten entering the world.

In April former tennis player-turned-presenter Sue Barker and photographer Koo Stark were born.

June saw the arrival of former Crystal Palace manager George Burley, along with tennis superstar Björn Borg and American novelist Patricia Cornwell.

Jerry Hall was born in July, as was one of my favourite male movie actors, Tom Hanks. I loved him in *Big, chapter 10,* and also in *Castaway*, where he makes a friend of a basket ball that he appropriately names Wilson.

Sex and the City's Kim Cattrall and vocal coach David Grant were August babies.

Former Crystal Palace player Ray Wilkins and athlete Sebastian Coe were born in September.

Highly acclaimed film director Danny Boyle, who was recently responsible for the amazing opening ceremony of the London 2012 Olympic Games, including a sequence with my favourite James Bond, Daniel Craig, and Her Majesty The Queen, arrived in October.

Another movie director, Richard Curtis, responsible for *Four*

Weddings and a Funeral, as well as my favourite film of the moment, *Love Actually, chapter 10,* and the film *Sixty Six,* which forms my *chapter 66,* was born in November, as was the star of the movie *10,* Bo Derek.

And celebrity violinist, Nigel Kennedy, just made it in 1956 by arriving on the 28th of December.

There will also have been many deaths in 1956, but one of particular relevance to me was the poet Walter de la Mare, who died less than two weeks after I was born. Odd to think that nine or ten years later I was winning Speech and Drama festivals with his poetry . . . a piece called 'Rachel' springs to mind.

So those are some of the key events of my year of birth, not that I can remember any of them taking place, of course!

Fifty Seven

It is approximately fifty-seven miles to drive to
Littlehampton from where we used to live on
Ross Road, London SE25.

This was a journey we used to do fairly often in the summer-time when the children were small. Although Brighton was closer and we all enjoyed the hustle and bustle of going on the pier, there was no sand at Brighton and the pebbles shelved quite steeply into the sea. It made it very tricky for paddling so we usually drove further afield to the wide expanse of beach backed by the dunes at Camber Sands or, most often, Littlehampton.

The children really loved their days out playing on the beach, paddling in the sea, going to the fun fair or taking a ride on the little train that ran along the sea front. Then there was the ice cream and sometimes, on the way home, a bag of chips! We had never had a family holiday so these days out were the closest thing to it and you had the bonus of sleeping in your own bed.

We arrived home after one of our excursions and Chris started unpacking the cool box and wind break out of the car whilst I went to open the front door. I unlocked the Chubb lock and put my key in the Yale lock. Nothing happened. I couldn't understand what was wrong so I called Chris. He tried the lock and realised straight away what the problem was.

'Take the children to Eric and Bruni's,' he said.

They were our next-door-but-one neighbours who used to

babysit for us sometimes when Chris was gigging and I was teaching fitness classes. I still didn't get it. The children were tired and ready for bath and bed why did he want me to go socialising?

'I think we've been burgled and they could still be inside,' he said in a low voice so as not to alarm the children, 'and I think you had better call the police.'

It was a complete shock. I did as instructed and went to my neighbours, and when I told them what was going on, Bruni rang the police and Eric went round to our house with some tools to force the front door open.

We had indeed been burgled but the intruders had long gone. They had broken in through the patio doors, which was odd in itself as they must have climbed the fence from one or other of our neighbours' gardens to get round the back of our house.

Everything was a complete mess, with all our clothes pulled out of the drawers and lying in a heap. They had stolen all my jewellery, including my mum's eternity ring that she had given me a few years before, which was very upsetting. They had taken our video recorder but although they had unplugged the TV they had left it behind, probably deciding it was too bulky and heavy to hoist over the six-foot fence.

They had even been through our food cupboards and helped themselves to the children's Jaffa Cakes and orange squash. I felt like throwing everything away, just in case they had touched it.

Chris and I slept downstairs that night, barricaded in, just in case the perpetrators decided to come back for a second attempt, although I don't think either of us actually slept much at all.

The police were very helpful and dusted for fingerprints, but no one was ever caught and nothing was ever recovered. They reckoned it was probably kids and said we were lucky they hadn't smeared everywhere with excrement.

We had a visit from a Crime Prevention Officer who recommended better locks for the patio doors, and a visit from the locksmith to fix those locks and the damaged front door.

It was a horrible experience and one I hope you never suffer, and I will never have again.

I simply don't understand how some people think it is OK to take things that are not theirs. They don't know or care how hard their victims have had to work to save up for little luxuries.

We weren't rich, far from it, and we both worked very hard to make ends meet. How dare they break into our home and steal our things.

Fifty Eight

I think every woman, if asked, would admit to having an ideal weight. Mine is fifty-eight kilogrammes or 9st 4lbs.

I haven't actually been as light as that since I did the Weight Watchers commercial in early 1989, although I did get down to 9st 6lbs on my last diet, which you read about in *chapter 28*.

I really liked the new svelte me, but I did have a few comments saying I looked a little gaunt in the face, so maybe I am better being a few pounds heavier at my age?

That's my excuse anyway!

Fifty Nine

It was in 1959, when I was just three years old,
that I went for my first dancing lesson.

Mum chose the Sissie Smith School of Dancing because Sissie was the choreographer for the Nottingham Operatic Society, which both Mum and Dad were active members of.

It was a long journey from where we lived in West Bridgford to Derby Road, where the school was located, and it was all done by bus. We caught the number 24, as mentioned in *chapter 24*, to the Market Square in the city centre, and then we took a trolley bus to the top of Derby Road before walking down the hill to the school.

Just to digress for a moment, do you remember trolley buses? They ran off overhead power cables via a trolley wheel, hence the name, so they were probably quite eco-friendly. The problem was they were always breaking down and causing traffic jams. They were a bit like trams, really, but they could go up bigger hills. I quite liked them as they didn't smell as bad as normal buses and they didn't vibrate as much.

Anyway, back to my first dancing lesson. The class was called the 'baby' class as it was for children under school age. If you went to dancing class as a very small child, I am sure you will remember that there is precious little dancing involved, it's more about acting out stories. My favourite was 'Little Red Riding Hood', particularly running away screaming from the big bad wolf at the end.

There was one bit in the story that I didn't enjoy so much, the bit where we had to skip through the wood. I couldn't skip. Although I could walk fairly evenly with the help of my built-up shoe, I wasn't yet able to spring off my left leg. So I adapted it to do a half-skip, half-walk movement which had the overall effect of me looking like a wounded animal. I did master skipping eventually, as my leg got stronger through swimming and dancing, but it is still a very vivid recollection.

We also used to do 'Ring a Rosie' in a circle and all fall down at the end so that we could do our 'good toes and naughty toes'.

I had been at Sissie's for about a year when we did our first show. The baby class was only involved in one scene, the skating scene. The senior girls did a ballet and at the end of it the 'babies' came on to do a simple little routine, and to 'feed the birds'.

The costumes were beautiful. We had red needlecord jackets trimmed with ruffled white net to simulate fur (although I think one girl had the real thing), white, mid-calf-length full skirts with tiny red dots on, ear muffs and a hand muff. We must have looked so cute, although I don't know for sure as I've never seen any photos.

The music started and we began our little dance, and then disaster struck. It might only have been a simple little routine but I forgot the steps! I guess it must have been stage fright but the routine had completely gone from my mind. To my credit I didn't just stand there or cry or run off the stage. I skipped the dance and moved to the front of the stage to scatter the imaginary crumbs in the direction of the audience. Even at that age I could think on my feet, something which has stood me in very good stead for the career path I chose!

The only other show I remember doing while I was at Sissie Smith's was one for the Operatic Society. They were putting on a production of *The King and I*, so of course needed the Siamese children. I have a vague recollection of going for an audition with my brother Richard but I think we were more or less selected because of our parents' involvement. There wasn't any dancing involved, but we did have to sing 'Getting to Know You' and sway in time to the music.

I was only seven so wasn't allowed to do all eight shows due to the performance rules governing children, so each group performed in four shows. My group did the Monday night, Wednesday matinee, Friday night and the coveted last night of the show on the Saturday. My only individual action was to pull the King's pantaloons and be shooed away by him.

The costumes were very elaborate and we had to wear brown body make-up and wigs with little top knots on the top of our heads.

At each of those four performances I cried my eyes out when the King died – not pretend tears, the real thing! Even at the tender age of six I was an emotional human being!

My brother went on to 'star' with my sister and my dad in the Nottingham Operatic Society's next production, *South Pacific*, but that was our family's final involvement. My maternal grandma had been diagnosed with terminal cancer and she moved into our house so that Mum could nurse her. There simply wasn't time for Mum to take us to any of our extra-curricular activities. Thank goodness we lived opposite the school.

After my grandma died, followed nine months later by her husband, I went back to dancing but to a different dancing school, as I explained in *chapter 6*.

Sixty

In Western astrology we have an annual cycle of
twelve star signs, starting with Aries towards the end
of March and ending with Pisces. My birthday is on the
10th of June, so I am a Gemini. In Chinese astrology it
is a sixty-year cycle.

There are twelve animal signs which are each allocated a year.
The year doesn't start on the first of January; it corresponds
with the start of the Chinese New Year, which changes from year
to year.

As an illustration I will use my daughter's birthday of the 8th
of January. If the animal had changed on the first of January,
Sophie would be a Dragon. The Chinese New Year started on
the 17th of February in 1988, so Sophie is a Rabbit.

If you have a birthday in January or February you need to
check the start of the Chinese New Year in the year you were
born to accurately ascertain which animal sign you are. As a June
birthday mine was easy to work out. I am a Monkey . . . no
comments please!

But it doesn't end there. As I mentioned it is a sixty-year cycle
and there are only twelve animals, but there are also five 'elements',
which are on a twelve-year cycle, so the same animal sign born
twelve years apart would not have the same ruling element. The
five elements are fire, water, earth, metal and wood.

Again I will give you examples from my family. My late dad and I are both Monkeys, but as he was born in 1920 and I was born in 1956 we are not the same type of Monkey, as we were born thirty-six years apart. Dad was a 'metal' Monkey, and I am a 'fire' Monkey. My mum and my son, Daniel, however, were born sixty years apart, so they are both 'fire' Tigers. There are similarities in their personalities, but Mum is Leo and Daniel is Sagittarius in Western astrology, so there are differences too.

I have always been interested in astrology but only became aware of the Chinese system when I worked in Hong Kong in 1979. I bought myself a book on the subject, which I found fascinating, and I used to take great pleasure in working out friends' and family's birth signs to see if I could recognise any of the supposed character traits.

So what are the Monkey's characteristics? Well here is what it says on a 'monkey mug' that I drink my fruit tea from:

> The Monkey is imaginative and inquisitive, with a good memory: a good organiser, he or she is charming and confident. A survivor in life, the Monkey is successful and competitive and good at solving intricate problems.

I would say that is pretty accurate and when you add the fire element it also brings extra energy and determination, along with stamina, daring and a uniquely inventive mind. There are also negative traits but I'd rather not draw your attention to those!

In my Chinese Horoscopes book there is also a section called 'East meets West', which talks about the influence of our Western sign on the animal character, and I think the summary of the Gemini Monkey is probably the most accurate description of me. I'm not being conceited with some of the things I recognise in myself, just honest:

These people are doubly versatile and mercurial – able to process information at the speed of light. A hyperactive handful, they have such energy and verve that they go through life like whirling dervishes. Emotionally, they are miserable without an adoring partner.

I count myself as very fortunate to have the aforementioned adoring partner, even though I don't always show it.

He is the wind beneath my wings.

Sixty One

This is the number of Waitrose and
Sainsbury's recipe cards I have collected.

I don't know why I do this as I have at least thirty recipe books, most of which rarely get opened. It's not that I don't cook, I do, and I really enjoy it. It's just that I'm usually a bit pushed for time and I don't want to spend the little time I have available experimenting on something that might not be very tasty.

I first started collecting these cards from Sainsbury's as I always used to do the weekly shop there. They had them positioned near the entrance/exit to the store. I suppose the idea was that you would pick up a card and then proceed into the shop and buy the necessary ingredients. I would pick the card up on my way out of the shop, drive home, unpack the groceries and put the card in a kitchen drawer, never to see the light of day.

When I changed supermarket to fit in with the location of the children's secondary school and began regularly shopping at Waitrose, I continued my addiction to these cards.

It wasn't until I was shopping with the children's nana and she bought me a holder for these recipe cards that I actually sorted through all the cards I had collected and started making the appetising-looking offerings. The really funny thing is how many of the cards I had duplicates of, not realising I had already picked them up on a previous supermarket trip.

Most of the recipes I have tried have worked out really well, but I still reckon I have tried fewer than half. The first time I try something I will follow the recipe to the letter, but then I might tweak it a bit for personal taste the second and subsequent times I make it. I have a Waitrose recipe for Dorset Apple Cake but the recipe suggests mixed spice. I prefer it with just cinnamon, only a small adaptation but, to my palate, it makes a big difference.

Our two favourite and most used cards are Spinach, Tomato and Chickpea Curry as mentioned in *chapter 98*, and Asparagus and Bean Strangozzi, which I usually get Daniel to do. The recipe requires the use of a chilli and I will always remember the first time Daniel made it when he was fifteen or sixteen. He had followed the instructions very carefully and was just about to dish up when he complained that his eyes were burning. I had omitted to tell him to thoroughly wash his hands after chopping the chilli and he had obviously rubbed his eyes. Thank goodness he hadn't needed to go to the loo if you get my drift! He is now very meticulous after chopping chilli.

Thankfully, as I am a vegetarian, there are only a certain amount of cards that are suitable for me, or I think my collection may well be in the many hundreds!

Chris and I became vegetarian as 1985 ended and 1986 began. We were hoping to start a family and after reading newspaper articles and watching television documentaries about the steroids that were being fed to animals to increase 'yield', we decided that we wanted to bring the children up as vegetarians so that they could make their own decision later in life on whether or not to eat meat.

In fairness, we had gradually been eating less and less in the way of meat. I hadn't eaten red meat for a number of years, so it was mostly just about giving up poultry and fish.

We had turkey for our Christmas dinner and, like most families, for the following few days, and tuna spaghetti on New Year's Eve and then we just stopped eating any animal flesh, although we do still have eggs and cheese.

I can honestly say I really don't miss it and I don't think my health suffers because of it as I always make sure we have suffi-cient protein from other sources. Earlier this year Chris and I decided to try some fish as we were concerned that maybe we weren't getting enough omega oils in our diet. We had a piece of salmon between us and, although we both managed to keep it down, neither of us enjoyed it so we haven't repeated the experience.

As for the children, well, Daniel does now have fish at least once a week and he also has chicken and some meat. Sophie however is still vegetarian, although she may well have experi-mented with tasting meat over the years. I guess I should have known she was likely to stay veggie after I overheard her, at a very young age, explaining to a friend eating a chicken sandwich that she was eating a fluffy little yellow chick. I don't remember if the friend finished the sandwich!

I have no problem with other people eating meat around me, except possibly a very rare steak, but I am not fond of the smell of it cooking, which is why you rarely see me on kitchen shows on QVC!

Sixty Two

In 1962 I bought my first record with pocket money I had saved up in my windmill money box, a present my mum and dad had brought back from a trip to Holland.

There was a programme on television at the time called *Dr Kildare* and, at the age of five, I had a massive crush on the star of the show, Richard Chamberlain. I really wanted the instrumental version that they played at the beginning and end of the show but I don't think it was released as a single. However, due to the popularity of the show, Richard Chamberlain recorded a vocal to the theme called 'Three Stars Will Shine Tonight', and that was the first record I bought. It reached number 12 in the UK charts in June 1962, but was a definite number 1 in the Roberts household, with me at least!

The second record I bought was 'Softly As I Leave You' by Matt Monro. I went onto YouTube to listen to it while I was doing little bits of research for this book and it still had me in floods of tears. Although Richard Chamberlain was undeniably the better-looking of the two to my five-year-old eyes, Matt Monro was undoubtedly the better singer in my opinion.

I also loved to listen to an EP of my dad's by Nat King Cole. It had 'Unforgettable' and 'For All We Know' on it, and even though I was only five my dad would talk to me about the amazing orchestration and the string arrangements by Gordon

Jenkins. I have always loved music but it surprises me that as such a young child I had such sophisticated taste. I think my children were still listening to 'The Wheels on the Bus' when they were five.

They have both inherited the musical genes, though. Daniel loves to listen to music, all types of music, and his knowledge on the subject is quite incredible. Definitely worthy of a 'phone a friend' on *Who Wants to Be a Millionaire!*

Sophie, on the other hand, loves to perform rather than listen and has been in two girl bands. She got a taste for it aged about two and a half when we made a recording of her singing 'Twinkle Twinkle Little Star' very sweetly. We also have a recording of her singing 'Baa Baa Black Sheep', which is not quite so angelic. She was doing well until she got to 'one for the dame', and then, like her mother in the 'feeding the birds' dance routine in *chapter 59*, she forgot the last line. It is very funny to listen to a three-year-old saying, 'Whatever', before it ever became a comedienne's catchphrase!

I keep reminding Sophie that I have the tapes if she ever makes it big in the music world!

Sixty Three

We all played 'when I grow up I want to be' when we were young children, but what did I want to be in the summer of 1963, a professional tennis player or a high-class call girl?

Let me explain. I have already mentioned that we lived opposite the Jesse Gray Primary School and when the school was closed we used to climb over the gates to play in what was the car park during term time. The caretaker knew us, as we all attended the school, and I think he just turned a blind eye to our trespassing, so long as we didn't do any damage.

My mum and dad were both very keen on tennis so during Wimbledon fortnight we would gather around our black-and-white television set to watch the play, particularly if there was British involvement, as there very often was in the early 1960s.

With Wimbledon still fresh in our minds, we children decided to have a tennis tournament, and to make it more fun we each had to pretend to be one of the professional players.

My brother and his friend were going to be Mike Sangster and Roger Taylor, my sister was Ann Haydon-Jones and I announced that I was going to be Christine Keeler!

If you are of a certain age you will recognise the name, but in case it is unfamiliar to you, she was the 'call girl' at the centre of the Profumo Affair that almost brought down the government of the day. Obviously, it was a huge news story at the time and I must have heard the name and got it confused with the British tennis player Christine Truman.

My sister, who is five and a half years my senior, was in hysterics and even my brother thought it was funny, although I'm hoping that at seven years old he didn't actually understand what a 'call girl' was! I know I didn't!

Suffice to say I didn't grow up to become either, although I did make it into the school tennis team at West Bridgford Comprehensive School.

I still play occasionally but I'm not very good, except for one blinding shot. It's a very low forehand down the line, and even I'm amazed when it actually clears the net.

Sixty Four

I am five foot four inches tall, which is
sixty-four inches.

Although this is a fairly decent height I often claimed to be five foot five inches. This probably started when I was a dancer and I would be looking for job advertisements in the back pages of the *Stage* newspaper. Usually there was a minimum height requirement of at least five foot five inches but I would go along for the audition anyway and tell a little fib when asked for my height.

Most of the time I got away with it, but sometimes they would get twenty girls at a time to stand in a line across the front of the stage and anyone who didn't measure up was sent home without dancing a step. I can understand why they did it – so there was some kind of uniformity on the stage. I just wonder if they would be allowed to put a minimum height requirement in adverts now? In this day and age of 'political correctness' would it be regarded as 'height-ist'?

I was the tallest female in my immediate family until Sophie grew up. My sister is five foot, and the tallest of her three girls is Rachel, at five foot three. My mum used to be five foot two but I think she has shrunk a bit with age, even though she is the most upright eighty-six-year-old I have ever seen.

As I have mentioned I am five foot four but Sophie is at least five foot six. Clearly she gets it from her dad's side of the family as Chris is six foot one, but Daniel would claim the height prize in our family at a very lofty six foot four . . . and I'm not convinced he's stopped growing yet!

Sixty Five

In 1965 I was entered into the Nottingham Speech and Drama Festival for the first time, and I won my class, 'verse-speaking for nine-year-olds'.

I had begun taking elocution lessons the year before. I think my mum was trying to dissuade me from going back to dancing lessons, as my previous dancing teacher had told her I would not be able to take examinations. It was also a lot easier to get me to the lessons as, rather than dragging an eight-year-old across to the other side of Nottingham on buses, my elocution teacher, Mrs Swann, was based in West Bridgford, where we lived.

At first I found it a little boring, as you had to do exercises to make sure your mouth formed the right shape to make the perfect vowel sounds. When I started to learn poems to recite out loud I became a lot more interested.

The first poem I learnt was called 'Donkey', and it was about the first staggering steps of a newborn foal. Even though I had only been going to lessons for a couple of months Mrs Swann decided she wanted to enter me for my Grade I examination in December 1964. This required me to learn a set piece to say alongside a poem of my own choice. As time was short, Donkey was my choice and I had to learn a poem called 'Rachel', by Walter de la Mare who, as I mentioned in *chapter 56*, died the year I was born.

The Examiner's Report said: 'A lovely clear voice. You lost yourself so well in the poem and so it sprang to life quite vividly. I really saw Rachel.'

And of 'Donkey' they wrote: 'Spoken with sympathy and understanding. Let the face reflect the thought as well as the voice.'

I passed my first Speech and Drama examination with eighty points out of a hundred, gaining me a Merit certificate.

Seven months later, in July 1965, I took my Grade 2 examination and passed with Special Honours, gaining the highest total of marks for my grade at the Nottingham Centre.

Just prior to that, I had won my first Verse-Speaking Festival, and a year later, in 1966, I won first place again in the older age group of ten- and eleven-year-olds. I was probably the youngest entrant as I had only turned ten in June. I was particularly thrilled as I was awarded the Lillian Bowles Trophy, the first trophy I had ever won.

Later that year, in December, I took my Grade 3 examination, and once again was awarded the Special Honours certificate. The two poems I recited for that examination were a very forgettable poem called 'Flamingo', which was the set piece, and a beautiful poem called 'Imagination', by G.F. Bradby. It was about the way we 'misremember' our childhood, and I am sure I have a much better understanding of it now than I did as a ten-year-old.

Not only did it help me to attain my Grade 3, and win me the Lillian Bowles Trophy, I also won my only prize at West Bridgford Grammar School Speech Day by reciting it.

I have tried to find the poem online for you to read, but without success I'm afraid. It could possibly feature in a recent G.F. Bradby poetry anthology entitled *Broadland & Other Poems*.

I was showing a real aptitude for Speech and Drama, however I had also restarted dancing classes. My dad was then made redundant from his job so there simply wasn't enough money for me to have lessons in both. I had to choose between drama and dancing.

There was no contest. I had always loved dancing.

Looking back now, perhaps I should have stayed with something that I had an obvious natural talent for and who knows, maybe I would have been Julia Roberts the actress!

Sixty Six

Do you believe in fate? I do. I thought about having
chapter 66 based on England's World Cup victory in
1966, but this really didn't seem quite right, as at the
age of ten I was not the least bit interested in football.

I can honestly say I don't remember crowding around a black-
and-white television set watching history being made!

The only thing I knew about football was how annoyed my
mum or dad used to be trying to get me home from dancing
class across Trent Bridge in Nottingham when Forest had been
playing. So the World Cup victory didn't seem particularly
relevant to my own personal history.

So back to fate. Whilst I was writing this book, I turned on
the television one night and a film was about to start called *Sixty
Six*. I didn't know what the plot was about and I only kept it on
because one of the stars was Helena Bonham Carter, who I was
fortunate enough to meet and interview in 2011 when I was in
Los Angeles at the QVC Red Carpet party. She had been nomi-
nated for an Oscar as Best Supporting Actress in *The King's Speech*
and was doing the round of parties in the run-up to Oscar night.
She seemed really genuine and even admitted to watching QVC
occasionally. I thought I would just watch a few minutes of *Sixty
Six* to see Helena Bonham Carter in a different type of role.

The film is about a soon-to-be thirteen-year-old boy, Bernie, planning his own bar mitzvah and is set in 1966, hence the title. He wants his bar mitzvah to be a grand affair, better than his brother's, as his brother bullies him. He chooses a flash venue and plans on having 250 guests and even writes to celebrities in the hope that they may attend.

His dad and uncle run a grocery store and are reasonably well off until a Fine Fare supermarket opens up a few doors down the street. From that moment things start to conspire against Bernie and his grand plans, including a house fire that destroys the attic of his house, where his dad had stashed all their savings. Things go from bad to worse as it transpires that Bernie's birthday is the same date as the World Cup Final, the 30th of July . . . not really a problem, England were never going to feature in it anyway!

I won't spoil the rest of the story, but suffice to say I watched it through to the end and surprised myself that sometimes I laughed out loud and the next minute had a tear rolling down my cheek.

It was a well-written human story and when the credits rolled at the end I guess I should have expected to see Richard Curtis's name there. There were a lot of similarities with *Love Actually*, which I have already confessed in *chapter 10* is my favourite film of the moment.

For the record, I thought Helena Bonham Carter gave a pretty good performance as Bernie's mum, Esther.

Sixty Seven

67 Priory Crescent was my first proper address
in London.

I say proper address because, prior to that, whenever I lived in London it would usually be courtesy of someone's generosity in allowing me to use their sofa.

This was a small, self-contained studio-style flat that I shouldn't really have been living in as it was a Housing Association property and my name was not on the tenancy agreement. The flat was actually rented to a singer who I had worked with on the cruise ship and she was once again away working. The flat was lying empty, I needed a place to stay and it helped her out financially, so although technically it might not have been the right thing to do, it seemed like the right thing at the time.

I was coming to London from Guernsey, where I had spent the summer of 1977, to attend the DJ course at Juliana's that I wrote about in *chapter 45*. I'm not sure that my mum and dad were thrilled that I was going to be living in the big city on my own; however, to their credit, they didn't say as much.

The flat was purpose-built and was one of only four built over four garages. All the other flats on the crescent had communal entrances, but these four had their own front door opening to the outside world.

It was really a big square with a small bathroom to the right as you came in, and the rest of the flat was open plan, with a small curtained-off area acting as the bedroom. The big bonus was that it had huge picture windows that offered up a far-reaching view down towards Croydon. I didn't realise at the time but it also faced south-west, so I could watch the sun setting, now one of my favourite things to do.

Another plus was that it was on the bus route. This is very important in south-east London as most areas don't have the luxury of being on the tube network. I could catch the number 68 to Croydon in one direction, and all the way to Chalk Farm in North London in the other. I never went to Chalk Farm, but it was a useful route through Norwood, Herne Hill, Camberwell Green and Elephant and Castle, before crossing the river and passing Holborn, Russell Square and, I think, Camden. It was a really good bus route but in rush-hour traffic it could take hours.

The other bus that went past the end of my crescent was the 248. It went to Crystal Palace in one direction and Streatham in the other. It wasn't such a useful bus, but you could catch either the 68 or the 248 to Crown Point and change to a 137 which would then take you all the way to the West End.

So I had my transport worked out, I had a job, I had a nice place to live, I was just a bit lonely living on my own. My loneliness was thankfully short-lived as I met Chris, *chapter 21*, a mere four months after I moved in.

I hadn't planned for Chris to move in with me, particularly after going out with him for only two weeks, but circumstances dictated and actually it worked out really well. The flat itself was big enough for two people; the bedroom, however, was a bit snug. There was only room for a single bed, so we used to sleep curled up together like spoons. That may be OK for a few weeks, or even months, but we lived there together for nearly two years! It was probably a good job we were both quite slim.

It was the first time I had lived with anyone other than my family or girl dancers when I was doing various shows. Although we got along most of the time we did have a few 'moments', but thankfully they never lasted long and we would always kiss and make up eventually. It was great to be young and in love and have someone to share my life with.

I think Chris's parents must have known he had moved in with me more or less straight away because of his change of address. I didn't tell my mum and dad that we were living together for a couple of months, although I had told them I had met Chris and they probably realised he was pretty special to me. They might have had their suspicions earlier than that though. On one occasion I remember the phone ringing and I was busy so I called through to Chris to answer it.

'Are you sure?' he asked.

'Yes,' I replied.

I heard him say 'Hello', followed by, 'I'll just get her.' You've guessed it, it was my mum. Apparently she had paused momentarily when she heard a man's voice and then said, 'Oh . . . you must be Chris. Is Julia there?'

Chris was quite cross with me for putting him in that position and to this day is reluctant to answer the phone when it rings!

When I did eventually tell them that we were co-habiting they probably weren't too surprised, more relieved that I was no longer on my own.

Chris continued to work at the Peacock Club in Streatham and his new home was even closer to his work than his former one. The other two members of the band actually lived in Streatham and I became good friends with Sharon, the girlfriend of the bass player, Paul. She was from Bristol and shortly after Chris and I met she gave birth to their baby, Christopher. She couldn't get out much as she didn't have family on hand to babysit so I would often spend the evenings with her if I wasn't working, or I would offer to look after Christopher if she wanted some time to herself.

I didn't go away for a summer season in 1978 as I wanted to spend my time with Chris.

When the advertisement for the Ashcroft Theatre pantomime auditions appeared in the *Stage* newspaper I went along. It was a different production company from the previous year but I managed to get hired again, which meant that Chris and I could spend our first Christmas together.

The show was *Dick Whittington* and starred Barbara Windsor and Norman Vaughan. Barbara played the title role, and I was her understudy. This meant I had to learn her lines, songs and stage positioning, and had to attend understudy rehearsals each week in case she was off sick. She would often come into the theatre and say to me, 'I've got a sore throat, I might not be in tomorrow.'

I think it was just to keep me on my toes as, true professional that she is, she never missed a performance.

Funnily enough, in the very early days of QVC we used to sell a range of nail-care products called Supernails. The regular guest and Supernails salon owner, Carolyn, would sometimes bring celebrity clients on air with her to endorse the brand, one of whom was Barbara Windsor!

I had also auditioned around the same time as the pantomime for a nightclub show at the Stork Room in the West End. I was offered that too, and somehow managed to juggle both jobs. I did matinee and evening performances at the theatre, then, in my beloved Snowdrop, who I told you about in *chapter* 16, drove straight into the West End for a midnight and 2 a.m. show. There is no denying that it was pretty exhausting but Chris and I both have the same philosophy regarding work: don't turn it down if you are physically able to do it. Anyway, I was young and had no other demands on my time so I just got on with it.

It didn't really bother me driving home on my own so late at night. I remember on one occasion being followed by the police as I drove through Brixton and then being pulled over for a routine check. I've often wondered what they must have thought when I wound my window down and they were confronted by a young curvy woman fluttering her false eyelashes at them! No, it was never a problem until the night it snowed.

When I had set off for the theatre, around 1.30 p.m., it had been a beautiful sunny winter's day. For some reason, I was wearing the new toe socks I'd had for Christmas, with a pair of Scholl sandals, and no coat. The weather was fine when I left the theatre in Croydon heading for the West End, but when I came out of the Stork Room four hours later it was snowing, and I mean really snowing. The further south I drove, the worse it got.

Brixton was a nightmare with cars slithering around like Bambi on ice. The trick was to try not to stop as even on a slight incline it was almost impossible to get any traction to move forwards. As well as the snow getting heavier it also gets very hilly approaching Upper Norwood, and although Snowdrop did her best, she finally gave up the ghost going up a steep hill, about half a mile from home. Luckily, I managed to roll her backwards into the kerb, rather than leaving her in the middle of the road. The other piece of good fortune was that she had died within fifty yards of a telephone box.

I rang Chris on our home number and at the first attempt there was no answer. I left it a few minutes and tried again. This time he picked up. He had just got in after walking back from Streatham, about two miles, because his car wouldn't even start!

He came to meet me through the snow, which was at least two feet deep, like a knight in shining armour, bringing with him a pair of boots and my coat. Both were very welcome, even though I had wrapped myself in a blanket I kept in the car for emergencies. We eventually arrived home around 4.30 a.m., freezing cold but safe, and I still had to get up the next morning to go in for the matinee performance of the pantomime.

Chris was also very good at helping with the chores and he even liked to share the cooking. I remember once we had been preparing spaghetti Bolognese together. Everything was ready to dish up and I was draining the pasta while Chris grated the parmesan cheese. We didn't have a colander so I was just using the saucepan lid. I'm not sure how but the next minute the spaghetti was sitting in the kitchen sink. I was not amused but Chris diffused the situation by starting to laugh, which set me off too. We ate it anyway, after retrieving it from the kitchen sink, and it tasted pretty good from what I can remember.

We were very happy at Priory Crescent and it was a great base not only for our work, but also for day trips down to the south coast. On Sundays, during the summer months, we would get up early, stop off at a bakery for supplies, then head down to Brighton or Littlehampton to spend the day on the beach.

After the drive back neither of us would fancy cooking, so we would collect a Chinese takeaway and a bottle of cider for Sunday dinner . . . happy times!

Sixty Eight

Number 68 Bath Street, St Helier, Jersey, was my
address in the summer of 1974 when I was appearing
as a dancer in the summer season at the
Hotel de France.

It was a flat above a restaurant called the Yankee Diner, and
was home to four of the dancers from the show and two
musicians from the Ivy Benson Showband. There is a good chance
that I was there by mistake, but it was a happy mistake from my
point of view.

There were six dancers in the show and two of us were under
eighteen at the beginning of the season. Beverley was sixteen
about to turn seventeen, and I was seventeen, soon to be eighteen.
Because of our tender years I think the intention was for Beverley
and I to share an apartment in the grounds of the big house
belonging to the owner of the Hotel de France for him to keep
an eye on us. The apartment was lovely and we would be able to
use the swimming pool in the grounds but I hated the idea of
being watched over.

As it happened, there was another dancer called Julia in the
show. She was much older than me, twenty-six I think, and when
the accommodation was allocated, it was her name that was
announced to stay at the big house while my name was on the
list for the Bath Street flat. I kept my mouth shut, particularly

as one of the girls in the Bath Street flat was Kathy, who I had worked with the previous summer.

The other Julia didn't seem to mind so we just went with the flow. I suppose it could have been the intention to partner Beverley with the most senior dancer to kind of 'mother' her a bit. Anyway I think the hotel owner was probably quite relieved that he didn't have a 'criminal' living in his apartment — if you skipped *chapter 7* please read it now and you will see I am not really a criminal.

With the benefit of hindsight I feel a little bit guilty about the mix-up. Julia had a boyfriend in another show, which meant that Beverley was on her own a lot, so I guess she was pretty lonely, particularly as she had no transport. This is maybe the reason I haven't rung her despite her being a regular in the Butler & Wilson shop and giving her phone number not once but twice to the girls in the shop to pass on to me because she watches QVC. OK, now I feel doubly guilty. I promise I will ring her as soon as I have finished writing this book! I'll even give her a signed copy if she wants one.

The flat on Bath Street wasn't exactly the lap of luxury but it was a fun place to live. Kathy and her friend Susie shared a room, and a girl called Debbie and I shared another. The Ivy Benson girls lived on the top floor but we all shared the bijoux kitchen, the lounge and the bathroom. Yes, there was just the one bathroom for seven girls, but somehow we managed, and at least there was a guest cloakroom just off the lounge.

At first we didn't mix much with the girls in the band — they were very worldly wise and kept very late hours — but once we got to know them we all got on really well. I got on particularly well with a young saxophonist called Gilly, so well in fact that I flew back from Ireland to go to her wedding in 1986, she came to my fortieth birthday party in 1996 and we still send each other birthday and Christmas cards. My mum and dad loved her too and even named a goat after her when they were living on the Isle of Skye.

The flat was a kind of open house really. It was so central that friends would just drop in for a cup of tea at all times of the day or night. We were often up in the wee small hours when the bakery across the road was loading up its delivery vans.

One night we had friends round and had run out of bread to make toast, so we called down to the drivers and asked if they could sling up a loaf to keep us going. They obliged, and this then became something of a ritual. If we were up when they were starting their day we would lift the sash cord windows and lean out to catch the doughy missiles. It must have looked hysterical for anyone at street level, but at that time in the morning there were precious few people around, and those who were would possibly not be in a fit state to comprehend what was going on!

Occasionally we would have the extra treat of a tray of jammy doughnuts with the jam still warm inside. I'm happy to say we used to go downstairs and collect them rather having them hurled up at us. I have no idea how the missing bread and cakes were explained away but fortunately no one got into trouble over it.

One of the regular visitors to our flat was a musician called Rod. We had met him at St Ouen's, the famous five-mile surfers' beach, where he used to sit in the sun strumming his guitar and singing. I think I actually recorded one of his late-night sessions on my cassette recorder – I'll bet the sound quality on that was great!

Jersey is a beach lover's paradise and I did my best to visit as many beaches as I could. They were so varied too.

St Aubin's Bay was on the south side of the island and was the other end of the bay from the town of St Helier. That was good for just sitting around on the beach or going for long walks. My failed attempts at water skiing were also at St Aubin's.

Moving west there was the stunning Portelet Bay. This was

at the bottom of a steep set of steps and I knew it from when we had visited Jersey when I was a child, as we had stayed at the Portelet Hotel.

Next to that was Ouaine Beach, which was at the unspoilt end of St Brelade's Bay, and then you had the buzzy St Brelade itself.

The whole of the west side of Jersey is made up of St Ouen's Beach and then you rounded the corner onto the north coast for bays like Greve de Lecq and Plemont, which I wasn't so familiar with.

The east side housed sandy Rozel Bay and rocky Bouley Bay, where they did a hill-climb race around hairpin bends in the road. And that brings us down to Gorey Castle and the lovely sands of St Clement. I wasn't keen on that beach at low tide though as you could see all the treacherous rocks that had claimed so many ships down the ages.

Down to Grouville and round the corner to St Helier. There were loads of other less well-known beaches, but let's keep them less well known shall we?

I loved Jersey so much that I went back for a second summer season, as you will have read in *chapter 22*, but I have to admit, although it was good, it wasn't quite the same.

Sixty Nine

There is a theory in bookish circles that you can judge
a book, any book, by reading page 69.

Apparently if you like page 69 then you will like the book. As I am writing this chapter before I have finished writing my book, I have absolutely no idea what page 69 of this book is going to be. I don't even have an idea which chapter it is likely to be.

All I do know is that if you have read this much of my book, you will have gone a long way past page 69 and I am hopeful that this means you have found it interesting and intend to finish it.

If you have just flicked back to page 69 and decided it wasn't actually that great, then thanks for sticking with it – after all, the page 69 rule could be just an urban myth!

Seventy

This is the number of seconds I sat behind a row of taxis in Croydon, thinking that I was at the back of a traffic jam!

And that is only the length of time my son Daniel actually timed me waiting after he had realised my error, so I would estimate that we actually sat there for at least twice as long.

We were both a bit miserable as we were on our way back from a Crystal Palace home game and once again we had lost. Even so I should probably have been paying more attention to the traffic.

In my defence, the taxis waiting in line along the roadside, before they turn into East Croydon station, do stretch quite a long way, and the back of the row is usually on a bend in the road so you can't see what is happening ahead. That said, you would have thought I would have realised that the cars going past on the outside of me were fairly free flowing whilst we were totally stationary.

I often wonder quite how long Daniel would have let me sit there waiting if I hadn't realised I was in the taxi queue.

Seventy One

Considering how much travelling I have done since, you
may be surprised to learn that I had never been abroad
until I went on a holiday with my parents in 1971.

I was fifteen, and we went to Austria, a little place called Igls,
near Innsbruck, to be precise. It was just the three of us. My
sister had long since moved out of the family home, and had her
hands full with her husband and three children under the age of
five, and my brother simply didn't want to go.

I think it was my mum who particularly wanted to visit Austria.
She has always preferred the cooler holiday destinations of
Norway and Switzerland to the heat of the Mediterranean. It's
probably to do with her colouring. She has very fair skin and as
a young woman had coppery red hair.

It was very exciting looking through the holiday brochures
and choosing where we were going to stay. Eventually the Hotel
Iglerhof was selected which was on the outskirts of the village
of Igls. I think it may well be a skiing destination in the winter
months, but we were travelling in August, to tie in with the
school holidays, so there wasn't any snow around apart from the
peaks of the surrounding mountains. The weather was surprisingly hot and sunny, but every afternoon there was a heavy
downpour of rain for thirty minutes or so and then the sun came
back out again.

Although the nearest airport was Innsbruck, for some reason

we flew to Munich and then had a rather long coach transfer. At least it gave us the opportunity to appreciate the stunning scenery.

We were all in one room, which I realise, now that I am an adult, might not have been ideal for Mum and Dad. I do recall that Mum sometimes used to 'have a rest' in the afternoons while I was out by the swimming pool, if you get my drift.

The hotel itself was very grand and I think my parents really enjoyed their stay, but there weren't many other teenagers there, apart from a French boy called Bernard, who I think I had a bit of a crush on. So the evenings were a little dull, but the days were fabulous.

As well as having its own outdoor swimming pool, the hotel also had tennis courts. I have already mentioned in *chapter 63* that Mum and Dad were keen tennis players and I was in the school tennis team, so I was able to give them a decent game. I had made my own tennis dress, along with most of Mum's wardrobe.

Although I say so myself, I had done a pretty good job. I had taken three patterns that Mum liked and by using all the different fabrics, putting sleeves in some and not in others, and making some knee length and some full length, I had created a good variety. I'm guessing I probably made all my own clothes too, which I had been doing for a couple of years. I think I started when my dad was made redundant and money was very tight, as that was the cheapest option, but I liked having unique clothes so I just carried on after our financial situation improved.

I didn't make a tennis dress for Mum as she preferred to wear shorts. Mum and I still have a joke about her wearing shorts as she has the whitest legs you have ever seen, but they're not in bad shape for a lady in her eighties!

We played tennis most days, but we also found time to walk from the hotel to a huge lake, which I think may have been Lanser

See, where they had stone table tennis tables, another sport my parents were very fond of!

We also walked halfway up the Patscherkofel mountain – well, I say halfway, maybe that is a slight exaggeration! There was a cable car to take you further up but we all decided to give that a miss.

All this activity, and I still had to find time to fit in my ballet practice, as mentioned in *chapter 6*. The timing of this holiday could have been better, as I was about to take my Royal Academy of Dance elementary examination. My dancing teacher, Miss Morrison, had only allowed me to go on holiday if I promised to do ballet practice every day, and Mum was on hand to make sure I did.

The hotel were very accommodating as they allowed me to practise on the huge landing outside our room. It was perfect as I was able to use the banister as my ballet barre, and it just happened to be the right height. Goodness knows what the other guests thought as they went up and down the staircase!

I have looked on holiday websites to see if this hotel is still in operation but I haven't been able to find it under the name Iglerhof. Maybe it's been redeveloped and renamed, or worse still knocked down. I hope not as one day I would like to revisit, and maybe even pluck up the courage to go on the cable car.

Seventy Two

I left school in July 1972, shortly after my
sixteenth birthday.

School for the preceding month had consisted of only attending on the relevant days to sit my O level examinations. It had been a particularly stressful time for me as, along with studying for my GCEs, my mum had decided to hold her dancing school show at the end of May, and I had a starring role. Not only did I have lines to learn and dance routines to learn, I was also making all my own costumes. I nearly managed it, but there was one costume that was supposed to have an elasticated puffed sleeve to the blouse and I simply ran out of time, so I improvised by putting rubber bands around my upper arms. It's a good job I didn't need to wear it for long as they were a bit tight and I could feel my hands going tingly.

So I had all the preparations for Mum's show and all my revising to do. To say I didn't have much of a social life is an understatement!

Looking back, it was probably all too much for me because as soon as I picked up my exam results in the August, I went to visit my sister in Scotland for a two-week holiday and I ended up staying there for months.

It's not as though it was particularly relaxing, as my sister had three children under the age of five and no spare bedroom, so I slept on the sofa. It's just that it was different, less pressured, and I think I was a bit burnt out.

Being a mum and recently having gone through the trauma of my daughter Sophie leaving home, I now understand how dreadful it must have been for my mum, particularly as I taught a lot of classes for her at her dancing school. She pleaded with me to go home, but I wasn't ready. I needed my own space, however selfish that seems to me now.

My sister didn't have very much money but, despite that, she didn't seem to mind having an extra mouth to feed. She and her husband Geoff had recently moved to a place called Bridge of Allan so that Geoff could take up the place he had been offered at Stirling University to study for a degree in Biology. Lynda was not working as she had to care for the children.

As I've mentioned a couple of times, I was a dab hand with a sewing machine, and I had made Lynda's girls, Toogie and Becky, a really pretty sundress each. We were out with the children one day and popped into a little shop called Quintessence, which sold candles, mirrors, shawls and other bits and bobs. The girl in the shop remarked on the girls' sundresses, my sister said I had made them and suddenly I had a job making clothes for a boutique!

We are not exactly talking haute couture here, but I was experienced enough to be able to adapt patterns to different sizes, although I think it was just small and large. In the early seventies smocks were very fashionable. They had no shaping and were very easy to sew. I did elaborate by adding little details like pintucking to create some variety.

Lynda wasn't really much of a seamstress at this point, although she was brilliant with knitting needles and a crochet hook, but she soon picked it up and between us we created some very wearable clothes. When I did eventually go home to Nottingham, Lynda carried on with our little cottage industry to earn a few much-needed pounds. She also began making most of her own and her children's clothes, which will have saved her a fortune down the years.

I also continued to make most of my own clothes and, when my children came along, I sewed and knitted garments for them too, as I mentioned in *chapter 32*. For me it wasn't only a cost issue; I really liked being able to create something original for them to wear.

I did try to supplement my small dressmaking income by getting a job, but it wasn't easy as I didn't know how long I would be staying at my sister's. A bit of babysitting was about all I could conjure up and, as you can imagine, that didn't exactly pay big bucks.

Although to my parents it must have seemed that I was throwing away my education and all my dancing training and aspirations that wasn't the case. I was still intent on being a professional dancer and made sure that I kept up with my dancing practice. Every couple of days my sister and I would roll back the carpet in the children's bedroom and I would use baby Becky's cot as my ballet barre.

It was a funny little incident that finally triggered the return of the 'prodigal'. I woke up one morning to find my nephew Deryk, aged four, and niece Toogie, almost three, playing with my make-up bag. The contents were strewn all over the floor and smeared all over their faces. Between them they had gouged out all the blusher, broken the lipsticks and generally ruined everything. Because I was so hard up I knew I wouldn't be able to replace it. I was so angry with them that I shouted and in response Toogie said, 'You can't tell me off, you're not my mummy!'

It was that sentence that made me realise that I was living my sister's life and that it was time to get back to mine. I left soon after that and was home in time for Christmas. My parents simply welcomed me back with open arms and have never really referred to the whole episode.

The funny thing is, my niece Toogie is now a professional make-up artist.

I suppose you could say she owes it all to me!

Seventy Three

It was in 1973 that my dreams of becoming a
professional dancer became a reality.

I had been buying the *Stage*, a weekly newspaper for people in the entertainment industry with a jobs section at the back, for several months, and travelling to London for auditions, but without success. Then I saw an advertisement for a summer season in Guernsey, Channel Islands, and the audition was being held near Nottingham.

My mum drove me to the audition at a dancing school in a place called Burton Joyce. I was put through my paces, and the choreographer, Sally, could see that I had the ability, she was just a little concerned about my age. After speaking with my mum I think she realised I was a very 'adult' sixteen-year-old and so she offered me the job.

At the age of sixteen years and eleven months my career in show business began – I even got my provisional Equity Card! This was really important, as I had been unable to go for a lot of auditions, as the ads had stated Equity members only. Equity is the union for people in the entertainment profession, and to protect its members you had to work forty weeks as a provisional member, before you were granted full membership status, which I mentioned in *chapter* 7. Until you had full membership you weren't allowed to appear in West End shows or on television.

The season in Guernsey was a long one, starting in May and running to the end of September, so it was giving me half of the required forty weeks with my first job.

The rehearsals started a couple of weeks later, which is when I met the other two girls, Jacqui, who later changed her name to Honey, and Kathy. Together we became the Sally Ashworth Dancers.

I had thought it was ideal that the rehearsals were close to home, but actually it wasn't so great. Jacqui and Kathy were both from London so they were staying at Sally Ashworth's house. This meant they could get to know each other when we weren't rehearsing, so I had a bit of catching up to do when we flew out to Guernsey.

Kathy was the oldest of the three of us and was a brilliant dancer, having trained at the Bush Davies School in Romford. She became our 'head girl'.

Jacqui was eighteen and had not had the level of training that Kathy and I had had so struggled a bit with some of the choreography. She made up for it though with a lovely personality.

We only had five routines to learn. The opening and the finale were 'feather' numbers. What I mean by this is they were in a showgirl-style, so we wore sequins and feathers, and wafted big feather fans around, whilst singing 'C'est Magnifique'. It is a good job there were only three of us as the stage was tiny at the Carlton Hotel, our venue for the summer.

The rest of the show comprised of a magician, Bunny Neal, who was one of the nicest people I have ever met, a singing trio called the Song Spinners, a solo singer, Kevin Ross, and a little-known comedy double act, Cannon and Ball, who were brilliant even before TV discovered them. Part of their act was for Tommy Cannon to send Bobby Ball off the stage in disgrace and then go on to sing the Platters song 'My Prayer'. It was probably my favourite part of the show.

We were only on the Equity minimum wage, which was a meagre £12 a week, but it wasn't as bad as it sounds as we had a house provided for us rent-free. It was a little fisherman's cottage on the seafront in St Peterport and we each had our own rooms, a luxury that didn't repeat itself very often in later jobs!

We also had a small garden at the back, which I seem to remember accessing by climbing out of my bedroom window rather than going downstairs to the kitchen. And of course we had Bessie, the car, who I wrote about in *chapter 16*.

It was a wonderful initiation into the world of show business, but in some ways it raised expectations which were not always met in the jobs that followed.

Guernsey was a beautiful place to spend the summer so no wonder my mum and dad and my best friend from school, Annie, came out for a holiday.

One of my favourite things to do was to get the ferry across to Herm Island where there are no cars, only farm vehicles. The best beaches were on the other side of Herm from where the ferry docked so we would walk along wooded paths, which was a pleasure in itself. It's one of those places I almost daren't go back to in case they have spoilt it – after all, we are talking nearly forty years ago . . . crikey!

I mentioned earlier in the chapter that Sally Ashworth had expressed some concern over my age. I'm not really sure why, but she had asked me to lie and say that I was approaching my eighteenth birthday, when I was actually about to turn seventeen. I obliged, but imagine my horror when, after the show on my birthday night, they threw open the doors to the bar to reveal a surprise eighteenth birthday party! Everywhere was decorated with keys and banners and there was a huge pink eighteenth birthday cake! It was so lovely of them to organise the party but really awful for me. I couldn't possibly come clean after all the effort they had gone to so I just had to play along.

That night I vowed that I would never lie about my age again. OK, I haven't always kept to that vow, but I do now . . . I'm forty-five — only joking!

Seventy Four

When we moved house recently, I was astonished to discover that I have no fewer than seventy-four pieces of Butler & Wilson.

Most of it is jewellery, but I am including in that tally some handbags, one of which is in the style of the Union Jack created in Swarovski crystals, and I also have the matching mirror compact. What I am not including, because it would take me well over a hundred, are all the Butler & Wilson clothes I own, some of them genuine vintage pieces.

For those of you who don't know, Butler & Wilson is a British brand that has been going for over forty years, specialising in costume jewellery and vintage clothing. Originally the duo, Nicky Butler and Simon Wilson, were antique dealers but they diversified into creating their own original designs which have graced the covers and inside pages of glossy magazines around the world. Simon Wilson now runs the brand on his own. Well, I say on his own, but he has a team around him, including his sister, Margaret, and you often see his designs without realising it on shows like *Strictly Come Dancing* and *The X Factor*.

There are two Butler & Wilson shops in London, one on South Molton Street that has jewellery, bags and clothing, and the Fulham Road shop, which specialises in vintage. It is also sold on QVC, which is how I first met Simon Wilson, although not the first time I had come across his jewellery.

By the late 1970s and early 1980s, Butler & Wilson had already reached cult status, and anyone who was anyone wanted to own a piece. In 1983 I was working on *The Price is Right, chapter 34*, and Jacqui, one of the other hostesses, was wearing the most amazing pair of earrings. They were crystal and virtually covered the whole ear, with a little chain and a clip onto the top of the ear as well as the lobe. When I remarked on them, Jacqui simply said, 'They're Butler & Wilson'.

She assumed that I would know what that was. I didn't let on that I had no clue, but it did help me many years later when, in QVC UK's first year, our fashion jewellery buyer wanted to feature the brand and wanted me to be the presenter of the first show.

I will never forget how nervous Simon was – difficult to imagine when you see him on screen these days. He had brought his neighbour's dog, Paddington, with him to make him feel more at ease, and to his credit Paddington was extremely well behaved under the studio lights.

The first show was very popular and Simon soon became a regular on QVC and, as we had hit it off so well, almost always worked with me.

My first piece of Butler & Wilson was a pair of clip-on crystal earrings, not quite the size and spectacle of the ones Jacqui owned, but gorgeous nonetheless. I think the iconic 'dancing couple' was next, followed shortly after by a big lizard brooch.

We had established our friendship before QVC asked Simon if he would fly out to the Bahamas for a live broadcast we were doing from the Atlantis Resort on Paradise Island. He arrived with his assistant, Anna, who still works for him, looking very bronzed. I remarked on his fabulous tan and he simply said, 'St Tropez, darling.'

I assumed he had been on his holiday before coming out to do the show. I did start to think it was a little odd that Simon had such a great tan and yet I never saw him sitting in the sun, he was always in the shade. Even stranger was while the rest of us were developing a bronzed glow, Simon seemed to be getting paler and paler. That would be the St Tropez fake tan gradually fading. He hadn't been on a holiday to St Tropez at all!

One of the reasons that my 'on air' relationship with Simon works so well is the banter between us. It started when I used to tell little stories associated with some of the designs we were selling, particularly the animal designs. That is how the ladybird saga that I mentioned in *chapter 50* started. Simon had designed a ladybird piece of jewellery and it had prompted me to tell the story of how my family and I had once been attacked by a swarm of ladybirds. I can feel that you are as disbelieving as Simon was, so let me elaborate.

Chris and I had taken the children on holiday to Norfolk. We had spent the morning at a 'petting farm', where the children had been stroking the animals and playing in the playground. We decided to have some lunch before heading back to the coast for an afternoon on the beach. We were just finishing eating when Chris touched my arm and indicated for me to look over my shoulder. There was a huge black cloud heading in our direction, but it wasn't of the weather variety, it was some kind of swarm. We paid the bill hastily and rushed the children towards the car where the first of the ladybirds was starting to land. I am not kidding, there must have been millions of them and we watched in horror, from the relative safety of our car, as people who hadn't been as quick off the mark as us were getting covered in the little creatures. I know they don't sting like wasps or bees but it was awful to watch little children screaming because the ladybirds had got tangled up in their hair. We had to put the windscreen wipers on so that we could see to drive away.

After telling this story on air, it became something of a running joke between Simon and I, and every time I got him a gift for

Christmas or birthday it would be ladybird-related. I even hand-stitched a ladybird soft toy for him on one occasion.

That was the start of the daft presents. I couldn't compete with the beautiful pieces of jewellery that would come my way, so I would get something funny instead. I particularly liked the rear end of a Westie that you position in the garden to make it look like it is digging a hole!

I'm not sure that Simon has kept any of his 'jokey' presents from me. I do know that he passed the bejewelled computer mouse I gave him to Anna. I know I have kept all the pressies that have come in the opposite direction.

I have lots of acquaintances who I really like, but only a few people who I would consider real friends.

I'm pleased to say Simon falls into the latter category.

Seventy Five

I got my first passport in 1975 but it was not quite as
straightforward as it might have been.

I had finished my second summer season in Jersey, *chapter 22*, at
the beginning of October and all the dancers had gone their
separate ways, as is usual at the end of a season. Jo had gone off
to Majorca, Gwen was staying on in Jersey, Irene and Linda were
going to work on a cruise liner and Tricia and I had returned to
the UK to begin auditioning for work, although neither of us
was particularly hopeful of getting a pantomime as most of them
had already been cast. That was the only downside of working
in the Channel Islands. The season was so long, May to October,
that by the time you got home to England all the best jobs had
gone.

I had only been home a few days when, out of the blue, I had
a phone call from Irene. I was quite surprised as we hadn't exactly
been 'bezzie mates' in Jersey, mainly because she and Linda were
virtually joined at the hip! So what was the reason for the call?

It turned out that Linda had decided she didn't want to go
on the cruise ship after all, as it would have meant she would
have been away from her boyfriend for another six months, hot
on the heels of six months in Jersey. The company were short
of a dancer, and Irene had suggested me. No audition, no photograph, nothing: just Irene's assurances that I was a good dancer.

The call was on the Thursday evening and the train to Italy, where the rehearsals were taking place, was leaving first thing Saturday morning, which would not normally have been a problem for me as I always leave things to the last minute. There was, however, the slight issue of me not having a passport, which I don't think I mentioned to Irene.

First thing next morning my dad rang the Passport Office to find out how I could get a passport in a hurry. The only way it could be done that day was for me to go to our nearest passport office in Peterborough to complete the paperwork on the spot, but even then there were no guarantees. I also needed to take two passport-sized photos, one of which needed to be signed on the back by someone upstanding in the community who could verify the likeness.

Remember, this was in the days before digital cameras and instant pictures, so first stop was the photo booth located in Woolworths in Nottingham. For some reason, in those days I used to wear a pink headscarf over my hair, tied at the nape of my neck. Obviously my hair had to be visible in the photo so I quickly whipped it off and brushed my hair. Despite my best efforts it was flat as a pancake and looked as if it hadn't been washed for a week! So lanky hair and no make-up, I was pretty as a picture . . . not!

I was always terribly embarrassed when I had to show my passport for anything. On subsequent passports I always used professional head shots that had been done for publicity shots for work. Actually, there is a downside to that too as you never look as good as your picture when you are standing at border control, although no one has ever said as much. They don't need to really as you can see what they are thinking: 'Crikey, she's photogenic!'

So, strip of not-very-glamorous photos in hand, it was hot foot to the bank for the manager to sign the back of one of

them. He already had his morning fully booked up with appointments, so Dad and I just had to wait until he could squeeze us
in.

~~I was starting to get a little edgy as it was lunchtime by the~~
time we got on the road to Peterborough and we needed to be
there before 3 p.m. to have any chance of getting the passport
issued before they closed at 4 p.m. I can't really remember all the
form-filling-out, but I do remember that at one point we were
told that the passport couldn't be issued that day. That's when
my dad mounted a charm offensive. He was a very handsome
man and was a salesman for a living, and somehow he won them
over. I am pretty sure if I had been there by myself I wouldn't
have been clutching my brand-new passport at five minutes to
four that Friday afternoon.

Mild panic then ensued, as I had been so focused on obtaining
my passport that I hadn't given any thought to what I might
need for three weeks in Italy in late October, followed by six
months cruising around the Caribbean.

Somehow I managed to pack and be at Victoria Station in
London to meet up with the other girls early the following
morning for our twenty-four-hour rail, then boat, then rail again
trip to Rapallo on the Italian Riviera.

The dance group was called Les Darling Girls, and was run
by an Italian woman, Carla Bonavera, hence the rehearsals in
Italy, although some of the time she lived in Mold, Wales, with
the group's choreographer, Joyce. As well as Irene and myself,
there was our 'head girl' Judy, who I still exchange Christmas
cards with, Joan, Carol and Kirsten. We were joined a few weeks
later by a girl called Jackie and with the benefit of hindsight I
wonder if she was brought in to replace me as I will explain later
in the chapter.

The journey to Italy, although long, was a real adventure for
me as I hadn't done any travelling in Europe apart from the

holiday to Austria with my parents. The train left Victoria heading for Dover, where we all got off with our mountains of luggage and boarded the ferry to Calais. From Calais we headed down to Paris, where we had to change trains to an overnight sleeper to Rapallo. It was very reminiscent of the film *Murder on the Orient Express*, without the luxury and thankfully without the murder. We were all pretty tired by the time the train pulled in to the station in Rapallo twenty-four hours later. We were met and taken to the *pensione* that we would call home for the following three weeks. They had laid out an early lunch for us so, after dropping our bags off and having a quick wash, we headed downstairs to eat.

About halfway through lunch, which can be quite a long affair in Italy, comprising of several courses, I needed the loo. I was directed upstairs to the toilet which had this old-fashioned chain pull flush. I did what I needed to do and then pulled on the chain. I was horrified when it came off in my hand.

Now if it had just been a wee I would probably have left it, presented the receptionist with the chain and tried to explain what had happened. What is that saying to encourage us to save water? 'If it's yellow, let it mellow; if it's brown, flush it down'! Well, what I had done needed flushing down, so I decided to try and reattach the chain to the lever by standing on the seat lid. Disaster – my foot went straight through the lid! I won't elaborate any further but as you can imagine it was all terribly embarrassing! Welcome to Italy!

Rapallo is a lovely little Italian town and somewhere else I would like to revisit. Every morning we would walk the mile or so to rehearsals, walk back for lunch and then go back in the late afternoon for a second session of rehearsals. The rehearsals were really demanding but I can honestly say, in terms of the choreography, it was probably my favourite dancing job.

I was very supple, and we had to dance the cancan, which I

loved, as well as some showgirly stuff in bikinis and feathers, the Charleston, national dances and some modern jazz. Everything needed to be learnt and practised before we flew out to New York. We also had to have costume fittings and publicity photos taken.

There was a lot to pack in, but we did have some spare time for exploring Rapallo itself and we were given a day off to visit nearby Genoa, which was very beautiful.

It was in Rapallo that I experienced proper hot chocolate for the first time. I had always had cocoa made with hot milk and a spoonful of sugar prior to this, but in Italy hot chocolate was thick and sweet and chocolatey with froth on the top and decorated with hearts or flowers in liquid chocolate. It was heavenly, but it was a good job we weren't there for too long or I would have been piling on the pounds before I even got on the ship!

The flight to New York was from Milan, and was long and not very comfortable. We arrived in New York in late November and it was already bitterly cold. I can remember thinking during the drive from the airport to the docks, where the SS *Doric* was waiting to set sail, that this was like a different world. The architecture of the Manhattan skyline was like nothing I had ever seen before.

The first cruise was just a short hop to the island of Bermuda, yet another place I would definitely like to revisit one day. I think it was a kind of 'dress rehearsal', and not just for us but for all the new crew joining the ship.

After that, each cruise was two weeks' sailing around the Caribbean, initially from New York, before moving our home port down to Fort Lauderdale in Florida from January. We only performed four nights per cruise, although we did do two shows on each of those nights, and we did a different show each of those nights, so we never got bored. But that's all we did. Unlike other cruise liners, we did not have to perform any other duties.

The rest of the time was our own, apart from rehearsals, to go sightseeing and shopping.

I remember doing my Christmas shopping that year in Macy's department store, which I must confess I had never heard of prior to the job. I also went to the famous Radio City Music Hall, to watch a show featuring the Rockettes dance troupe who were sort of an American version of the Tiller Girls. They are still going strong, albeit with different dancers I would hope, whereas the Tiller Girls have long since hung their fishnet tights out to dry. Although, I think I remember seeing them in a reunion for a big charity event fairly recently?

We visited all the popular Caribbean islands, Barbados, Antigua, Grenada, St Lucia, and also some lesser known ones, like St Thomas, which is popular with the Americans, St Maarten, Aruba and Curaçao, all of which I listed in *chapter 41*. We also went to Venezuela and Haiti, where I nearly missed getting back on board. Haiti, as I'm sure you will have realised if you saw the pictures of when the earthquake hit in 2009, is very underdeveloped. Not only the buildings, but the roads too, which leads to big traffic problems. Not every port we visited could accommodate a big ship like the SS *Doric*, so sometimes we would anchor out and get on little boats, called tenders, to be ferried to the quayside. There were very clear signs for passengers and crew alike that it was our responsibility to be back in time to catch the last tender.

Crime was a bit of a problem in Haiti, so some friends and I got in a taxi and went to a fabulous hotel just outside of Port-au-Prince. We told the taxi a time to come back for us which gave us a couple of hours' wriggle room. We had our lunch at the hotel, enjoyed swimming in the pool — the first time I had ever seen a swim-up bar — and were ready to be picked up at 3 p.m. The taxi wasn't there. By 3.30 p.m. we were starting to get nervous, so asked the hotel to book us another taxi, which they did, and it duly arrived half an hour later. Still plenty of time to make the last boat at 6 p.m., you would have thought. Well only just.

The journey back to Port-au-Prince was fine, but as we reached the outskirts the traffic started to build up and soon we were at a total standstill. We got out and ran the last few blocks but even so we didn't get to the quayside until gone six. Fortunately they had held the tender for a few minutes, but another ten minutes and they would have had to go, otherwise the *SS Doric* would have missed the tide. There were the four of us and two other people on the boat, and the minute we were on board they lifted the tender back to its position as a lifeboat and hauled anchor. Apparently if we had missed the boat we would have had to make our own way to the next port of call at our own expense.

Every place we visited, I bought a silver charm to go on a bracelet, which I still have now. The charm I bought in Haiti was a bongo drum, and I'm not entirely sure it is silver, although they assured me it was at the time. I had a nutmeg from Grenada, maracas from Barbados, a horse and carriage from Bermuda and a tropical flower from Martinique. There were only a couple of islands we visited where I couldn't find silver charms. In the Dominican Republic I bought a piece of amber, which is probably more authentic anyway, but unfortunately it came off my bracelet and I lost it. I also bought a shark's tooth. It is a genuine shark's tooth and is a bit on the yellow side now, though not showing any signs of decay!

We spent Christmas Day at sea, en route from Nassau in the Bahamas, and to date it's the only time I've ever been away from the UK for Christmas.

By this time Jackie, the seventh member of the troupe, had arrived and we began rehearsing her into the show before Carla and Joyce joined the ship for a cruise and to check up on us, I guess.

Do you remember earlier in the chapter I mentioned that I wondered if Jackie was meant to be my replacement? Well, the reason I say that is because as soon as they arrived I was called in to see them. They asked me if I had anything to tell them. I wasn't sure what they meant so said nothing. It transpires that the ship's captain had noticed that I walked with a slight limp, which was exaggerated when the ship was rolling in stormy seas. I had rehearsed with these people in Italy for three weeks and they hadn't noticed, nor had it affected my dancing, but apparently there was some question as to whether I was covered by the ship's insurance policy in case of an accident. Obviously I had to come clean and tell them about my polio. I don't know how it was resolved but I stayed on board for the whole six months and nothing was ever mentioned again.

Irene and I had originally shared a cabin, but when we knew Jackie was joining us Irene volunteered to move in with Joan who was in a smaller cabin next door to ours. I thought this was a little odd until I realised that Joan was hardly ever there as her boyfriend on board was an officer, and she spent most of her free time with him.

Jackie and I got on very well together but it was possibly a mistake having us share a cabin. We both loved our food and, let's face it, there are plenty of opportunities to eat on board ship. The day started with early breakfast, probably the only meal I didn't attend, followed by breakfast, morning coffee, lunch, afternoon tea, dinner and, just in case you were still peckish, the midnight buffet. I'm sorry to admit that both Jackie and I had zero willpower, so when we arrived back in the UK, at the end of April, we both had excess baggage, and I'm not talking suitcases!

Seventy Six

If you programme your satellite navigation system with the code NG7 6NX it will take you to the site for Nottingham's annual Goose Fair. Do you see what I have done there to come up with seventy-six? I've removed the code's letters!

Goose Fair is quite a big deal in Nottingham and some historians think it dates back as far as 1284 when it was actually used to trade geese and other livestock. I must have visited it several times as a child, but that is not why it is in this book.

Do you remember in *chapter 23* when I listed all the different jobs I had done, I mentioned I had been a fish and chip salesperson? You possibly wondered why I didn't just write that I had worked in a chippy. That's because I didn't. I worked on a stall at Goose Fair selling fish and chips.

I had came back from Jersey after my first summer season there and was on the lookout for fill-in jobs to tide me over to my next dancing job. There was an advert in the *Nottingham Evening Post* for casual workers for the food concessions at Goose Fair. I rang the number, got the job and a couple of days later received a few minutes of basic training before the fair opened to the general public.

I didn't have a uniform as such but the one requirement was to cover your hair as it was a food outlet. I wore a red spotted head scarf and probably looked more like a gypsy than most of the travellers themselves. I don't know if I wore gold hoop earrings – probably not, they may have fallen off into the deep fat fryer!

I do remember it was jolly cold though, even with all the cooking going on – well, it was November.

It was very, very hard work, and very long days, but it was quite a laugh too, especially when people I had been at school with recognised me and asked me if I had joined the fair permanently.

The worst thing was the smell of fish and chips lingering on my clothes and in my hair. UGH! I think I stayed in the bath for a week to get rid of the smell. Still, it was a few quid in my pocket and another life experience.

Seventy Seven

It takes approximately seventy-seven minutes to drive
from London SE25 to RAF Duxford, depending on
traffic, of course, and on which route you take.

I have only done that precise journey once, although I have
passed the turn-off on the M11 motorway many times, en
route to Chris's parents' home in Lincolnshire.

The reason I made that one specific trip was to film an episode
of *Beadle's About* in 1987. I'm hoping you remember the show? It
was a series of set-up situations that a friend or family were 'in
the know' about, but that the main participant was unaware of.
It was not dissimilar to the American *Candid Camera* show, but
with a bit more of an edge.

The scenario at RAF Duxford involved a man and his wife
on a day trip to the air museum, which was home to a life-size
Concorde aeroplane. Once he and his wife, who was in on the
joke, had parked their car in the car park and gone inside the
museum, the *Beadle's About* team sprang into action. They swapped
his car for a dead ringer and then blocked him in at the front
with other cars and positioned an enormous tank behind his car.

I was playing the part of a young mum, which was quite
appropriate really as Daniel was five months old and I was pregnant again with Sophie. My car had also been blocked in by the
tank and I was getting panicky because I needed to get to nursery

322

school to pick up 'my child'. My job, with the help of his wife, was to persuade the guy that he could move the tank backwards and so let all the cars out that were blocked in. Although he was reluctant at first, he eventually climbed up onto the tank to attempt to move it. Of course the inevitable happens, and he ends up crushing several cars in the process . . . all dummy cars, I might add. He was actually quite upset, and then angry, when Jeremy Beadle revealed himself, although he did see the funny side of it eventually.

That was the second episode in which I had appeared that series. The first was more enjoyable to do and, in my opinion, funnier. It was set in an office where a temp secretary has been employed for the day. The prank was being played on her.

After settling her in, her new boss says he has to pop out for a few minutes but also tells her that he is expecting a visit from his wife.

Minutes after he has left the office, there is a buzz on the office doorbell but it is not his wife, it is me, playing the part of his mistress. I want to see my 'boyfriend', but the secretary tells me he is out, so I say I'll wait for him. She is obviously uncomfortable with this, as she is expecting the wife to arrive at any moment. I proceed to be quite indiscreet about what is going on between her boss and I.

There is then another buzz on the office bell and it is the wife. The secretary doesn't know what to do, so I volunteer to hide in the cupboard.

The wife is very angry when she comes into the office and starts accusing her husband of having an affair. The secretary denies all knowledge, saying she is only a temp, but looks on with horror as the wife insists she knows the mistress is hiding on the premises and starts searching around. She averts her gaze as the wife approaches the cupboard and yanks the doors open . . . the cupboard is empty.

Following her fruitless search the wife leaves, at which point the temp secretary's curiosity gets the better of her, and she goes over to the cupboard to have a look for herself. Of course, Jeremy Beadle springs out, microphone in hand.

I did one other 'hit', which we filmed in the Covent Garden piazza and I can't actually remember what the prank was. By this time my pregnancy was beginning to show, so my career as a member of Beadle's Hit Squad was cut prematurely short.

Seventy Eight

In 1978 a commercial artist named Syd Brak came to
the UK from his native South Africa to work for a
well-known poster company called Athena.

You will remember Athena if you were in your teens or
twenties around this time, as we all had their artwork
plastered on our bedroom walls. Do you recall the girl dressed
in tennis gear with her back to the camera, exposing the cheeks
of her bottom? Well, that was one of Athena's best-known posters
and, before you start wondering, that was not me!

However, I did sit for Syd Brak, from which he produced two
posters which were on sale in Athena shops around 1984. Maybe
you even owned them?

I didn't know him, it was just a job. I had been rung up by
one of the agencies I worked for and asked if I would like to
do it. They didn't normally ask if you wanted to do a job; they
just told you when you had been chosen, but this type of work
was particularly poorly paid so they used to check with us first.

Apparently Syd Brak wanted to draw two posters to represent
the fitness boom in the eighties, so he particularly wanted someone
who looked like they were fit and, more importantly, who had
their own fitness gear.

Over the course of a couple of hours he did a lot of sketching
and he may have taken some photos too, and that was that.

A few months later I was looking through some posters in an Athena shop, probably for something to hang on our walls, when I came across the posters he had drawn of me, but they are not called Julia. One is called Sally and the other is Debbie. I bought them just as a keepsake but never put them up on my wall so the story kind of ends there. Well, not quite.

Chris always struggles for presents to buy me for Christmas and my birthday, particularly since I have worked at QVC and everything is available to me at a discount. It was approaching my fiftieth birthday, which I wrote about in *chapter 50*, so he wanted to get me something really memorable.

He found the folder I kept the posters in – no mean feat I can tell you – and took them to a local print shop to be enlarged and framed. While I was out at work he put them up on the wall of my home gym and on my birthday morning surprised me with them . . . how thoughtful is that?!

Seventy Nine

This is the approximate number of calories in a
small banana.

I'm not crazy about bananas, but over the years, rather than
reaching for a bar of chocolate or a biscuit, they have satisfied
my sweet cravings. I am very picky though when it comes to
their state of ripeness. I don't like them very green because usually
they don't have so much flavour, but I will eat them. I really can't
eat them when they are very black and the skins have gone thin.
I find the texture of the fruit then is almost starchy.

The only thing they are then good for, in my opinion, is
cooking . . . banana loaf or banoffee pie spring to mind. I told
you I have a sweet tooth! So I like my bananas just yellow with
maybe a few black spots.

They are often considered to be a 'fattening' fruit, just as peas
are a 'fattening' vegetable, but it all comes back down to the
quantity of them that we eat, and surely it is better to eat a
banana than a jammy doughnut, or some peas rather than a plate
of chips. I'm not saying I don't eat doughnuts or chips, just not
very often.

They are also quite a good source of the B vitamins, in particular
Vitamin B6, and a moderate source of Vitamin C, potassium
and manganese. They are approximately 75% water, 23% carbo-
hydrate, just over 1% protein and a tiny amount of fat.

I always thought that most bananas were grown in the

Caribbean or Costa Rica, and probably most of the bananas we eat in Europe are. However, on doing a bit of research, it turns out India grows approximately 28% of the world's banana production each year, though mostly for domestic consumption. I also found out that bananas and plantains come in all shapes and sizes, and in a variety of colours, including my favourite, purple.

Did you know that they make paper from the banana plant too, and that in Japan they have been using it to make fabric since at least the thirteenth century?

Isn't the internet amazing?

Eighty

1980 was the year I started teaching exercise classes.

The eighties was the decade that fitness became a multi-million-pound industry. Everyone suddenly got very interested in going to exercise classes or working out at home, along with Mad Lizzie on ITV and the Green Goddess on BBC.

Personally I wasn't the type to turn on the TV at breakfast and do a workout, but I did buy the *Green Goddess Exercise Book*; in fact, I still have it, and I also invested in the *Jane Fonda Workout Book* – again my copy is still intact and on my bookshelves.

I didn't intend going into the fitness industry, it was born out of necessity – the need to eat and pay rent. I was doing bits of extra work, which when you got them could be quite lucrative, but it was very erratic, and bills don't wait! I didn't want to get a 'proper' job, because then it becomes awkward getting time off for auditions and castings, so I was looking for something part-time. That's when I saw an advert in my local paper, the *Croydon Advertiser*, for a fitness instructor to teach body-conditioning classes at the Sundance Centre in Croydon.

I'd never even been to a body-conditioning class, let alone taught one, but with my background in teaching dancing, and the sudden availability of fitness books, I decided I could put a class together, so I applied for the job.

The lady that co-owned the Sundance Centre asked me to

take a trial class, which she would assess, and if she approved, there were a couple of slots a week I could take on.

I had about three days to structure a class and put together a music cassette – how dated does that sound?! It was before CDs, let alone iPods, had even been thought of! Luckily, with Chris being a musician, we had recording equipment, and between us we sorted out a tape with the right beats and tempos to do the exercises to. Thanks to Jane Fonda and the Green Goddess I managed to plan out an hour's class.

Looking back now, I can also see more than a hint of Pilates in a lot of the exercises I favoured, although back then I, along with most of the country, had never heard of Joseph Pilates and his fitness regime, which I write about in *chapter 100*.

My hour-long class consisted of a warm-up, some stretches at the barre, lots of floorwork, a short jog and a cool down.

I arrived at the Sundance and was taken downstairs to a very small studio with only just enough headroom for tall girls to stretch their arms above their heads. It didn't trouble me, being only five feet four inches, and it did have the saving grace of mirrors along the length of one wall. I would say it could comfortably hold six girls, and that's how many awaited me on my body-conditioning teaching debut!

I must have done something right, probably my energy, enthusiasm and novel approach, because I got the job, and was soon asked to do more than the original two classes a week.

I was also asked to diversify into teaching teenagers modern jazz, which I found really enjoyable, and adults ballet, which I did not! Having grown up with ballet and seen it beautifully performed at the highest level, it was sometimes difficult to recognise it as the same art form. Still, the girls I taught seemed to enjoy the classes, and it is a brilliant way of improving strength and flexibility.

At the height of my teaching stint at the Sundance, I was

teaching between ten and fourteen classes a week, sometimes as many as three back to back in one evening. I used to do the entire class with the girls so I was incredibly fit, probably the fittest I've ever been in my life.

Sundance were very amenable when it came to me having time off for auditions and other work. It didn't happen very often but, when I landed the job working as a hostess on *The Price is Right*, I was filming all week in Nottingham and only able to teach at the weekends. They simply arranged for other teachers to take the classes I couldn't, on the understanding that I would have the classes back when I finished filming.

I had told them it would be a month of filming, but due to a union dispute, we were unable to film a lot of the time, and one month stretched into three. My job was still held open for me.

With the benefit of hindsight, I think it might have been beneficial to have someone 'off the TV' teaching at your fitness studio. I say this because they used me as a model for the advertisement they ran in the local paper.

My 'girls' and I were also involved in a fitness display held in the Whitgift Shopping Centre in Croydon. It was around the time that *Fame*, the television series, was at the height of its popularity, and there we all were in our leotards, footless tights, leg warmers and compulsory headbands, looking like a bunch of extras from the show – it was great fun though!

I had to have more time off to do the second series of *The Price is Right*, and then I discovered that I was to have a little production of my own. In April 1986, I found out I was pregnant with my son Daniel. I was over the moon, as I really love children, and hadn't wanted to leave it too late before starting a family.

Again, Sundance were brilliant. They kept asking me how long I wanted to carry on teaching for, and I just kept saying, 'As long as I feel OK.'

My doctor actually encouraged me to keep exercising, she just advised against jogging, lying on my front, which was pretty impossible the bigger I got, and overstretching in the latter stages.

I was also very fortunate to have an obstetrician, Dr Marion, in my class, so she kept an eye on me. I continued teaching up to thirty-eight weeks, and towards the end I must have looked vaguely ridiculous. I had an enormous bump, but I hadn't really put on much weight anywhere else.

Daniel arrived a week late, so I had three weeks off prior to his birth at the end of November, and I started back at Sundance the following March. It was a great way to earn a bit of money whilst getting myself back in shape and not being away from my baby son for too long.

Sometimes, if Chris was gigging and I couldn't get a babysitter, I would take him with me. Luckily, he was a really good baby, and he would sit in his car seat watching the girls fling themselves around – I think he enjoyed the music.

I had only been back teaching for a couple of months when I discovered I was pregnant again, and 'discovered' is the right word, as you will have read in *chapter 43*. I had to take it easy for a couple of months after my 'scare', but once I was past twenty-four weeks I became more actively involved in the classes again.

Daniel was still occasionally coming in to Sundance with me but as he got older and more mobile it became trickier.

He never actually crawled, he just went straight from bottom shuffling to walking at age ten months. He would sit quietly and play with 'Truck', his favourite toy, eat his raisins and drink his juice, and then he would get bored. This was the dangerous bit, particularly if the girls were doing floor work, as he would wander around with me, almost as though he was checking they were doing it properly, and out of the blue 'whack' them with Truck! It's a wonder they kept coming back.

Again, I taught up to thirty-eight weeks with Sophie, but it was more of a struggle, as I had put on over three stone in weight.

I did go back to teaching at the beginning of April, but it was much harder with two babies in tow. Unlike Daniel, Sophie didn't seem to enjoy watching the girls. When I did have to take her with me, I would leave her at the reception desk with the new owner, Anita, but I could often hear her crying. I decided it wasn't fair on anybody so on the days when I couldn't get a babysitter I arranged for someone else to take the class. I had also started teaching at a couple of other fitness studios, where they ran daytime classes, and this was a lot easier for me as Chris was generally around in the day.

To be honest, until I started writing this chapter, I hadn't realised quite how long I spent in the fitness industry. It must have been ten years on and off, alongside bits of acting and modelling, being in a band, and television appearances – in fact all through the 1980s.

By the end of the decade though, because of the continuing obsession with fitness, standards started to be tightened in terms of qualifications. I didn't have a fitness teaching qualification, partly because I hadn't needed one, and partly because when I had started out there weren't really any relevant qualifications to take. However it was getting increasingly difficult to work without one, as the studio owners couldn't get insurance against any potential client injuries unless all the teachers were fully qualified.

I had two options. I could study for a qualification to continue what I had been doing for years, or I could stop teaching.

The decision was made for me really. My presenting career had really started to take off, so I was too busy to study for my fitness qualification, teach, work and bring up two young children.

After a decade of 'keep fit', I hung my leotard and footless tights out to dry!

Eighty One

This was the number of candles I put on my mum's
birthday cake on her eighty-first birthday.

I know it sounds obvious – she was eighty-one so there were
eighty-one candles – but trust me, it is not as straightforward
as it sounds!

My mum and dad had come to stay with us for a week to
coincide with this very special event and, as has become
something of a tradition in the Roberts family, I had baked a
chocolate birthday cake. I do them in a heart-shaped tin, and
it is a simple chocolate Victoria sponge with chocolate fudge
icing. To make it extra special, and also for a bit of fun, when
I had finished icing the cake I decorated it with eighty-one
birthday candles – it was a bit of a tight squeeze as you can
probably imagine.

I made sure Mum and Dad were both in close proximity to
the kitchen before I started lighting the candles as I knew we
wouldn't have long before the first ones lit would burn all the
way down. Sophie helped me to light them all and Daniel ushered
Jojo and Bobbie (their pet names for their grandma and grandpa)
through to the kitchen. If we hadn't closed the kitchen door
really quickly I'm pretty sure the smoke detector in the hallway
would have gone off – it was always very sensitive to me frying
veggie bangers for some unknown reason!

We sang a very snappy 'Happy Birthday to you' to my mum

before urging her to make a wish and blow the candles out before the house could catch fire.

I managed to get a photo of Mum just as she was in the act of extinguishing the candles. It's not a very flattering shot of her but it's one of my favourite photos as in the background Dad was literally splitting his sides laughing. I think it was the last photograph I ever took of him.

It wasn't a moment too soon for the cake. As it was I had to pick little bits of melted wax out of the almost liquid icing but it was absolutely worth it for the happy memory it has given me.

Eighty Two

According to the BBC News website and in particular a page called '7 billion people and you: What's your number?', I am likely to live to the ripe old age of 81.7 years, which I have rounded up, optimistically, to 82.

I had thought that this age was specific to me, as the website had asked me to enter my date of birth, country of birth and gender. However, when we entered my daughter Sophie's information a few minutes later, it came up with exactly the same life expectancy for her, so obviously it is just a generalisation for females currently living in the United Kingdom, and it doesn't take into account age, lifestyle or health.

I am apparently the 2,821,095,482nd person to be born in the United Kingdom since records started, and the 76,271,926,109th person to have lived since history began.

The page had come about as the world's population was due to hit seven billion in the following weeks and in the short space of time I was entering mine and Sophie's data and checking the results, the world population had increased by a staggering 148 people.

The estimate is that the population of the world will reach 10 billion by 2083. I'm quite relieved that I won't be around to see it, unless of course they have discovered the 'secret of eternal youth' by then, in which case the world's population will be considerably more than 10 billion!

Eighty Three

In 1983 I finally signed a recording contract with our
band Jools and the Fools.

From the name you have probably guessed that I was Jools.
The 'fools' were my partner Chris and his bass-player mate,
Paul.

We had actually been trying to get a record deal for a couple
of years without success, and during that time had changed our
name twice. The first name couldn't have been very good as even
I can't remember it, but for a while we went under the name of
I Would.

Chris was really the mastermind behind the band. He wrote
the music, we wrote the lyrics together, and then Chris produced
the tracks.

We had bought a four-track 'portastudio', which was a fancy
cassette recorder that allowed you to record separate things like
drums, bass and keyboards on three of its four tracks, then
'bounce' them on to track 4, so that tracks 1, 2 and 3 were free
to record vocals and backing vocals. It was reasonable quality
and allowed us to hear the finished versions of songs, or to change
things we didn't like, but we didn't think it was good enough
to send out to the record companies.

When he was working with Jim Davidson, Chris had recorded

some tracks at a facility called Rock City at Shepperton film studios. He also used the studio to record a song he had co-written for Iris Williams, called 'Don't Make My White Christmas Blue', which he co-produced with the engineer Nick Smith.

Nick's dad had also been a recording engineer and was working for EMI when the Beatles first recorded there. He was famously quoted as saying, 'Visually they made quite an impression, but musically we didn't really hear their potential'!

I think that quote was probably applied to us by a lot of the A & R departments who received our material, and unfortunately we were not given enough of a chance to prove otherwise.

Nick's dad was also a recording artist in his own right. If you are of a certain age you may remember Hurricane Smith, who had a big a hit with 'Oh Babe, What Would You Say?'

In order to create the best impression and to produce decent demonstration tapes to send out to the A & R departments of record companies we decided to self-finance some sessions at Rock City.

Recording studios in those days were very different from today's. These days almost everything is recorded digitally onto a hard drive, without the use of tape. In those days everything was recorded onto two-inch-wide tape, so if you needed to edit anything, the engineer literally had to cut lengths of tape out of the recording, and then splice the two ends back together. You really needed to have faith in your engineer!

There was no auto tuning, so if you sang something flat or sharp it had to be done again and again and again. We also did all the harmonies and backing vocals ourselves. They were very long and expensive days in the studio but when we walked away with the first three tracks we had recorded, 'In My Car', 'Gigolo' and 'Telephone', we were all elated.

We had also paid for a photo session with a photographer I knew, so that we could give the aforementioned A & R departments an idea of our image. There was a great shot of the three of us crammed into a telephone box, which must have amused the passers-by immensely.

A & R stands for Artists and Repertoire but they were often referred to as the 'um & er' department as they needed a great deal of convincing before they would commit the record companies' money to develop a new artist.

The investment in ourselves paid off as we managed to get plenty of interviews on the strength of the demos and photos. These days very few companies accept unsolicited material, due to plagiarism law suits, but we had appointments with some of the big players like EMI, RAK and MCA, as well as loads of the smaller 'indie' labels.

We did come close with a couple of major companies, in particular MCA, whose head of A & R at the time was a guy called Charlie Eyre. He liked us enough to send us along to meet a record plugger called Pete Waterman. I'm sure you recognise that name, as he went on to produce the likes of Kylie Minogue and Rick Astley, and appeared as a judge on music talent shows. In those days, though, he was a plugger, responsible for getting new releases played on the radio. The walls of his office were covered with photographs of him and various Radio 1 DJs of the time. I don't think he disliked us, but we didn't make a huge impression on him either.

One of the problems was that we were a studio band, and didn't do any live performances. It goes through phases in the music industry, and we had just missed the boat in terms of studio bands, as most of the record companies wanted bands that had a good live following so that they already had a fan base. The nineties saw lots of studio-created bands, but now it is back to bands that can perform live, as that is just about the only way to make any money with all the free downloading that goes on.

As well as A & R departments, we had also sent the demos and photos out to the *Melody Maker* newspaper, to the 'playback' page, which was where the journalist Colin Irwin reviewed tapes sent in by 'undiscovered' bands. I kept a copy of his review from the 18th of September 1982 edition, and this is what he said:

> Being inexcusably sexist about all this, the most fetching photograph of the week came in from a London band called I Would whose lead singer Jools Roberts looks like a *Vogue* cover shot. Unfortunately she sings in a breathless Minnie Mouse voice that instantly has me cringing while the rest of I Would are just too knowing for comfort.
>
> They seem to have their art well sussed. Neatly constructed songs with cutesy choruses and singable punch-lines, and a sound just modern enough to catch the ears of ageing producers who think they are being hip by liking it. The sort of thing EMI will probably sign and Radio 1 will love; it's already inspired me to start hurling bricks at windows.

Even though he was a bit mean about my voice – although probably accurate, as I am definitely no Adele, more a less good version of Sophie Ellis Bexter – I thought it was a great review.

Unfortunately, we didn't get signed up by any ageing producers at EMI, but, after changing our name to Jools and the Fools, we did manage to catch the attention of music industry veteran Tony Calder, who was involved in several independent record labels at the time.

He had started his career with Decca in the early 1960s and was instrumental in promoting the Beatles track 'Love Me Do'. In 1978 he had become manager to Eddy Grant and helped him set up and develop Ice Records. In 1982, around the time we had our first meetings with him, Eddy Grant released a track called 'I Don't Wanna Dance', which became a massive worldwide hit, selling over 14 million copies.

We were really excited to be signed up to one of his labels, G.C. Recordings, as he obviously knew the business and must have thought we 'had something'!

After we signed, the record company paid for us to go into the recording studio to master some more tracks, and two of them, 'Boys Will Be Boys' and 'Television Heroes', were on the point of being released as singles.

We had done the final mix at Sarm Studios, which was one of the first studios in London to install a Solid State Logic mixing console, making it a studio choice of huge music industry names like Queen, Madonna, Yes, ABC, INXS and Seal. One of the UK's top record producers, Trevor Horn, whose own band the Bugles had a massive hit with 'Video Killed The Radio Star', recorded an unknown band he spotted on the music show *The Tube* there. Anyone remember Frankie Goes To Hollywood? We were in very illustrious company!

Once we had the final mix, we had to have something called an acetate cut, from which eventually the vinyl discs would have been pressed. Apparently they were very fragile, and we were instructed to keep them in the fridge. The idea was to let a plugger listen to it 'as a record' before trying to get radio airplay for us.

Speaking of *The Tube*, we had sent them a cassette of a couple of our tracks for the section of the show where they played up-and-coming new bands. The producers of the show contacted us and asked us to send a reel to reel and some photographs, so that they could play the track under a montage of pictures. They even gave us the date of the show it was to be featured on.

We sat and watched with great anticipation but for some reason, maybe an interview or performance overran, the new talent section was axed that week, and our tape was returned unplayed.

It was very disappointing, as maybe that would have been our big break, but at least we still had our record deal, and everything was ready to go.

Then we were called to a meeting at Tony Calder's office in Eton Square. He explained that another of his labels, KR, was heavily involved in the UK release of a track called 'Saddle Up', by David Christie, which had also become a huge hit. With that and the success of Eddy Grant's latest release, 'Electric Avenue', which got to number 2 in both the UK and US charts, he simply didn't have the time to devote to Jools and the Fools to break us as a new band. So, within a year of signing our deal, we were dropped.

It was a devastating blow, but we didn't give up. We wrote some more songs, 'The Parting' and 'Kicking a Can', recorded them as demos, and began the foot slog of visiting record companies all over again.

By this time though I was working on *The Price is Right* and I'm not sure my heart was in it, so gradually Jools and the Fools took a back seat in terms of my priorities.

Chris and I did have a track called 'Caught in a Trap' picked up by EMI Publishing as a potential Eurovision Song Contest entry, and I had another 'near miss' in 1985.

I had seen an advertisement in one of the trade papers for a girl singer to front a band for potential TV appearances. I had sent one of our demo tapes and a photo of myself to a P.O. Box address. We were just about to move into our first house, *chapter 46*, and so I had given my new address as I wasn't sure how long it would take to get a response, and I didn't want anything being sent to the old address.

A couple of days after sending my stuff off, I had a phone call from the people. Almost unbelievably it transpired that they actually lived two roads away from my new house, and they had gone to drop off a backing track that they wanted me to put a vocal on, only to find an empty house with a 'For Sale' sign outside! Goodness knows what they must have thought. Thankfully they had rung, so I went to fetch the tape and, courtesy of our 'portastudio', I was able to lay a vocal down on their backing track.

They liked what I did and it looked like it was all systems go until, at the last minute, the guy decided to use his wife as she had sung on the demo.

The song was called 'Clouds Across the Moon', and the band was The Rah Band. It was a top 10 hit, and I must admit to a hint of envy when they appeared on *Top of the Pops* a couple of weeks later.

So, I had been close several times, but 'no cigar', as the saying goes.

But that isn't quite the end of my recording career, as I do have a gold disc to hang on my wall if I want to.

In a very unlikely twist of fate, QVC decided to celebrate their fifth anniversary, in 1998, by having the presenters record a CD in conjunction with Mungo Jerry of 'In the Summertime' fame. We sang our version of 'The Locomotion' on our own, and also joined in the chorus of a track penned by Mungo Jerry called 'Partyland'.

The plaque on the gold disc reads:

Congratulations
JULIA ROBERTS
Now 20,000 QVC Customers
have received your CD
1st October 1998
EMG

Eighty Four

Eighty-four degrees Fahrenheit is the average daily
temperature in the Bahamas in May.

Believe it or not, I was lucky enough to go there for work,
although I almost missed the opportunity.

QVC were going to be broadcasting live from the recently
opened Atlantis Resort on Paradise Island, Nassau. They needed
two presenters to go and asked me and Clare, one of my colleagues.
Of course I was thrilled to be asked, but there was a slight
problem with a clash of dates.

The day after we were due to fly out with the crew, my
daughter Sophie had a ballet exam. I have always prided myself
on being a mum first and career girl second but this was a tough
decision.

Eventually, after much soul-searching, I told QVC that I
wouldn't be able to go because of the dancing exam, but I did
offer to travel out on my own a couple of days later, not believing
in my wildest dreams that they would let me. Imagine my surprise
and delight when QVC agreed.

Everyone else had taken a direct flight to Nassau, but there
weren't any available on the Sunday. It meant I had to fly to
Miami, then get a flight across to Nassau from there. It was a
bit of a trek through Miami airport to get my connecting flight,
but I made it to the departure gate with a few minutes to spare.
I couldn't see the aircraft waiting, so presumed it must be running

late, particularly as there didn't seem to be many people waiting to board. A couple of moments later they opened the gate and walked us onto the tarmac towards a very, very small plane.

I should mention at this point that I am a bit of a nervous flier and my heart sank as I climbed the steps. It was such a small plane you couldn't even stand upright in the gangway. I was convinced I was going to die. I tried to concentrate on the fantastic view from the window but even that couldn't distract me for long. Is it possible to hold your breath for forty-five minutes? It really felt like I did. I was so relieved when we landed, even when I discovered that although I had arrived safely from Miami, my luggage hadn't.

That evening there was a welcome party for both the English and American broadcast teams. All I had to wear was what I was standing up in, which was not very fresh after a transatlantic flight, a dash through Miami airport and a nervous onward journey. Everyone rallied round, lending me shoes, clothes and even make-up. From that day I have never again travelled by plane without my cosmetics in my hand luggage. My clothes eventually caught up with me the next day.

The Atlantis Resort is pretty impressive, complete with casino, a wealth of restaurants, beautiful gardens and a huge swimming pool. It was to the latter that I went on my first day to sleep off the jet lag and prepare for my first show the following day. The sun was rather warm, as you can imagine, so I decided to take a dip in the pool. With the benefit of hindsight I should have used the steps, because as I slid off the poolside into the water I realised too late that I was in the shallow end. I remember thinking, 'Ouch, that hurt' (or something similar!) as I stubbed my toe on the bottom of the pool. About two hours later I knew I was in trouble – my big toe had doubled in size.

Imagine the embarrassment of being driven through the Atlantis Resort and along the road to the doctor's sitting on the bonnet of a crew vehicle, which bore a striking resemblance to a golf buggy. Fortunately it transpired that I hadn't broken my toe, merely badly bruised it, but I was advised to keep it in ice for ~~the rest of the evening. Shame I didn't know about Arnica gel~~ in those days!

My first show was with Simon Wilson from the iconic British jewellery brand Butler & Wilson, which I wrote about in *chapter 74*. We were positioned on high stools with a backdrop of steps and fountains leading down to the infamous pool and the ocean beyond. It was very hot and although my toe didn't feel too bad to start with, about an hour into the two-hour show it really started to throb. Thank goodness we didn't have to get up and walk anywhere. As it was I had to be carried back to my room.

The next day I had an Elemis beauty show, and then Clare and I presented a 'Gems of the Sea' show together.

My final show was with Joan Rivers and her collection of costume jewellery. I have always enjoyed working with Joan Rivers because, despite the fact that she is undoubtedly a worldwide star, she is never condescending towards her QVC presenters. She just gets the whole concept. People who watch regularly get to know and trust the presenters, and she is a guest, albeit a very famous one, and she behaves like one. She also has the most wicked sense of humour and is as sharp as a knife.

The show was being broadcast from the lawns of the Atlantis Resort, with a live audience, so obviously Joan didn't want to arrive too far in advance. She was also doing a show later that evening for QVC US using the same location. Unfortunately the location manager had not realised that for our show Joan would need some kind of shade. It was 4 p.m. and very hot and sunny, at least eighty-four degrees.

When she arrived on the set, with literally minutes to go to the live broadcast, she pointed out that we couldn't possibly sit in direct sunlight for two hours, we would melt! The crew sprang into action and improvised by dragging over two garden pagodas, strapping them together and then sawing off the middle legs, which were creating a 'pole' effect right in front of the two of us. This created the desired shade with moments to go before the start of the live broadcast. Talk about skin of your teeth! Joan, as you would expect from the true professional that she is, was totally unfazed, so I still had to be on my toes to make sure that none of her witty remarks went too far!

She was also great fun when not on air, going paragliding with the American crew. It's something I have always fancied doing, but I haven't been brave enough – yet! I wouldn't even do the 'Leap of Faith', a vertical drop water slide. Mind you, after the toe incident I think everyone was quite relieved that I declined.

It was such a fantastic experience that I could not stop talking about it when I got home, and this ended up costing me money, as the following year I had to take the family there on holiday.

I had a friend who worked for a travel agent and she found me some reasonably priced flights, and through a contact I had made at the Atlantis Resort I was able to get a discount on the room rate, but even so it was the most expensive holiday we ever had. It's a good job we all had such a fantastic time.

Our days started with a walk on the beach, before breakfast at the Marketplace Restaurant. It was lovely to sit out on the terrace and watch the fish and the stingrays in the series of pools surrounding the dining area. Most days consisted of sitting by the swimming pool in the morning so that the children could enjoy the various water-based activities available to them, and going to the beach in the afternoon.

Their dad doesn't swim so it was down to me to join in with playing games in the pool and even joining in the aqua aerobics. The children tricked me on one occasion, when they had asked if I wanted to go on the Lazy River. This sounded all right, sitting in an inflatable ring and meandering along a current-driven waterway, so I agreed to go. We started climbing up steps, quite a lot of steps, and I asked them if it was right.

'Oh yes,' they both chorused.

~~They were giggling so I should have guessed something was~~ afoot!

Eventually we got to the top of the steps and although there were inflatable rings there was no 'Lazy River' in sight, just a tube curling downwards at an alarming angle. It was my first and last experience on a water slide. I think I had my eyes closed most of the way down, and to top it all as I splashed into the water, having been expelled at speed from the tube, my bikini top came off. Very embarrassing!

Despite much cajoling from the children I still declined the 'Leap of Faith', as mentioned earlier in the chapter, so the children went off on their own. It is some climb to the top as the drop is an almost vertical sixty feet.

Of my two children Sophie has always been the leader and the daredevil, even though she is the younger of the two. I stood at the bottom of the slide, camera poised, waiting to record for posterity the moment each of them started their descent. I saw Daniel wave and captured the moment on camera, albeit with slightly shaking hands as I was nervous for him.

As he was travelling through the tube at the bottom of the slide, sharks swimming around him I refocused on the top of the slide waiting for Sophie to appear. No sign of her. It turned out that she lost her nerve at the last moment and wouldn't jump.

Here's the question, who was braver: Daniel, for doing the Leap of Faith, or Sophie, for having to face all the people on the steps on the long climb down?

Eighty Five

Eighty-five is the average daily temperature in the
Maldives in April.

Is this starting to feel like déjà vu from the previous chapter? Don't worry, the story is quite different!

We were looking for somewhere lovely to go on holiday in the Easter break in 2002. My friend Denise, from my *Price is Right* days, had recently returned from a holiday to Sun Island in the Maldives, and she said it was the closest thing to paradise on earth. So the destination was decided upon, we just needed to select a resort.

The Maldives resorts are all individual islands. Some are really tiny, some are more suited to couples on honeymoon and some are quite touristy with lots of organised activities. There was also an issue of cost. Some of the five-star islands were way beyond our budget, particularly as there were four of us. So yes, location was very important but we also had to make sure the 'price was right', if you'll excuse the pun!

In the end we opted for quite a large island, in the Lhavayani Atoll called Kuredu.

When I rang to make the booking I was asked how we would like to travel from Malé airport, where the international flight landed, to Kuredu.

There were two options. We could either take the seaplane, which was a journey of forty-five minutes, or we could opt for a cruise through the islands, which would take six hours. I thought it would be lovely to see some of the other islands en route to Kuredu, and to be able to stretch our legs a bit after the twelve-hour non-stop flight, so I booked the cruise.

The flight was uneventful, if a little cramped, and we landed at Malé in the mid-afternoon. It was very warm, warmer, I suspect, than the average of eighty-five degrees, and a little disorganised, but eventually we were in a queue to get onto a dhoni, a traditional Maldivian fishing vessel, to be transferred to our cruise. I was starting to feel a little nervous at this point as we seemed to be the only tourists choosing this method of transfer. I was even more alarmed as we approached a rusty old miniature version of a cross channel ferry. OK, maybe we should have taken the sea plane!

In fairness, the first couple of hours were not too bad. We sat on the top deck, in the gradually cooling sun, watching numerous beautiful islands slip past. The waters were calm and the only real issue was dodging the smoke from the funnel which was single-handedly polluting this stunning island nation!

As dusk started to fall we headed below deck, which more or less coincided with hitting the open waters of the Indian Ocean. The relevance of this? It was a lot choppier than you might imagine the Indian Ocean to be!

There were no plush sofas and chairs, just rows of plastic-covered benches, and there was no restaurant, not even a bar, just a machine in the corner for soft drinks and snacks. It was not exactly what I had imagined when I had booked the cruise transfer.

To their credit, the children did not complain too much and even managed to get a little sleep, which was probably just as well as the vessel heaved and creaked in the open waters. It was an immense relief, approximately eight hours later, to head back on deck and watch the welcoming lights of the jetty draw near.

It may not have been a particularly auspicious start to the holiday but what was to follow more than made up for it. Having been assigned our two adjacent beach bungalows, we followed the porter along sandy paths and I remember him saying, 'This is the last time you will wear your shoes for two weeks.'

He wasn't joking. They had marketed the holiday as a 'no shoes, no news' destination, and that is precisely what it turned out to be.

The no shoes applied to everywhere, even the restaurants and bars, and the no news was personal choice. There was a television room that we went into once to watch a football match, but we were more or less the only people in there. I think it has changed now with the advent of WiFi, which in many respects is a terrible shame. Holidays really should be to get away from it all.

The following morning, after walking along the beach to the restaurant for our breakfast, we went to the welcome meeting. It was there that we learnt that there were a few available seats on the sea plane for the transfer back to Malé at the end of our holiday. There was a list in the reception area, and it was strictly on a first-come first-served basis. You have never seen me move so fast . . . our names were top of the list!

The holiday itself was everything I had hoped it would be. Our bungalows opened directly onto a white sand beach with the clear warm waters of the ocean beyond. The bungalows were very basic with the only 'mod con' being the telephone to connect you with reception. The beds were interesting – a mattress on top of a cast concrete base – but every day our 'manservant', Mohammad, would make a decorative display with the top sheet.

If the beds were interesting, the bathrooms were even more so. You opened the door to the en-suite and you were outside in a little walled garden. The basin, the shower and, yes, even the loo, were open to the elements. It was a little surreal and yet somehow liberating to bathe out in the open without fear of being overlooked.

As I mentioned earlier, Kuredu is one of the larger islands. Some of the islands you can walk the whole way round in a matter of fifteen or twenty minutes, but Kuredu took about an hour to circumnavigate, depending on how much time we spent paddling, or in some instances wading through the water where the sand gave way to the overhanging vegetation. We did this most days, usually just after breakfast, before settling down to a lazy morning on the beach.

The Maldives is one of the only holiday destinations where my partner Chris has been tempted into the sea. He doesn't swim so isn't fond of big waves and cold temperatures, but in the Maldives it's almost like being in an enormous bath. The children and I took advantage of the warm water by going for long swims, sometimes as far as the jetty about half a mile distant.

We also went canoeing, which I discovered I am useless at as I just can't seem to get the hang of the paddling technique, and the children had a go at water skiing. I say had a go, but in truth neither of them was a natural. Daniel persevered until he fell off quite far out and realised he wasn't alone but was splashing around with creatures with fins. They were actually dolphins, but Daniel was convinced they were sharks and just wanted to get back into the boat. None of us had a go at diving, which is a shame really as the Maldives are famed for the tropical fish and clear waters.

After lunch each day we would keep out of the sun until around four in the afternoon and then walk to the furthest west point of the island and out onto the sand spit which stretched towards the reef. We always made sure we were back in time for the sunset ritual, deck chairs and a cocktail, the children's non-alcoholic, as the sun dropped in the sky before slipping over the horizon. I love to watch the sunset and when I do eventually retire, it will have to be to a house that allows me to watch that fireball of energy retreat for another day.

The two weeks flew by, and it was with great regret that we squeezed our feet back into our shoes before boarding the seaplane bound for Malé. That in itself was an adventure, skimming along the surface of the water before taking to the sky. It was a fabulous bird's-eye view of all the atolls and low-lying islands and probably the happiest I've ever felt in a plane because at least you know if it has to make an emergency landing in the sea it will float!

We made the mistake of returning to Kuredu for a holiday a couple of years later. It wasn't the same. They had demolished the old beach bungalows we had stayed in and put swanky new timber beach huts in their place. There were water bungalows on stilts with all the mod cons that had been lacking previously. I know it is progress, but it had lost a little of its rustic charm.

Needless to say we took the seaplane in both directions on that visit, although that wasn't without drama. We were booked onto the seaplane that would get us to Malé in time to make our connecting flight back to the UK.

We knew the pilot was a bit of a joker as there was a sign adjacent to the gang plank that said, 'The madness starts here'. We climbed aboard with our minimal hand luggage (those planes really are tiny) and the pilot started the engines. Next minute he was on the intercom: 'Everybody off, this plane's going nowhere.'

For a split second we thought he was joking, but no, there was a mechanical problem, so we all had to disembark. There was a nervy wait of an hour or so as they had to send another seaplane from Malé to pick us up but we made it in plenty of time to connect with our flight back to the UK.

Much as I love the Maldives I don't think I would visit Kuredu again. I wouldn't want to see any further 'improvements' they have made in the name of luxury.

Eighty Six

As I listed earlier in the book, I used to appear in a lot
of television commercials. In May 1986, although
I had just discovered I was pregnant with my first baby,
I was still going to auditions, or 'casting sessions' as
they were called, as I wasn't 'showing' at all.

My agent at that time, who shall remain nameless, called me
to go for a casting for a commercial for Harp Lager. The
advert was to be shot over the course of a week in Dublin at the
end of May.

The production company were looking for five young actors
to play a group of footloose and fancy-free friends. I was thrilled
when I got the job as it would be potentially my last opportunity
to earn some decent money before my bump got too big. I went
along with the other actors for a costume fitting and we were all
set to head out to Ireland the last week of May.

Imagine the look on my face when the call came through that
the shoot had been postponed. Normally this would not have
been a problem; however, I was already eleven weeks pregnant
and naturally enough would begin to thicken around the waistline
fairly soon.

A couple of weeks went by and I heard nothing then, in the
middle of June, I was contacted to say the shoot was back on
for the first week of July. Fortunately, because of all the exercise
classes I was teaching at the time, I had very strong abdominal

muscles so I still didn't look pregnant, although I had put on a couple of inches around the middle. We had already had the wardrobe fitting and I didn't want to draw attention to my weight gain so I said nothing and hoped for the best.

The five of us flew out to Ireland at the beginning of July and set up home for the week at Jury's in Dublin.

There were three boys and two girls, myself and Francesca, daughter of the *It's a Knockout* presenter and football commentator Stuart Hall. We hit it off instantly, which is always a good thing when you are going to be living together for a week. The boys were Robin, Jim and Peter. Peter was best known at that point for his role as Joey in the BBC comedy *Bread*, although now he is a successful film producer. Again the boys were really easy to get along with so it wasn't only on screen that we were a group of friends.

The shoot started with no problems as we were filming mostly interior scenes, although any exterior shots we were doing were often rain-interrupted. Although it was a commercial for Harp Lager, I wasn't required to drink any of the golden liquid, which was just as well in my condition!

As the week progressed we started to fall behind on the schedule because of the weather. I remember spending a whole day in a minibus with the windows steamed up and all we achieved was one shot of Peter. That was the day they asked us if we could stay over the weekend and into the beginning of the next week.

That was problematic on two fronts for me. One was quite clear: my tummy was starting to protrude slightly. The other was that I had a wedding to go to on the Saturday back in England.

You may remember in *chapter* 68 that I said I flew home to go to my friend Gilly's wedding? Well, this is where I flew home from.

Fortunately I was not the only one with plans that weekend

so it was agreed that we would fly home on the Friday night after filming, and back out again on the Sunday night ready to start filming again on Monday morning. Poor baby: already a jetsetter and he wasn't even born yet!

Thankfully the weather was kind to us the second week and everything went off without a hitch. There was one shot where I nearly had to divulge my pregnant state. We were filming at a lovely old railway station which had an iron bridge to get from one platform to the other. My action was to run up the steps and across the bridge to meet my friends. Our director was a bit of a perfectionist as we had already learnt earlier in the shoot, and I must have run up and down those steps fifty times or more. Again, thank goodness I was a fitness teacher and in really good condition. I kept thinking, 'If we do this one more time I'll have to tell them', but we got the desired take before that was necessary.

The final shot we filmed was all the friends sat outside a pub bathed in the golden glow of sunset. That meant we had to wait for the sun to set to get the desired effect, but at least I was sitting down.

By the time we got back on the minibus for the drive back to Dublin I was starting to feel a bit unwell so I had to ask the driver to pull over to the side of the road for a few minutes. That's when I told Francesca my 'secret', which I'm pleased to say she kept to herself. We finished filming the next day and all headed to our various homes, but not before I had done a bit of matchmaking for Peter and Francesca, who fancied each other like mad.

I met up with them a couple of weeks after the filming and they couldn't believe that my bump had appeared so quickly – those abdominal muscles had finally succumbed to pressure from within!

They were also the first friends to visit after I had taken Daniel home from the hospital. I have a great picture of Peter with the five-day-old baby in his arms, and he is laughing but with a slightly distasteful expression. Maybe Daniel had just done a poo!

Peter and Francesca didn't stay together but I kept in touch with them both for a while. I went to see Peter in a stage play a couple of years later and then he made the move into film production. His first film was *Sliding Doors*, a good movie if you haven't seen it, and he was also behind the first *Johnny English* film starring Rowan Atkinson. If you watch carefully he makes a cameo appearance à la Alfred Hitchcock.

Francesca and I stayed friends for years but seemed to lose touch after she had her first baby. I'm not surprised; it's very difficult to keep up long-distance friendships at the best of times let alone when you have your hands full with nappies and steriliser units. Hopefully we may catch up with each other's lives in the future.

So all my efforts were worthwhile and eventually a satisfactory ending with a few quid in the bank to tide me over until I could work again. Well, not exactly!

I had been waiting for quite a while for the money to come through for the shoot and, despite many phone calls to and promises from my agent, I didn't receive a thing – ever!

I think my agent declared himself bankrupt so even after getting Equity, the actors' union, involved, I never got a penny piece for the actual filming. It was all very stressful for someone who was about to give birth.

I did, however, contact the production company and explain the situation regarding my agent. They were very understanding and agreed to pay all the repeat fees directly to me.

It was certainly better than nothing!

Eighty Seven

My beloved dad was eighty-seven when he left
this world.

He would be the first to say that he had a good innings, a very appropriate expression as he was a massive cricket fan, but nevertheless it was a huge shock and very sudden.

I was in Spain checking on the progress of the building work to my house when I received a phone call from my brother. I hate conversations that start with 'there's nothing to worry about', which are the exact words my brother uttered.

Apparently Dad had been looking after Mum, who was ill in bed with the flu, and he had passed out, falling backwards and banging his head on the kitchen step. Mum had stumbled out of bed to find him prone on the floor with blood pouring out from a cut to his head. She immediately rang for an ambulance, even though he had started to come round from the faint.

The paramedics arrived quite promptly and continued to dress the wound that Mum had already started bathing. Despite Dad's protestations the ambulance team decided to take him off to hospital to do a few tests as they wanted to know the reason for the blackout. Mum wasn't well enough to go with him in the ambulance so she had called my brother and he was ringing me from the hospital.

I had been scheduled to fly back to London Gatwick the following day but decided to change my destination to East

Midlands so that I could go and see Dad and take care of Mum.

My brother picked me up from the airport and we went straight to the Queen's Medical Centre, in Nottingham, where Dad had been kept in overnight for observation. The preliminary tests hadn't shown anything conclusive so they were planning to do a few more tests. Richard was upset as Dad had had another blackout at the hospital and he had thought we had lost him.

My dad's face was a mixture of surprise and pleasure when he said, 'What are you doing here, I thought you were in Spain.'

It was so good to be able to hug him and to assure him that I was only checking up on him before going to look after Mum.

They moved him onto the ward where he was to spend another night under observation just as dinner was being served. He selected fishcakes, followed by yoghurt for dessert. He chose the yoghurt as he thought it would be healthier for him than the alternative offering of ice cream. When his dinner arrived they had given him ice cream by mistake, but when I asked him if he would like me to change it he said no as he didn't want to be too much trouble. He made Richard and I laugh when he said the fishcakes weren't a patch on my mum's home-made ones; it just surprises me that he thought they might be! He enjoyed his guilty pleasure of his ice cream and was having a cup of tea when he got a sudden shooting pain in his right temple.

'It hurts,' he said, 'it really hurts,' and then he passed out.

They were the last coherent words he ever spoke and he never fully regained consciousness.

Richard rushed off to get the medical staff while I held Dad's hand, then, while they were trying to resuscitate him, I rang Mum and told her to ask her neighbour if he could drive her to the hospital immediately.

I like to believe that Dad hung on until Mum got there and that he could hear her voice even though he didn't respond, and I have assured Mum that this is the case. Although the doctors were summoned it was too late for any kind of surgery to save him as an aneurysm, which we didn't know he had, had burst, causing massive bleeding to the brain. He died two hours later.

I had already rung Chris to ask him to come and be with me as things were not looking too good, but I also needed to let Daniel and Sophie know what had happened.

Daniel was watching an England match on television with his friends and thought I was ringing to talk about the football. I made sure that Sophie also had a friend with her before I imparted the awful news. The strange thing is they both said exactly the same thing, 'Oh, Mum, I'm so so sorry, do you need me to come?'

Neither of them wanted me to be on my own. I reassured them that their dad was on his way and anyway there was nothing they could do really.

Mum was in a state of shock, as you can imagine, so I sent her home with my brother and I stayed with Dad, stroking his hand as I waited for Chris to arrive from London. I knew he had gone from his body but I just couldn't bear to leave him all alone and I couldn't believe that this would be the last time I would touch him. I sat with him for two hours trying to imprint that kindly face into my brain so that I would never forget it, and then I went and sat in the foyer of the hospital to wait for Chris. I think it was one of the worst and loneliest hours of my life. Chris took me back to Mum's and eventually I managed to get her into bed although neither of us really slept much.

The days that followed were a blur of tears and arrangements, as you will know if you have been in this situation yourself. I stayed with Mum for a few days then my sister replaced me as I had to go home for Daniel's twenty-first birthday.

It was a very difficult day. It should have been a celebration of his coming of age but, despite our best efforts, it was terribly overshadowed by my dad's recent passing.

My friend Simon Wilson organised a table for us at a restaurant he had taken me to a couple of times, San Lorenzo, near Harrods. He also treated us to a bottle of champagne. We had walked through Harrods as I hadn't even been able to buy Daniel his present and he had expressed interest in a new coat. We didn't find one that he liked, but I did buy him a green Armani Jeans T-shirt with an eagle on it which he still wears, despite having to have it patched after it got caught in the drum of the washing machine. It's funny how that T-shirt has so much significance and I think of Dad whenever Daniel wears it. The top I was wearing at the hospital I still have, but cannot bear to wear, even though it was one of my favourites.

My brother and I organised the funeral and in the process learnt of a Garden of Remembrance in Radcliffe-on-Trent, where Dad had lived when he first met Mum. We would be able to scatter Dad's ashes and have a shrub planted in his memory. With the help of my mum and sister we selected a winter jasmine as it would flower each year around the time of his death, and would provide some colour in the garden when most other plants are not in bloom.

A few weeks after the funeral just the immediate family gathered to plant our special shrub. We each said a few words, scattered some of the ashes and filled in the earth around the roots.

When it was my turn, I patted the earth down and something caught my eye. On the bush to the side of me was a single white feather and you may be wondering as to its significance? Well, I have a belief that white feathers are a sign from the departed. I carry this feather with me in my purse at all times. There have been other white feathers that I have found both comforting and reassuring but none quite so special as the one that appeared that winter day.

There have been other 'signs' too. About a week after his death, Chris was doing a function at a venue he works at fairly often. It's not unusual for people to approach the band and request their favourite song, however, on this evening, a request was passed to the band anonymously by one of the bar staff. It was for a song called 'Some Enchanted Evening' from the musical *South Pacific*, and it was a song my dad had sung when he played the lead role in the show for the Nottingham Operatic Society.

On another occasion I was helping Mum with the *Times* crossword, which she and Dad used to do regularly. Chris is not a crossword fan and would admit that he very rarely, if ever, gets the answers to the clues. He walked into the room as my mum was reading a clue out for me.

'Inferno,' he said.

We both just stared at him. It was the correct answer and I think we all knew where the answer had come from.

It took me a long time to come to terms with losing my dad. I know he was 'a good age', and I know he didn't suffer a prolonged, painful illness, but knowing these things doesn't make the loss any easier.

With the benefit of hindsight, I think my dad was ready to go, but we certainly weren't ready to lose him. I am just so grateful that something made me change my flight destination so that I was with him at the end of his mortal life.

I think of him often and with love, and I hope and believe that occasionally he looks in on us.

Daniel was already standing at five months old. This was taken in April 1987, and although I didn't know it I was already pregnant again with Sophie.

My favourite picture of Daniel and Sophie as toddlers – it sits on my desk so I look at it every day I am at home.

The four people I love most in the world and my darling dad who we lost in 2007.

My first presenting job for Vauxhall Motors at the 1989 Motor Fair at Earls Court – it was a baptism of fire.

The Roberts family at Mum and Dad's surprise Golden Wedding Anniversary party.

Daniel's third birthday party, where he and I both caught chicken pox off one of the other children. Centre stage is the traditional Roberts family homemade chocolate birthday cake.

My first day at QVC, the 6th of September 1993. People often say I haven't changed a bit but I would beg to differ – I look so young!

Beautiful Daisy, my birthday present in 1999. She survived a fifteen-foot fall as a kitten but couldn't survive being hit by a car in 2008.

I love to watch the sun set into the ocean and what a place to do it: the Maldives on a family holiday in 2002 – Chris was pointing the camera.

I feel so blessed to have such a happy and close family unit. I am very proud of the adults my children have grown into. I have needed their support over the last couple of years and they have been there for me.

Denise and I have been best friends since our *Price is Right* days. I would do anything for her and I know she would do anything for me.

Casa de las Aguilas, my house in Spain that was the inspiration for this book. You can see why it was nicknamed 'Hotel Guatla' during the rebuilding – it ended up far too big for our needs. I hope the new owners love it as much as I did.

Me with Simon Wilson just prior to a Butler & Wilson show on QVC. I have known Simon for over seventeen years and he is a true friend.

Eighty Eight

In October 1988 I was cast to be the main featured artist in a Weight Watchers television commercial.

I was ecstatic as I had been struggling to lose the final stone or so of weight that I had gained during my second pregnancy. Not only would I be getting useful advice on how to shift the extra pounds, I was going to be paid for the privilege.

I have always had minor weight issues and in fact I was put on my first 'diet' when I was only seven. My mum had to have a major operation, so my brother, sister and I were sent to stay with relatives. Lynda and Richard went to stay with our paternal grandmother, who was an OK cook, but I went to stay with my mum's aunt, Auntie Agnes, who was a fabulous cook . . . Oh dear!

I used to love visiting Auntie, not just because she was a great cook, but because she was a genuinely warm and kind human being. She lived in Swanwick, near Ripley, in Derbyshire, which was about twenty miles from where we lived in West Bridgford, but we would see her most weeks. When she visited us she would call into the baker's as she changed buses to buy bread rolls, which in Nottingham are called 'cobs', and potted meat for us to have for our tea.

Before I started at infant school I used to accompany my mum when she made the reverse bus journey to visit Auntie. We would arrive just in time for elevenses, have lunch with her and then catch the bus to be home for when Lynda and Richard finished school.

Auntie had an old rocking chair that I loved, but was only allowed to sit in it if I had been well behaved. On one occasion I was happily rocking in the chair when there was a knock at the front door. It was the vicar. Auntie brought him through to the sitting room to say hello and for some inexplicable reason I decided to lift my skirt up over my face and in the process flash him my knickers! I don't think I was allowed to sit in the rocking chair for some time after that.

I had stayed with Auntie Agnes previously, however it had only been for a few days at a time. When Mum was recovering from her operation it was agreed that I would stay for two weeks. Although we would walk to the shops most days I had no one of my age to play with, so I used to fill my time trying to learn how to type at Uncle Eric's big old typewriter, reading my Famous Five books and 'helping' Auntie bake. She made lemon meringue pie to die for, lovely little sponge cakes, and, my absolute favourite, egg custard.

It's a good job I was only there for a fortnight, because during that short period of time I put on so much weight that some of my clothes didn't fit me! I'm serious. So my first diet was to get me back on the straight and narrow and, quite literally, get me back into my clothes. And it wasn't so much a diet, more a sensible eating plan, with no puddings, and the occasional treat. To be honest, it's more or less how I eat nowadays.

Christmas is always a particularly problematic time for me as I make my own mince pies, pastry and all, and my own Christmas cake, which I absolutely adore, so, like a lot of people, it is the time of year I tend to put on most weight. The timing of the Weight Watchers commercial couldn't have been better. The last thing I wanted to do was put on any more weight, and the incentive of a big pay day made sure that I stuck to the diet plan over the Christmas period.

It's funny, but if I hadn't had Sophie eight months prior to the audition for Weight Watchers, I probably wouldn't have been carrying enough weight for the advert to have had an impact. I had just been through the summer feeling very unhappy at my inability to lose the baby weight, even though I was back teaching fitness classes – about six a week, actually.

When the phone call came through from my agent that I had got the job, I couldn't believe my luck. It was the perfect job at the perfect time. There was just one proviso: we all had to make target weight to actually feature in the commercial. We had ten weeks to achieve our weight-loss goal, before shooting the commercial in early January, so the period ran right across both my son's birthday and Christmas.

I enrolled at my local Weight Watchers class in Croydon. After the initial induction meeting, where we received our diet programme, we had to go back weekly to get weighed.

Usually I would dash there after teaching my fitness classes, and usually I had the children in tow, as Chris worked evenings. I never stayed for the meetings because of the children; it was just to make sure the weight was coming off.

My target weight loss was one and a half stone, and as I was starting at 10st 5lbs, it meant getting down to 8st 12lbs, which was actually slightly less than I'd been before having the children.

The first week I lost 5lbs, and the second week a further 3lbs, but the third week it was a very disappointing half a pound. This was probably because most other people introduce exercise in week three, but I was already doing all my fitness classes. The weight loss was less dramatic after that, but steady, and I even lost half a pound during Christmas week, despite having a small slice of Christmas cake and a mince pie or two!

I reached my target weight with a couple of weeks to spare so my role in the advertisement was secure.

The campaign that year was the 'Weight Watchers Quick Success Programme' and involved the six 'actors' bursting through life-sized posters of our former 'fuller figured' selves and doing a bit of a dance routine to a jingle that said, 'Breakthrough to weight loss.' How appropriate, if a little obvious.

There were five females, of varying ages, and one male, Eddy. One of the girls was called Jodie, and during the breaks in filming I discovered that she was a singer. Not long after the Weight Watchers campaign she appeared on *The Des O'Connor* show on television. She had a really good singing voice and looked amazing. Not long after that, I read in the papers that she was going out with Des O'Connor, and she went on to marry him in 2007. I bumped into her a few years ago, in a hairdressing salon in Covent Garden, and we exchanged telephone numbers with a promise of keeping in touch, but neither of us has . . . so far.

As the main feature in the commercial, I also did all the talking and had a little sequence of twirls in different outfits to represent the different seasons of the year. My outfit for the summer was a bathing costume, which I was very self-conscious about wearing, despite the new slimline me. I needn't have worried, it was only on screen for a flash!

The photos for the posters that we burst through had been taken prior to our weight-loss efforts, and, as you might expect, we were asked to wear very unflattering clothes, slouch a bit and relax our tummy muscles to make us look even chunkier than we were. I didn't feel too bad about this minor deception as I had genuinely lost a lot of weight, and besides, the 'chunky Julia' photo only featured right at the beginning of the advert for a fraction of a second.

However, a few months later the *Sun* newspaper ran a promotion offering free enrolment to a Weight Watchers class and to advertise it they did an editorial piece on yours truly and asked me to do a photo session. I had asked what I needed to take to wear, but was told that the stylist had something for me. The 'something' was the tightest short red dress you have ever seen, but at least it wasn't a bathing costume!

The promotion ran for a week, so my before and after photos featured in the paper every day, and they also used me for the television commercial to advertise the promotion. There was no escaping the 'chunky Julia' photo with the miserable face!

I learnt a lot of good habits from the Weight Watchers diet programme, and the bonus was that while I got thinner, my bank balance fattened up a bit!

Eighty Nine

In 1989 I got my first job as a presenter, fronting a live
presentation for Vauxhall Motors at the Earls Court
Motor Show.

I had decided I wanted to be a presenter shortly after Sophie
was born. The time I had spent sitting up through the early
hours whilst feeding first baby Daniel, then a year later his sister,
had not been wasted. I usually had the television on for company
and I would watch some of the presenters and think, 'I could
do that.' Thinking something and doing something are two
different things, but as soon as I started to get myself together,
when Sophie was a few weeks old, I began to put my plans into
action.

I already had a showreel of the work that I had done before
having the children, but this was mostly television commercials
and was aimed at getting acting roles rather than presenting work.
It was all a bit of a catch-22 really, as you needed to do the
work to put on your showreel, but you needed a showreel to
secure the work.

As luck would have it, while I was doing an acting job in
Bournemouth for a corporate video, I happened to mention my
aspirations about becoming a presenter. I have seen the corporate
video in question, and maybe that is why one of the crew members
told me about a studio that could shoot several clips of me
'presenting' that could be edited onto a showreel.

A couple of weeks later I was back in Bournemouth filming my pieces to camera, which, although not awful, were not very good either! Fortunately, the technician who had edited my previous showreel was a bit of a whizz kid and he managed to extricate enough material to make a half-decent showreel. His name was Vadim Jean, and he went on to direct the film *Leon the Pig Farmer*, which coincidentally had a scene in it shot at Marco Polo House, the home of QVC UK for nearly nineteen years.

It was this showreel that had landed on the desk of the producer for the Vauxhall Motors job, and on the strength of it I was called in for an audition, and was then offered the job.

Landing the job had been comparatively easy, but the reality soon hit home when a huge script arrived for me to learn as they were not going to be using autocue. I'm sure most of you know that autocue is what newsreaders and politicians use, and it is your words projected onto a screen in front of the camera for you to read. The problem is, it is quite expensive to hire the equipment and the operator, and we were going to be live at the Motorshow for the best part of a week, so financially it simply wasn't viable.

Not only was it a large script to learn, it was also full of technical data for the two cars that Vauxhall were launching, the Calibra and the Cosworth. The whole presentation lasted about seven minutes, so as you can imagine there was a lot to remember, and it was to be repeated on the hour, every hour, throughout the opening times of the show. Not only was I presenting to the people gathered around the Vauxhall stand, but every performance was also going to be shown on a huge video wall behind me. Talk about a baptism of fire!

The run-through on the night before the show opened was dreadful. I kept forgetting my lines, and I also had to learn the action, when to get in and out of cars, and where the cameras were going to be positioned for me to talk to. I thought I had bitten off more than I could chew, and I think the producer was having his doubts too, but it was too late for either of us to do anything about it!

~~I must admit the first couple of presentations were pretty ropey~~ but as the first day went on I started to improve, in part thanks to one of the camera operators, Gill, who would whisper prompt words to me if it looked like I had 'dried'! Another coincidence here, as she did some freelance work at QVC many years later.

As the days rolled on, I got more and more confident, so by the time Chris brought the children to see 'Mummy on the stage', I was virtually word perfect. Actually, I was able to get a copy of the footage Gill filmed on the show where my family were spectators, and she got some great shots of them looking really cute, but totally uninterested – the children that is, not Chris!

I had got to know some of the people on the other stands who had watched and sympathised as I struggled with the first few performances. Across the aisle from Vauxhall was the Audi stand, and on the final presentation all the salesmen stopped what they were doing and just stood and watched. It was a little unnerving, but at the end they all held up cards like they do in the ice skating adjudications . . . it was a row of perfect sixes. How kind was that?

It was while I was doing the Motorshow, that Chris organised for me to audition for the local cable television channel, which you will have read about in *chapter 17*.

I passed my audition and my television presenting career was launched.

Ninety

It was a goal in the ninetieth minute of the 1997
play-off final at Wembley that saw Crystal Palace
promoted to the Premiership.

I remember it well, as I was sat in the stand at the end where the goal went in. David Hopkin controlled the ball with his left foot and struck a 'worldie' with his right into the top corner of the net. There was a moment of silence before the red-and-blue end of Wembley erupted in celebration.

The supporters of the opposing team, Sheffield United, were stunned into silence, and I knew exactly how they felt because that had been us the year before.

You have probably realised by now, if you didn't already know, that I am a football fan, and my team are Crystal Palace, as mentioned in *chapters 38* and *49*.

I became a Palace fan almost by default as, although I am a long-time lover of 'the beautiful game', I didn't really support any one team. I have never supported my hometown team of Nottingham Forest and only dabbled briefly with Leeds United when I was in pantomime there.

My affection for Palace grew after I had been asked to do a reporting piece for *Cable Today*, mentioned in *chapter 17*, about the fans travelling to Wembley by coach for the 1989 FA Cup Final against the mighty Manchester United. I couldn't believe how passionate and dedicated the fans were, following their local team rather than one of the 'big' teams.

At the time I lived quite close to Selhurst Park, Palace's home ground, so they were my local team and I started to take an interest in them, even though we lost the aforementioned Cup Final after a Wednesday-night replay.

When I was subsequently asked to present the Friday-night slot called 'Palace Chatback' on *Cable Today*, I didn't give it a second thought and as part of my research I became a regular at the home matches. My son Daniel was four when I took him to his first Palace match. It was a freezing cold afternoon and we were playing Coventry City. It was not the most exciting game, ending in a goalless draw, but Daniel stayed until the final whistle, despite me frequently asking him if he would like to go home. In all the years I have been taking him to watch football I can only remember us leaving before the end on one occasion. It was when we used to ground-share with Wimbledon, before they became the MK Dons. We had to sit in the away fans' stand, which felt a little weird anyway, and we just had a really bad game. We were 4–0 down with ten minutes still to play when we trooped dejectedly towards the exit.

It is certainly never boring supporting the 'Eagles' as they are usually battling relegation from the top flight, or trying to win promotion back to it. Add to that boardroom battles and administration, not once but twice, and you will begin to understand what I mean about it not being boring.

In *chapter 49* I related the dubious honour we hold of the team to be relegated from the Premiership with the highest number of points. I was out filming Irish dancing with the *Cable Today* crew when I heard the news from Highbury Stadium, Arsenal's old home ground. Crystal Palace had lost 3–1 and as a result were relegated. It was devastating.

Unfortunately we have been a bit of a yo-yo team in recent

years, so 1996 saw us trying to climb back into the Premiership through the play-offs. For those of you who don't know, the top two teams in the second tier of English football, the Championship, gain automatic promotion, and the teams who finish third to sixth are handed the lifeline of the play-offs. Third plays sixth and fourth plays fifth over two legs, one home and one away, and the team who win on aggregate go through to the play-off final.

In 1996 Crystal Palace had had a good season and were unlucky to miss out on automatic promotion, finishing third. We made it to the play-off final where we had to face Leicester City. We took the lead, but Leicester equalised so the match went into extra time. With moments to go the match looked certain to be decided by a penalty shoot-out, so our manager made a substitution to have the best penalty takers on the pitch. Within seconds of the substitution Steve Claridge had scored the luckiest goal of his career off his shin pad. I still find it very difficult to watch him in his role as a pundit on the BBC.

So now you know how I knew what the Sheffield United fans were feeling a year later . . . gutted! Incidentally, they also hold a rather unwanted record. They are the only Championship team to lose a play-off final at three different venues: the old Wembley, the Millenium Stadium in Cardiff and the new Wembley.

We also featured in the play-off final of 2004 against West Ham. We had made the final by the skin of our teeth by beating Sunderland in the semi-finals. No one had given us a hope as Sunderland had managed to score two away goals in the first leg at Selhurst Park which meant that, although we were winning 3–2, they had the home advantage for the second leg.

I wasn't able to go to the away game as I was live on air at QVC selling jewellery – very bad planning on my part! Although they are not meant to, the guys in the gallery were keeping me up to speed with what was happening in the match. Sunderland scored to equalise, then scored again to take the lead. As full time approached one of our defenders, Darren Powell, got his head onto a corner and found the back of the net. It was 4–4 over the two legs, so the game went into extra time. At the end of the additional thirty minutes there were no further goals, so the game would be decided with penalties.

These are tense at the best of times, as any England fan will attest, but when you can't watch and the gallery have decided they can't risk giving you information any more, it was excruciating. Thank goodness for my camera man, 'H', who, unbeknown to the producer, was feeding me the scores using hand signals. We won 5–4 on penalties and it was all I could do to refrain from jumping up and punching the air!

The play-off final that year was played in Cardiff while Wembley was being rebuilt. It was a very long coach journey but thankfully worth it, as Neil Shipperley scored the only goal of the game to win us promotion. That was also a fluke goal as it went in off his knee . . . I thought this was supposed to be 'foot' ball!

There have been lots of other ninetieth-minute goals for Palace, some significant, and some not so. Definitely one of the most important of all was scored by our recently departed manager, Dougie Freedman, when he played for us.

Being relegated from the Premiership to the Championship is bad enough but in the 2000/2001 season we almost dropped to the third division, or League 1 as it is now called. We had had a torrid season, and for some time the fans had been calling for the manager Alan Smith to be sacked, even though he had been our hero by winning us promotion in the 1993/1994 season. Who would be a football manager? My son Daniel, actually, given half a chance!

Eventually, with just two games of the season to go, and with Palace six points adrift of the other teams in the relegation dog fight, Alan Smith went and Palace favourite, Steve Kember, took on the role of caretaker manager until the end of the season. We had to win both our remaining games, away from home, and hope that other results went our way.

To make the situation worse, the first of those two games was against Portsmouth, who were also relegation candidates. Unbelievably, we beat them 4–2, which meant we went into the final game of the season with a slim chance of survival.

That game was against Stockport County. It was a very nervy encounter, both for the players and for the fans, whether they had made the trip to Stockport or, like me, were watching on television at home.

My poor son Daniel couldn't watch at all as his Sunday League team had a match that day, so unusually his dad took him. Sophie stayed home with me and at times, when it all got too stressful, I had to go and sit on the stairs and Sophie had to call through what was happening.

It was still 0–0 as we moved into the final minute of the game, and a draw was not good enough for us to avoid relegation. The ball was cleared after an attack on our goal, and punted hopefully upfield for what would almost certainly be our last chance. Dougie Freedman ran the length of the pitch, stole the ball off a team-mate's toe, ran towards their goal and scored with seconds left on the clock.

I remember Sophie and I screaming and shouting and hugging each other, and she is not even a massive Palace fan! Goodness knows what the neighbours must have thought was going on!

No wonder Dougie Freedman is not just a Crystal Palace hero, he is a legend! In his capacity as manager he managed to lift us to the lofty heights of fourth in the Championship before departing for pastures new. Hopefully his successor, Ian

Holloway, will be able to continue the good work he started and who knows, maybe get us promoted back to the Premier League.

I can dream, can't I?

Ninety One

In 1991 we took our children on their
first proper holiday.

Sophie was three and Daniel was four. They had been to the seaside lots of times, to Brighton, Littlehampton, Camber Sands and Poole, but these had all been day trips, they had never stayed away from home for a whole week before, apart from visits with their grandparents.

The destination was the Isle of Wight, and this had been determined by Chris being offered a gig there. We thought it would be good for us all to go and stay for a week, but hadn't realised the week in question was Cowes week, which meant that everywhere was pretty well booked up. Finally, after dozens of phone calls, we were able to book a holiday bungalow on a managed site.

It was a bit of a tight squeeze in the car on the way down to the ferry, as not only did we have all our clothes for the week, we also had Chris's drums, and, of course, the four of us.

Mind you, it wasn't as tight a squeeze as when we used to go on holiday to Blackpool when I was a child. I'm not sure why we used to make the long trek from Nottingham to the west coast, when Skegness, on the east coast, was only seventy miles away. I think it was because we used to stay in a guest house, which was run by someone my Auntie Agnes knew, not far from the North Pier. It was called The Moorings, and while I don't have much recollection of the place, I can still recall the smell of soup that seemed to permeate the building.

The journey there used to take hours, in the days before motorways and fast cars. Although we used to break the journey with a roadside picnic I'm sure the phrase, 'Are we there yet?' must have been repeated hundreds of times from the back seat of the car. I can also remember the excited shrieks of, 'I can see the sea!' as we finally neared our destination.

The beach closest to the guest house was one of those where there is no beach when the tide is in. I'm not really fond of those as there isn't any soft sand to lay your towel out on, but in those days the adults all sat on deck chairs while we children made sand 'pies' with our buckets and spades.

If we were having a picnic lunch, which I don't think we did much as the guest house was full board, my dad used to lay out something he referred to as a 'ground sheet'. This seemed to be some sort of waterproof long cape in a khaki green colour, and I have a sneaking suspicion it may have been something to do with the army, and could well have dated back to my grandad's army days! This would then be covered with a tartan rug – didn't every family have one in those days – to make it more comfortable.

I also remember my mum and dad always had a flask of tea with our beach picnic, rather than cold drinks. And what was it with the flasks in those days, they didn't keep anything piping hot and always seemed to leak. My dad used to put a piece of greaseproof paper over the neck of the flask before screwing the stopper in, I guess to tighten the seal?

On the days when the tide was in, so there was no beach to play on for several hours, we would go to the boating lake or the pier, or take a ride on the famous Blackpool trams. There was also a public garden close to where we stayed that had huge rocks in it that my sister and brother were allowed to clamber over. I was not permitted, either due to my age or concerns over my weak leg.

We normally went to Blackpool for the Whitsuntide holiday, which was at the beginning of June. One year it actually coincided with my birthday. I think I was six, and I can still remember my presents. I had a pink hat and gloves, a faceted glass bead necklace with an aurora borealis coating so that it shone all the colours of the rainbow, and a shell-covered jewellery box with a dancing ballerina inside.

I even remember having a pink shop-bought birthday cake, which in itself was unusual, as if we had been at home my mum would have baked the traditional chocolate cake that we all had on our birthdays. The pink cake might have looked lovely, covered in pink fondant icing, but it didn't taste as good as Mum's home-baked chocolate cake! It is a tradition that I have carried on with my own family, and only occasionally vary if I get a request for a coffee and walnut or luscious lemon cake instead.

I have only been back to Blackpool twice since those family holidays: once for a dancing audition, and the second time just passing through on my way to film in its neighbour, Fleetwood, for Sky Sports, coming up in *chapter 94*. Maybe it's time for another visit?

Anyway, back to the Isle of Wight.

We still had quite a long drive after we got off the ferry, as we were staying on the west of the island near Freshwater, but it was a beautiful sunny August day, and, to their credit, I don't think there was one, 'Are we there yet?' from Daniel and Sophie in the back of the car.

It was early evening when we finally arrived at the holiday village, which was situated on the cliffs above Colwell Bay. The holiday bungalows were semi-detached and were laid out in rows stretching towards the cliff edge. The receptionist showed us to ours, which was the last but one before a big wire fence and a sign saying something along the lines of: 'DANGER – CLIFF ERODING – KEEP AWAY'.

I asked if there was anyone in the adjoining bungalow, and was told that they weren't renting that one out any more as it was too close to the cliff edge. This did not fill me with confidence, as the bungalow we were staying in was attached to the one that was perilously close to the cliff edge!

It wasn't the most luxurious accommodation I have ever stayed in, and it did have a rather musty smell as though, like its neighbour, it hadn't been rented out for a while, but it didn't spoil our first family holiday and we were really lucky to find anywhere to stay during Cowes week.

We were also blessed with good weather, which is always a bonus with seaside holidays in the UK.

Ninety Two

In early October 1992 Sophie started primary school.

It had been a bit of a struggle to persuade the school, Cypress Infants, that she should start with the first intake of pupils for that particular school year, as her birthday was not until January, so technically she wasn't due to start school until the following term. I think it helped that her brother was already at the school and that I had been a willing parent in terms of helping in the classroom whenever work commitments allowed.

Both Daniel and Sophie had attended a Montessori nursery school prior to going to 'Big School'. I had discovered Montessori whilst I was researching a feature on local education for the cable TV channel I worked for. I really liked their approach, which was more than just 'playing' with the children as they do in most playschools – I suppose the clue is in the name!

They had both started at the Montessori school together, Daniel after a year of playschool and Sophie after only six weeks, which meant that Sophie had two years at Montessori. She absolutely loved it and they loved her, but it was only two mornings a week and she really was ready for school.

She had always been a very bright child, probably helped by having a sibling just thirteen months her senior. Whilst we were teaching Daniel his colours and numbers and alphabet, Sophie would be learning too, half the time without us realising. I do remember when we went to the doctor's for her three-year-old development check that they were rather surprised that she could already write her name, albeit with the S backwards, which apparently is quite common with left-handers.

So, after a little persuasion, the headmistress of Cypress Infants bent the rules a little to allow Sophie to start school with the final intake of that term's birthday children. She looked so cute in her grey pinafore dress, white blouse and red cardigan when I dropped her off with Daniel for her first day at school. I say 'day', but actually it was only mornings until the half-term break.

I returned just before midday to collect her and was standing in the corridor with the other mums when a mother who had been helping in class came out and said, 'You are never going to believe this, but there is a child in there reading to the rest of the class.'

Moments later the children spilled out into the corridor.

'How was your first day?' I asked Sophie, to which she replied, 'I liked it . . . I read to the children.'

What made me laugh then and still does today is the fact that she said 'the children' rather than 'the other children', almost as if she didn't view herself as a child.

Throughout her first year, her teacher, Miss Wilkins, encouraged Sophie to help the other children with reading and writing and it is a trait she has carried through into her adult life as she is always willing to help those who want to learn.

Ninety Three

The 1st of October 1993 was the first broadcast date
of QVC UK.

There was a lot of media attention, as you might imagine, and in fact it was even a news story on ITV's *News at Ten*. They ran the opening sequence, featuring myself and another of the original presenters, Jon Briggs, which had launched the channel at 2 p.m. that afternoon.

Funnily enough, although we were going to be broadcasting live, initially for eight hours a day, the opening sequence itself had been pre-recorded the previous day. I guess the 'powers that be' wanted to make sure it was word perfect, as it was a moment in history and they knew it would be scrutinised by millions of people over many years.

Every 1st of October, out comes that old piece of footage of me with my short curly hair, wearing a blue jacket and black skirt, with Jon towering above me, seemingly looking down my cleavage. He wasn't, it was just the angle it had been shot from, at least that is what he told me!

Incidentally, whenever people comment about it they always say, 'I remember you in the early days with your permed hair.' For the record, it wasn't a perm, I have naturally very curly hair, I just choose to blow dry it most of the time.

After welcoming everyone to the channel, Jon then went on to present the first full hour and I'm sure some of you will remember the first-ever product we sold. It was a 'Volkswagon Beetle alarm clock', which sold out. I wish I had had the foresight to order one, as I should imagine it is something of a collector's item now . . . isn't hindsight a wonderful thing!

As you can imagine there are thousands of stories and anecdotes about the job that literally changed the course of my life, but in the interests of keeping this book to a readable length, they will have to feature in a book of their own, if I ever find the time to write it.

Ninety Four

1994 was the year I recorded my favourite
piece of work.

The football season 1993/1994 saw Crystal Palace promoted back to the top flight of English football after their shock relegation a year before. With one game remaining of the season, and promotion a certainty, I contacted Sky Sports to ask if I could film a feature on 'my' team's winning season.

I hadn't previously worked for Sky Sports, but was an avid viewer of a programme called *Sky Sports Saturday*, which, as the name suggests, was broadcast on a Saturday. It was on for the entire afternoon and featured all sorts of sports, not just football. The presenter was Paul Dempsey.

I had rung the show's producer, Tony Baines, with the outline of an idea and he was interested.

'Fax me the idea over and I'll see if we can crew it,' he said.

Well, that was easier said than done. Notice I said 'fax' the idea and not email, because we are talking almost twenty years ago here. Isn't it amazing how technology has moved on in the last twenty years? Email is so quick and easy, faxing not so, particularly if, like me, you didn't have a fax machine!

Fortunately I knew my neighbour did have one so, after hurriedly typing up my idea on my trusty old typewriter, I nipped next door to ask if I could 'borrow' his fax machine to submit my hastily written idea to Sky Sports.

Within hours I had a phone call to say that they wanted to do it, and told me that a cameraman would meet me at Crystal Palace's training ground on the Thursday morning, and that I was booked in to edit on the Saturday morning before the piece would be broadcast in the afternoon.

I was a bit nervous about the tight time schedule as I had never done anything like it before. I'd never been in charge of what was being filmed, in other words, producing, and I had never set foot in an edit suite before. To say Tony Baines was taking a bit of a chance on me is an understatement.

I knew the people at Crystal Palace through the 'Palace Chatback' piece I hosted on my Friday *Cable Today* show, so getting access to film at the training ground wasn't a problem. I also organised to interview the then Crystal Palace manager, Alan Smith (no, not the one who used to play for Arsenal!), who had led them not just to promotion, but promotion as champions.

I had an idea of the sort of shots I wanted for the piece and I had planned the music I wanted to use, aided and abetted by Chris.

When I arrived at the training ground my cameraman was already there. Luckily I had been assigned someone with a lot of experience of filming football. He asked me what I wanted, and I explained I needed lots of shots of the lads training and some close-ups of all the individual team members, and he just got on with it.

We filmed the interviews and a shot of me with the team in front of a goal, and that was that for the training ground.

We then headed off to Selhurst Park, Crystal Palace's home ground, where I had arranged to interview Ron Noades, who was the chairman of the club at the time. We took a few shots of the old Holmesdale Road stand, which was to be demolished to make way for a new all-seater, two-tier stand, and we filmed a piece to camera in front of the entrance. All the filming was finished by mid-afternoon, and I just had to hope that I had enough footage for the piece.

My cameraman headed back to Sky with the Beta tapes, which he was going to have transferred onto video tape for me, with the time codes burnt into it, so that I would be able to do a rough 'paper edit' to save time in the edit suite.

The tapes were biked over to me on the Friday afternoon and, once I had put the children to bed, I set about viewing all the footage, picking out the sequences I wanted to use and writing down all the relevant time codes.

It was a very laborious procedure, particularly for a complete novice, and, although I had started at around 8 p.m., I was still working on it when Chris arrived home from his gig at around 3 a.m. He went to bed but, when I hadn't followed him an hour later, he came back downstairs and made me go to bed. He knew I had to be at Sky Television for the edit at 9 a.m. and I was going to need to be on the ball (excuse the pun!).

After just three hours' sleep I dragged myself out of bed and headed off to Isleworth, where the Sky studios were located. I was shown to the edit suite where my editor was already at his desk.

'Hi,' I said, 'I'm Julia, and I'm a bit nervous as I've never done this before.'

He smiled at me and replied, 'Hi, I'm Bob, and neither have I!'

Fortunately he was having a little joke with me. Again I had been assigned one of the most experienced editors. It seems Tony Baines was compensating for my lack of experience by surrounding me with his top people.

I explained that I wanted to start with my piece to camera, which was about Palace being crowned champions this season, but how it had been a very different story twelve months earlier.

Bob found some footage of the defeat at Arsenal that had seen Palace relegated the season before. The music I had selected was Bryan Adams, 'Please Forgive Me', and we found some very telling shots of former manager, Steve Coppell, with his head in his hands, as the Gunners put three goals past Nigel Martyn to seal our fate. It also needed some voiceover, but Bob said we would do that later.

The next sequence was the training ground and there was brilliant footage, shot from a low angle, of the team being put through their paces. Again it needed voiceover, but this time the music was much more upbeat, if a little obvious. I had chosen the Average White Band track called 'Pick Up the Pieces'. I particularly love the bit where the coach, Steve Harrison, was throwing balls to the players to run onto and practise headers.

Next it cut to the interview with Alan Smith and we needed a shot of a player called Paul Stewart, who had been instrumental in getting us promoted, but who had only been on loan so hadn't been at the training ground when we filmed as he had returned to his club. Bob had to search the archives to find a shot of Paul Stewart. It was such a short clip that he had to play it in slow motion, but it worked.

The next segment was the interview with Ron Noades, before cutting to a tracking shot of the Holmesdale terraces, which again required voiceover, which had the Bryan Adams track 'Everything I Do' bubbling under it.

I was starting to wonder when exactly we were going to be recording all this voiceover as time was ticking away.

The final section of the piece, still with 'Everything I Do' playing, which had to be back-timed so it finished with the final shot, was close-up shots of the players and management, again in slow motion, concluding with the shot of me with the team in front of the goal.

As we were editing this last series of shots, there was a phone call from the gallery of *Sky Sports Saturday*. It was almost I p.m., and the show was about to go live. They needed to know if the piece would be finished in time to be played out at ten past two, and they also needed a short segment for the top of the show to promote that it was coming up. Bob gave them a clip to play out, and confidently assured them that it would be finished in time. He then turned to me and said, 'We had better get that voiceover recorded.'

By this time I was running on adrenalin. My heart was thumping as Bob took me to the voice booth. Although I had done voiceover work before, this was a very pressurised situation. We both knew that it had to be one take for all of the voice sequences . . . no second chances! There was a piece in the script, referring to Palace's relegation the previous year, where I say, 'I'm not ashamed to say I cried.'

Everyone always complimented me on the way I delivered the line, as I had a slight wobble in my voice which sounded like emotion. It was emotion of a different sort, panic that we wouldn't be finished and would miss our 2.10 p.m. slot after all our hard work.

The finished tape was handed to the gallery just before 2 p.m., and I was shown to the green room to watch it being played out live. I was shaking. It was almost like giving birth, but not so physically painful. I sat on my own in that green room and marvelled at the way it had all come together, thanks in no small part to two very professional Sky Sports employees. Whether it was relief or pride, I'm not sure, but as the piece finished I realised I had tears rolling down my cheeks.

I left the Sky building feeling elated, and even being held up in the Twickenham rugby traffic couldn't dampen my spirits. I was still on a high when I got home, particularly after I had watched it again (and again and again).

Tony Baines must have been quite happy with my work as I did a few other features for Sky Sports.

I filmed two more features on Crystal Palace. The first one was a 'Fun Day' filmed the week prior to the start of the new

Premiership season. We had been drawn against Liverpool for our return to the top division. There were lots of activities for children, like five-a-side games and a bouncy castle, and also a Celebrity Charity Match, which included comedian Sean Hughes, DJ David Jensen and former Palace manager Steve Coppell. The end shot was of two seven-year-old Palace fans saying, 'We're back!'

One of them was my son Daniel.

The second one was focusing on how teams prepare over Christmas for their Boxing Day games. The Palace lads joined in the festive fun as I offered around the mince pies, and there was a great shot of Richard Shaw and some of the other players looking longingly through the manager's office window as Alan Smith, wearing a Santa hat, and I sipped sherry.

I also did some filming at the Wimbledon training ground as I knew their chairman, Sam Hammam. The feature was about the necktie business run by their goalkeeper, Hans Segers. I managed to get some good quotes from several of their better-known players, including one from their captain at the time, Vinnie Jones. I had asked if it was true that they were one big happy family, and Vinnie replied, 'Yes, it's true, but I wish Sam was more generous with the family allowance!'

I drove to Cardiff to film a piece on ice hockey, a sport I knew absolutely nothing about. If you think footballers like to pull a few stunts, they have nothing on the hockey players!

When I was trying to do some interviews in the changing room, they kept walking behind the interviewee completely naked to try and put me off. It didn't, but we couldn't use any of the stuff we shot for fear of falling foul of the obscenity laws! The final piece looked pretty good as I had selected 'Two Tribes' by Frankie Goes to Hollywood as the teams skated onto the ice and 'Cold As Ice' by Foreigner as we watched the action. I kept the puck as a memento and used it as a paperweight for years.

On the strength of the feature I was asked to be a reporter for the Benson & Hedges Cup competition, which saw me flying to Edinburgh, and also visiting the ice rink in my home town, Nottingham!

Another sport I covered for Sky was ladies' boxing. I must be honest here and say that boxing is about the only sport I really don't like, and I like ladies' boxing even less.

We were filming in Fleetwood, just north of Blackpool on the Lancashire coast, the hometown of boxer Jane Couch, who was known as the 'Fleetwood Assassin'. She later caught the eye of boxing promoter Don King, and went on to become Ladies World Champion.

The most memorable part of that day for me was having to stop for a two-hour sleep in my car at a motorway service area on the way back to London, because I was so tired.

So I did a few features on different sports for Sky, but my favourite was, and always will be, the Crystal Palace promotion feature in 1994 where I 'cut my teeth'!

Ninety Five

When I stepped off the plane at Kaitak Airport in Hong
Kong in 1979, the humidity was 95%.

It was like being hit with a wet blanket and there was a very
distinct smell of rotting vegetables. After a flight of more than
twenty hours, I was beginning to wonder whether the hasty decision I had made to travel halfway round the world, for a singing/
dancing job, was the right one.

I hadn't been looking for a dancing job abroad, after all I was
fifteen months into my first 'serious' relationship. I had attended
an open audition for a new dancing agency following a phone
call from my friend Pat, who I had met at the end of my 1975
summer season at the Watersplash in Jersey. We had kept in
touch sporadically after the season finished, as we had got on
very well, but I had gone on the cruise ships and she had taken
a job in Nigeria, so we hadn't really seen a lot of each other.

The audition room was teeming with girls when we arrived
as the agency were looking to place girls in a selection of different
jobs. In between learning the various step sequences and then
performing them, we were catching up with each other's recent
past.

Gradually the number of girls was being whittled down until
eventually there were just a few of us remaining. Nothing had
been mentioned at any point about who was being looked at for
which specific job, but when we were down to the last few we

were asked if we would be interested in going to Hong Kong for three months.

Pat, who, as I had learnt during our chat between routines, now preferred to be called Tricia, seemed quite keen to go, but didn't want to go on her own. The next thing I knew I had agreed to go with her, as they had offered me the opportunity to do a couple of vocal numbers and I was trying to break into singing at the time.

There is a distinct possibility that I took this decision not just to please Tricia and progress my singing career, but also to get my own back on Chris, who was away doing a two-week job in Dubai with the actor/comedian Derek Nimmo. I hadn't wanted him to go, which I admit was pretty selfish of me, but he went anyway.

He got back from Dubai a few days later, and I told him I was going to Hong Kong for three months. If he minded he didn't say so, but I suppose he felt he couldn't really. Who knows, maybe that is why we are still together; absence makes the heart grow fonder, so they say. He even wrote me letters, as I mentioned in *chapter 15*, and he hates writing letters!

We had two weeks of rehearsals in London, during which time we had to have the necessary inoculations, which included cholera. We had been warned that this might cause some immobility in our arm and they weren't joking. Why then had the agency arranged for us to have a photo shoot the morning after the jabs? You should have seen us trying do our hair and make-up, and change costumes without the ability to raise our left arms above shoulder height!

There were five of us in the group, which the agency had named 'Dynamite'! As well as Tricia and myself there was Suzanne, and the two Janes, one of whom was our 'head girl'. Jane, the head girl, was also doing some of the choreography and taking rehearsals. She was a really good dancer, as was Tricia, and I wasn't too bad, but the other two were a little slow at picking up the routines which became quite frustrating at times. It meant we had to go over and over the routines until they could remember them. In fairness, we had a lot to learn in a short space of time but it comes with the territory when you are a professional dancer.

Also during rehearsals we had become members of a Chinese Social Club. The sole purpose of this was to get discounted air fares, but it did mean that the five of us were sitting amongst a group of Chinese people who didn't speak a word of English on the plane. At least we had each other to talk to, and I think the air steward felt a little sorry for us as he organised for us to go up to the flight deck, a treat normally reserved for children with birthdays. It's such a shame that with all the fear of terrorist attacks and hijacks they don't allow it to happen these days.

It was a long flight with three touch downs, in Switzerland, the Middle East and Calcutta. We did get off the plane at Calcutta to stretch our legs but it was so hot and humid, almost to the point of suffocation, that we got back on the aircraft as soon as we were allowed.

So I was on board the aircraft and Chris was busy locking himself out of our flat. We were still sub-letting the Housing Association flat off my friend, which I told you about in *chapter 67*. Well, I say 'we', but she wasn't actually aware that Chris was living there too. Rather than risk losing our base in London, we decided not to tell her that I was going away for three months, so Chris would simply make sure that all the bills were paid on time. Sounds simple enough, but when Chris managed to lock himself out of the flat while I was still en route to the Far East, he had to phone my friend's parents, who lived in the Barbican, and tell them the whole story. They were OK about it, but he still had to go and meet them for their approval before they would hand over the spare set of keys!

Fortunately, I was oblivious to all this when the plane finally touched down in Hong Kong, which, as I mentioned earlier, had 95% humidity and was still very hot, despite it being quite late in the evening. We were checked in to a hotel for the night to get some rest before being taken to our apartment the next day.

Jane had been to Hong Kong before, so as well as being our head girl, she also became a bit of a tour guide for us in the first few days. If I remember rightly her brother was in the Hong Kong police and under his protection we visited some slightly 'dodgy' places where tourists wouldn't normally venture, but it gave us a taste of the real Hong Kong.

After a day to get over our jet lag it was time to get back to rehearsals with opening night only a few days away. Ideally the rehearsals would have taken place at the venue but there was a hitch: it wasn't actually finished, so we had to rehearse at the apartment.

The venue we were to be performing at was called the Cabaret Club, now there's an original name. It was on the lower ground floor of a shopping mall called the New World Centre and it was still very much a work in progress. There was no dance floor, no carpets, no furniture; in fact, it was pretty much an empty shell with hordes of people working 24/7 to finish it for the Grand Opening ceremony to be performed by Hollywood film star Vincent Price.

The night of the dress rehearsal arrived and we were able to perform on the dance floor, albeit with carpet fitters hard at work around us. All things considered, the dress rehearsal went really well, but in theatre there is a superstition that a bad dress rehearsal will lead to a great opening night, and vice versa. Unfortunately this came to fruition as some bright spark, who was probably only doing as instructed, polished the dance floor until it had a mirror-like finish. It looked beautiful but it was almost impossible to dance on. So, from our point of view, the Grand Opening was a bit of a disaster with us hardly able to move and when we did we kept slipping over, a bit like 'Bambi on Ice'. I suppose it was quite appropriate that Vincent Price was doing the opening night honours, after all, it was a bit of a horror show.

Somehow the club managed to dampen down the shine on the floor so it steadily improved over the next few nights. I don't remember all the routines we performed, but I do recall the 'Copacabana', and also the two songs I performed.

One was Neil Sedaka's 'Breaking Up Is Hard to Do' and the other was 'Last Dance' by Donna Summer. I had the distinct impression that the management of Cabaret had been expecting more of a showgirl-style group, parading around in bikinis and feathers, rather than the funky outfits we were in. They never let it show though as it's not the done thing to 'lose face' in Chinese society.

Whatever they thought of our dancing style they looked after us really well. The apartment, as mentioned in *chapter 15*, was spacious and in a nice area. The owners of Cabaret also had a little place called Bottom's Up, and if you are thinking the name sounds familiar it is because it featured in the Bond movie, *The Man with the Golden Gun*, starring Roger Moore. We were taken there a couple of times and also treated to dinner at the seriously posh Gaddy's restaurant in the Peninsula Hotel.

Talking of being treated to dinner, I can't remember actually cooking anything while we lived in Hong Kong, as we were constantly being invited out by different groups of people so we had lots of interesting culinary experiences. From the Jumbo floating restaurant in Aberdeen Harbour, to stopping at a shack at the side of the road on a day trip to the Chinese border, we tried most things.

One of the most surreal was eating on a small sampan in Hong Kong's typhoon harbour. After the shows one night we took the Star ferry over to Hong Kong Island. We always paid the extra cent to travel on the upper deck as Jane had warned us about 'spit' deck. We got a small boat from the harbourside out to an even smaller boat where we were going to dine.

This small sampan was actually somebody's home and was a bit like a floating caravan. We sat on seats, which converted into their beds at night-time, and after we had ordered our food from the selection on offer, they proceeded to cook it in a tiny kitchen area at one end of the boat, separated from us by a curtain. The food was delicious and the experience was quite gratifying as we knew we were helping to supplement their meagre incomes. I wonder if it is where the idea for 'pop-up' restaurants came from, where you go and eat at a complete stranger's house!

One of my favourite evenings out was dining on the veranda of the Repulse Bay Hotel, a beautiful old colonial building right on the beach, complete with silver service and ceiling fans. It was one of those occasions where I had to keep pinching myself to make sure it wasn't a dream. It made such an impression on me that, when I returned to Hong Kong a few years ago for a trip with our QVC buyers, I committed the mortal sin of going back to a special place from the past.

I was with Ali, one of the other QVC presenters, and we managed to get a few hours off from the hectic schedule for a bit of sightseeing. We went to Stanley Market, which was pretty much as I had remembered it, if a little more built up, but what a shock when I went in search of the Repulse Bay Hotel. A new skyscraper Repulse Bay Hotel had been built across the road from the original, and that beautiful colonial building, with steps leading down to the beach, is now a games arcade. I was utterly devastated. My trip down memory lane stopped right there, as I had no desire to see what they may have done to my favourite beach, Big Wave Bay.

I've always loved going to the beach, wherever I am in the world, whiling away a few hours with a good book and a walk along the shoreline. In Hong Kong I used to wake Tricia at about ten in the morning, regardless of what time we had gone to bed the night before, and we would go off in the TR7, which we had managed to 'borrow' for the duration of our stay, to Big Wave, Saints, Repulse or Clearwater Bays to spend the day, before getting back for another dinner date and our two shows in the evening.

After one such day at the beach we were running a little late for our dinner date. Our hosts for the evening had selected a restaurant quite close to the New World Centre, so everything should have been fine, except that the service in this restaurant was unbelievably slow. To save time we had ordered all three courses before our meal, but by the time we had finished our main course we simply had to leave or risk being late for the show. It must have been quite comical for any onlookers watching three European girls running down the road, each clutching a bowl of cherries jubilee. Our hosts had offered to pay for the glass serving dishes so that we could have our 'takeaway'!

All these dinners out and yet I never had a problem with my weight in Hong Kong. Maybe it was because we were always rushing around so that we didn't miss a moment of this incredible experience. Or maybe it was because we could often be found dancing until two or three in the morning at our favourite club, Disco Disco, as on the night of the typhoon described in *chapter 15*.

We didn't always head straight home when the nightclubs closed, we would sometimes go for a late-night coffee and snack . . . yes, more food! One night we had gone to an American-style diner and ordered burgers and iced coffee. When the food arrived it was the thickest burger I had ever seen. I picked it up to take a bite and the burger shot out of the back of the bun and landed in one of our hosts' cup of coffee, splashing it all over the table and him. There was a moment of nervous silence before we all started to laugh, which was a huge relief to me as not everyone sees the funny side of these things.

Hong Kong wasn't just about food and dancing though; there was lots of other socialising. We went to lunch with the film producers who made a lot of the 'Kung Fu' movies and with the benefit of hindsight I think the owner of the Cabaret Club was trying to get us featured in one of them as publicity for his club.

We spent the day on a Chinese junk, a large version of the sampan, before partaking in a midnight beach picnic. We went to the races at Happy Valley and up to the top of the peak, with its magnificent views over the harbour.

We even took the ferry to Lantau Island, which in those days was stunningly beautiful and relatively unspoilt. Sadly that is no longer the case, as it is now the location of the new Hong Kong airport and is connected to the mainland by a bridge. Another unwanted discovery from my trip with QVC.

There are plenty of stories to tell about that trip too, but maybe that's for a different book?!

Ninety Six

When we moved from our first house,
The Coach House, in 1994, we moved into a
house that was built in 1896.

It was in the Surrey village of Woldingham, and, coincidentally, it was also a former coach house, although it was called The Downs Cottage.

We had decided to move to coincide with Daniel starting junior school, and although we sold our old house within days of it going on the market, it was not proving quite so easy to find a house we liked, and that we could afford, in Woldingham.

We were only shown three properties in the village in our price range and none of them was ideal. The Downs Cottage was the best of the three, but it had two drawbacks. It was located on the main road through the village, and it had very little in the way of a garden. Apart from that, it had potential. It was detached, with three bedrooms, a good-sized kitchen, a dining room and a generous lounge.

Our offer was accepted, but we had to wait for the tenants who were renting to move out before we could move in. This wouldn't have been too much of a problem, except that we wanted Daniel and Sophie to start their new school at the beginning of the school year, and the tenants weren't due to move out until late September. We spent the first three weeks of term ferrying the children across from South Norwood to Woldingham in the morning rush hour, but at least it was only for three weeks.

It must have been a little strange for Daniel and Sophie on the day we moved, leaving one house in the morning to go to school, and coming home to a different house in the afternoon, but I'm sure it was quite exciting too.

We moved in to The Downs Cottage at a time when I was extraordinarily busy with work. I was working four days a week at QVC, I presented two *Cable Today* shows a week, plus any additional footage that needed to be shot for the shows, and I was picking up a little bit of work for Sky Sports. I wasn't working the day we moved in, but after that I worked every day for the next twenty days, sometimes working for two different companies on the same day. It was madness, but when you are freelance you have to take the work while it is there because it could all dry up in an instant.

The drawback was that Chris unpacked all the kitchen stuff, so I spent the next couple of years saying, 'I'm not sure I would have put that there!'

The first few months we accepted the house as it was, although we knew that there were lots of changes we wanted to make, and a few we needed to make.

Sophie had the smallest of the three bedrooms, and it was far from ideal as it had no window, just a glass door, which was the only access on to the roof garden.

There was a reasonably sized dining room, which had been converted from a garage, but we didn't use it as it was the other end of the house from the kitchen. And then there was the kitchen itself.

It was quite large and L-shaped, but there were no doors, just two arches, which made it open to the hallway and the front door. There was no table but it did have a breakfast bar built around the pillar that separated the aforementioned arches. This would have been all right for Chris and I, but it wasn't ideal for a six- and seven-year-old and anyway it wasn't big enough for us all to sit and eat together.

So that was where we started with the alterations. The breakfast bar was knocked out and the arches were filled in, one with a half-glazed kitchen door, and the other part bricked with an internal window above it to let in light. Chris did the work himself, with a little bit of help from me when I was around!

Next we tackled the waste of space that was the dining room. We decided to erect a stud wall to separate the space into a small office for me, and beyond it a music room for Chris. Again we did all the work ourselves, including removing all the wood-chip paper, which had seemingly been attached with superglue!

We also replaced the hideous metal shower cubicle in the downstairs cloakroom and replaced it with a modern corner shower, which turned out to be a godsend, as you will read later in the chapter.

After sprucing up the rest of the rooms with a bit of painting and decorating to make it feel like home, we left it alone for a couple of years while we hatched our major renovation plan. We also needed to save up some money, as we had completely blown our budget on the move to Woldingham.

It wasn't until four years later that we were ready to embark on our ambitious plan of turning this three-bedroomed cottage into a six-bedroom house, complete with gym, conservatory and games room. All the relevant planning permission was in place and we had remortgaged to bolster our finances for the work; all we needed now was a builder. Enter Vernon.

We had used Vernon's services when we had renovated our house on Ross Road and he had given us a very reasonable estimate. Unfortunately, one of his workforce had died in the period since the previous job, but he assured us he had a great team around him and at least we knew he would not rip us off.

I really liked Vernon. He was a 'salt of the earth' character and a hard-working family man. He didn't drive a flash four-wheel drive; he had a battered old Ford Granada estate. He had a glass eye and he was partially sighted in the other one, but that hadn't hindered him producing good work in the past so we decided to give him the contract. The work was due to start the last week of August and finish prior to Christmas, at least that was the plan!

I had slight misgivings the first day he turned up on site with his two 'lads', who must have had a combined total age in excess of 130! To be fair, things started off reasonably well, with them knocking out the old bay window in the lounge and replacing it with twelve-foot-wide patio doors that would eventually lead into a conservatory.

They did a great job demolishing the old roof garden and excavating into the hillside to make space for the gym and the games room. They had even managed to erect the retaining wall and get the steel RSJs in place to start building up from, and they had removed a segment of the roof of our bedroom as we were going up another storey. It was all looking very promising, and then the rains came. It started to rain around the end of September, and it just kept on and on every day.

The electric fuse box, which had been housed in the old garage, was now open to the elements, and despite being covered with plastic sheeting still managed to get wet and leave us without power on more than one occasion. The rain was so heavy and persistent that it leaked through the tarpaulin covering the bathroom so we had to dodge the various containers catching the leaks every time we wanted a bath. How grateful were we for the downstairs shower we had installed.

Our bedroom was the worst though. The builders had erected a temporary plywood 'wall' across the length of the room, leaving just enough room for our bed, the built-in wardrobe and a chest of drawers. Because it was the only moderately dry place on site they would use the other half of our bedroom as their rest area. They would arrive at 7 a.m., put on the kettle for their first cuppa of the day and then 'f' and blind about the appalling weather. I think they mustn't have realised I was the other side of a flimsy plywood partition trying to sleep, having quite often only crawled into bed at 3 a.m. following a late shift at QVC.

September turned into October and it was still raining every day and getting colder by the minute. It really was a miserable time, and then, to top it all, my mum was diagnosed with breast cancer. The saying 'it never rains but it pours' took on a real meaning for me. I will always remember my mum's first words to me when she came round after her operation. She reached her hand up and stroked my cheek and said, 'You have beautiful skin.'

Dad was an absolute rock, ferrying Mum back and forth to the hospital for her radiotherapy treatments and generally being there for her.

To keep Mum positive, I had managed to get hold of some tickets to go and watch the dress rehearsal of the Royal Ballet at Covent Garden from one of the boxes. It gave her something to look forward to and to get better for. The performance was in December but unfortunately our house was still a total building site. They came to stay anyway and slept in our 'half-bedroom', while Chris and I had the sofa bed downstairs. Mum didn't complain about the less-than-luxurious surroundings and I think the trip to the ballet lifted her spirits, as she still talks about it.

Slow progress had been made on the building work, despite the weather's best efforts, but there was no way the work could be finished by Christmas. On Christmas Eve, Vernon came to the house with a big basket of flowers in red and gold and apologised profusely that the works weren't finished. What a lovely thing to do, after all there wasn't much he could do about the constant rain.

The weather improved in the New Year, although I do remember we had snow that year as Chris found Vernon's phone under a snow drift after he had unwittingly dropped it. Within a couple of months we had the shell of our 'new' house for us to take over and decorate.

Although it had been a dreadful time, there were some lighter moments during the renovations, which almost inspired me to write a comedy series! As I mentioned earlier in the chapter, Vernon was partially sighted so he wasn't always aware of what was going on around him. One day he was carrying some long pieces of wood on his shoulder when one of the 'lads' called his name. He swung round in the direction of the sound and in the process almost decapitated another of his workforce, who ducked just in time! Vernon was totally unaware and the chap had to duck again as Vernon swung back to continue on his path.

I also mentioned Vernon's old Ford Granada, which he used to load up with building materials to bring to the house. The Downs Cottage was on a fairly steep hill and the poor old car gave up the ghost near the bottom of the hill a few yards up from a sharp bend. Instead of calling one of the breakdown recovery services, Vernon simply left it there with the hazard warning lights flashing. We had to pass it at least four times a day as we ferried the children to and from their school in Caterham, and we watched the lights grow dimmer and dimmer until eventually they stopped altogether. He did get it towed away in the end, but not before it had caused major traffic issues during the commuter and school 'rush hours'!

Then there was his two 'lads'! One of them managed to tread on a piece of wood with a rusty nail in it which went straight through his foot. He limped to the front door to ask if we had a plaster! Sophie had just started doing pointe work at ballet class, so she was able to offer him some surgical spirit, which she helped to administer, before suggesting he should pay a visit to the hospital for a tetanus jab!

The other old boy got in the way of a wall he was knocking down so he ended up in casualty too with cuts and bruises to his leg. There were loads of other small incidents with the three old boys that I really could have written a comedy show about and I already had the title in my head . . . 'Bodgit and Leggit'!

I am not saying that the building works were in any way bodged though as they were all capable builders, and we had specialists come in to do bricklaying, roofing, plumbing and electrics.

The specialist that did the roofing was one of Vernon's actual lads, in other words, one of his sons, Tim, and another of his sons, Paul, helped out from time to time with general labouring. As fate would have it we bumped into Paul at Alicante airport some years later on one of our trips to the Spanish house. Of course I asked after his dad and I was really upset to learn that he had died.

We were really pleased with the makeover we had given the house except for one room, our bedroom. It was nobody's fault, as it is always difficult to visualise the end result, but the room was a bit too small and it was quite dark, even though we painted the walls in light colours. We lived with it for several years before taking the decision to remove the stud wall which separated our room from the small single room next to it, which was only used occasionally for guests. This would then make a beautiful master suite, with French doors opening onto the roof terrace. I really wish we had done it before as it made such a difference to the house and was probably the reason we were able to get a buyer in a difficult market when we wanted to sell.

With no Vernon to call on, Chris and I did the construction work ourselves, but again called in the experts for plumbing, electrics and tiling. I am a dab hand at removing tiles with a hammer and chisel, and even contributed to putting up plasterboard when necessity demanded it. We extended our en-suite bathroom to include a walk-in shower, and we even installed a television at the end of the bath, which Chris often says is the only thing he really misses about the old house.

We were about halfway through the bedroom project when my dad died quite suddenly, which I wrote about in *chapter 87*. After staying with my mum for the initial few days and again after the funeral, we made it a priority to get the bedroom finished in time for Christmas, as I wanted Mum to come and stay and we were sleeping in 'her' room. The room had single beds and there were many nights when Chris reached his hand across to hold mine as I quietly sobbed in disbelief.

The work on the bedroom became feverish as we needed to finish all the painting before the carpet was laid and our new bed arrived. The children, who were both away at university, had come home for the holidays and they got stuck in as well. Daniel helped with the walls and the ceiling, and Sophie's job was gloss-painting skirting boards, window frames and doors. It was while she was doing this one day that she got soaked.

We were having a small problem with the newly installed shower. We later discovered that it was the position of the motorised pump that would sometimes prevent it from working due to lack of pressure, which was easy to fix once we knew what the problem was. Normally we switched the shower back to the off position, but on this occasion somebody hadn't. Sophie was busy painting when the shower randomly turned itself on, which frightened the life out of her. Paintbrush in hand and fully clothed, she reached for the lever to turn the shower off but mistakenly altered the flow from the overhead unit to the body bar so the jets of water hit her full on until she corrected her error. I rushed into the room, following her shriek, and couldn't help but laugh as both she and the bath-room were totally drenched! She started laughing too and it was a much-needed release of tension after the previous few weeks.

The painting was finally finished at about 2 a.m. with the carpet fitters due to arrive less than eight hours later. It was the 21st of December, so we were cutting it very fine, but it looked like it would be finished in time for Christmas.

When the fitters arrived they unrolled the carpet, but it didn't quite fit. Apparently it had been stored in a warehouse with no heating, and the temperatures had been sub-zero so the carpet wasn't flexible enough to be stretched in the normal manner. Minor disaster, as we had the bed arriving the next day! Thankfully the carpet fitters had a solution. We needed to have the heating on full blast for twenty-four hours to soften the backing and they would come back the next day, before starting their packed schedule, to try again. The trick worked, and two hours after they finished laying the carpet, the bed arrived. I am known for being a bit last minute, but even by my standards that was tight!

It wasn't the best Christmas, as you can probably imagine, but we looked after Mum and made sure she at least had some moments when she could escape the awfulness of losing my dad.

We had turned The Downs Cottage into a lovely, welcoming family home where the children were able to grow up and entertain their own friends. Their games room was just big enough to house a table tennis table, or that could be folded away and replaced with the snooker table. If they wanted a gathering we never had a problem with it, so long as they cleared up afterwards. The way I looked at it, they had to put up with the discomfort of having the house built around them so they deserved to enjoy the fruits of all our efforts.

I have however vowed that I will never again live in a house that we are renovating whilst it is a work in progress.

Ninety Seven

This is the number of medals I won for dancing in competitions and medal tests as a child.

It may seem like a lot but some of my friends from the Nora Morrison School of Dancing had many more medals than that.

We only really took part in two main dancing competitions a year as we were also training for examinations and the annual show, which took place in November. Most of us who were serious about dancing gladly gave up three or four nights a week and at least one day of our weekend to attend our various classes or private lessons in ballet, modern and tap. I have no idea how any of us ever got any school homework done, but I seem to recall that trying to learn German grammar over a cup of cocoa before going to bed was a fairly regular occurrence.

The Sunshine Festival, for which there were three stages, the heats in March, the semi-finals in June, and the finals in July, which took place in London if you were lucky enough to make it that far, was one of our annual festivals. I think I only made it to the finals twice and both times it was performing a duet.

These days it would probably be considered politically incorrect, and maybe it was, but my friend Teresa and I would apply dark face and body make-up for our performance of 'Old Man River' from *Showboat*. We were depicting slaves in the Deep South of America and we had to feel their pain with every fibre of our being as we sang and danced our way through the routine. It was such an unusual choice by our dancing teacher and almost always won us first place. I say almost always as at the finals of the Sunshine Competition we had to settle for third.

The other competition that we entered every year was the IDTA Festival which happened in Leicester in May. That was probably my favourite competition as the adjudicators seemed to be more into performance and less about technique, which suited me perfectly!

We occasionally also entered the Derby Arts Festival, and a festival that took place in Scunthorpe, the latter of which I can only remember participating in once, although I do remember it was a lovely modern theatre.

The other competition that only some of us took part in, as it was in the middle of the school summer holidays, was the Skegness Festival. It was a week-long competition, which meant you needed to stay in Skegness if you were competing in lots of categories.

The first year I did it was when I was eleven years old and it was to be regarded as our family summer holiday. My sister, Lynda, had given birth to her first baby, Deryk, only a week or so before, so imagine the scene. Mum, Dad, Lynda, Richard, newborn Deryk and me, not forgetting Paddy the dog, all cooped up in a caravan! Thankfully I was only in five or six dances that year, so I think maybe our holiday was cut short. I won two gold medals in that competition, and my parents were so proud that they had them engraved, the only time they have ever done it.

I think I did the Skegness Festival most summers, but it wasn't always a family affair. One year I stayed with my friend Susan and on the first evening we begged her dad to take us to the beach, even though the sun was starting to set. If you know Skegness at all, you will know the beach is vast and that when the tide is out the sea is barely visible from the promenade. Well, the tide was out that evening but Susan and I still wanted to paddle our toes so we went racing off down the sands. The trouble was that the tide was on the turn and it started to come in at quite a pace. Added to that and the failing light there was also a backwash which was threatening to cut us off. It was very, very scary, particularly as the sand underfoot was very soft and muddy, almost like quicksand. Susan's dad had to roll his trouser legs up and carry us across the rapidly rising backwash. He was not best pleased.

I usually did quite well in the competitions as I loved performing to an audience, but one year it was a totally different story.

I was fourteen and had just had a growth spurt. Most of the other girls in my age group had a typical dancer's physique, slender and willowy. I was voluptuous! From the very first dance the adjudicator took a dislike to me. I was used to being placed in the medal positions, or at the very least gaining an Honours certificate. This is not me being conceited, that was just how it was, but not in this competition. Dance after dance in all the different categories, Greek, National, Ballet, Character, Song and Dance, Modern and Tap, not a single place or Honours certificate. Even in the duet sections my partner and I were marked down.

All the parents from my dancing school were shocked and my dad was all for giving the adjudicator a piece of his mind – in fact, at the end of the festival, I think he did. The only section where I wasn't marked down was the group section. I guess even she realised it was unfair to penalise all the other girls just because she had taken a dislike to me. We used to perform a beautiful routine to 'Jerusalem'. The music, the choreography, the costumes and the performance from all involved really was mesmerising. The adjudicator had no choice, she had to award us first place.

What happened next is something I will never forget. Not

only had 'Jerusalem' won us all gold medals, it had also won us a trophy. Under normal circumstances the most senior member of the group would have been presented with it, however, these were not normal circumstances. The girls decided amongst them-selves that I should receive the trophy from the adjudicator.

It probably meant very little to that adjudicator, but it meant the world to me to receive such a show of support from my fellow dancers.

Ninety Eight

Aloo gobi is number 98 on the takeaway menu at the
Indian Palace Restaurant in Javea, which we like to
frequent when we are in Spain.

It is cauliflower and potato cooked with onions, tomatoes and
delicate spices. It is one of my two favourite dishes, the other
being chana masala, which is chickpeas, onions and tomatoes in
a rich tangy sauce, but that is number 105, so couldn't feature
as a chapter.

Both of these dishes are described on the menu as 'side dishes'
rather than main courses but usually, when Chris and I eat there,
we will have one of them with number 111, basmati rice, and
garlic naan, number 126, and that is dinner!

The first time we went in, I ordered and then the waiter turned
to Chris in expectation. He was very disappointed when he
realised that our order was so minimal. We're not even big
drinkers, so our bill is usually under twenty euros and yet they
still give us complimentary poppadoms to start, and always offer
us schnapps or moscatel to conclude. I hope the tip I leave is
big enough.

Because of the regularity of our visits the waiting staff became
very familiar with us, in particular a waiter called Lucky, whose
uncle owns the restaurant. One evening we fancied an Indian
meal but we weren't really in the mood for going out, so we
decided to have a takeaway. I rang the Indian Palace and as I

was coming to the end of our order the voice on the other end of the phone said, 'I think I know you.'

It was Lucky, and he had recognised me not by my voice, but from the order I had just placed!

We don't always have the same dishes, particularly if we are ordering a takeaway in the UK, which usually coincides with watching a football match on the television. In some ways I am such a 'lad', although I prefer sparkling water to wash it all down rather than lager. We'll try bhindi bhaji, stir-fried okra in carom seed and garlic, which is delicious, mushroom bhaji, which I'm not so keen on, and lentil dhal. Speaking of dhal, it always reminds me of an incident when we were on holiday in the Maldives. Although it really is paradise on earth, and we loved both our holidays there, there wasn't a lot on the menu that we could eat. Most evenings were themed in terms of cuisine. We were OK on Italian evenings as there were pasta dishes we could enjoy, and our other favourite was Indian night. It was a self-service restaurant and all the dishes were labelled. I was helping myself to some dhal when an elderly gentleman, who bore a striking resemblance to the Major from *Fawlty Towers*, asked in a booming upper-class voice, 'Dhal, what is dhal?'

I explained that it was yellow lentils cooked with garlic and chilli, and he turned his nose up and walked away. Ever since then none of my family can utter the word dhal without quoting 'the Major'.

I am a reasonable cook but I'm not very experienced at cooking curried dishes. I think you need to be given authentic family recipes to get the true tastes of India.

One of the best Indian dishes I have ever made was from a recipe sent to me by one of the contestants in QVC's Search for a Presenter in 2007. It was for Bombay potatoes and was actually pretty vague as she had written 'to taste' throughout. Maybe that is the key. Add the ingredients not by measurement but to your own personal taste and then you are more likely to enjoy the outcome.

There is one recipe for spinach, tomato and chickpea curry, which is on one of the Waitrose recipe cards featured in *chapter 61*, that the family enjoys but I don't do it that often. The reason? Preparing the spinach, all 250 grammes of it.

I only cook it when Chris is at home and guess who prepares the spinach?

Ninety Nine

On the 27th of August 1999, my mum and dad
celebrated their Golden Wedding Anniversary although
they had no idea that there was any kind of
celebration planned.

We had never really made a big deal of Mum and Dad's
wedding anniversary, although we always sent cards and
a present or flowers. Even their Silver Anniversary had gone by
relatively unmarked as I had been away in Jersey in a summer
season.

With the big day a few months away, Lynda, Richard and I
started to plan a surprise party for them. We know our parents
well, and knew they wouldn't want an extravagant do in a hall,
so Richard agreed that he would host a party for the family and
close friends at his house in Nottingham, as it was kind of a
central point.

This doesn't sound like it requires too much in the way of
planning, but with my sister's family dotted around Scotland,
including the remote Fair Isle island, a certain amount of precision
was required.

My brother's wife at the time, Ann, was a huge help. She rang
me to get a list of people that I thought my parents would like
to see at their party, and then she did all the contacting, swearing
everyone to secrecy.

It wasn't the longest list in the world – my dad's two surviving brothers, John and Joe and their families, and people they had met through Mum's dancing school and through my old dancing school, Nora Morrison's – but we wanted it to be a gathering of people who were special to them.

I had arranged with Mum and Dad that Chris and I would visit them for the day to help them mark the occasion. We arrived in the morning, and the plan was to go over to my brother's house 'for tea'. It took a bit of persuading to have Mum dress up a bit. She normally went over to my brother's in casual trousers and a T-shirt, but I knew she would be very cross with me if I'd allowed her to be 'in public' so casually attired. I suggested a pretty floral skirt and top and encouraged her to put on just a dusting of make-up as it was a special occasion. Dad took the hint and put on a smarter pair of trousers and we all headed off to my brother's.

I really don't think Mum and Dad had any idea of the surprise that awaited them, even after remarking on how many cars there were parked on Richard's normally quiet cul-de-sac. Richard opened the front door to greet them as normal and then led us through to his garden room. The look on their faces was price-less as the realisation dawned that we had secretly planned a small gathering for them.

My sister's family were all there, including grandchildren and great-grandchildren. Our two children were there, along with Richard's two, Sam and Lee.

Ann had done a fabulous job with the catering, and Richard and his children had done a little bit of decorating to give the party atmosphere. Although it was August, you can never take the British weather for granted, but luck was on our side and the sun was shining brightly, without being blistering hot!

It can't have been far off being the perfect day for Mum and Dad, surrounded by their family and friends and in comfortable, familiar surroundings. I had hoped it would be something we could repeat for their Diamond Wedding Anniversary but sadly my dad died just two years short of the occasion.

Writing about it now, I appreciate just how lucky I am that my parents stayed together all those years and gave us a solid base from which to flourish. I'm sure, like most couples, they had their moments, but thankfully they were very rare.

My dad was in some respects quite a placid person and didn't often raise his voice in argument. This may well have been helped by the job he did. He worked as a travelling salesman so he had to have great communication skills . . . that will be the Monkey and the Gemini in him, as detailed in *chapter 60*.

He also had to stay away from home a lot when we were quite young children and I think this probably helped Mum and Dad's relationship as they didn't argue about how to bring us up, it was mostly down to my mum. This was not always easy for her, as my brother and sister used to fall out a lot.

On one occasion I remember I had been poorly so Mum was obviously stressed looking after me. Richard and Lynda began playing up and Mum had just had enough. She packed a bag and walked out of the house! I was in floods of tears and neither of my siblings seemed to be doing anything to stop her from going, so in my pyjamas and slippers I ran out of the house after her. She was already halfway down the road to the bus stop, so I had to run to try and catch up with her. When she saw me she told me to go home and that Lynda would look after us until Dad got back. I wasn't having any of it. She started to walk to the next bus stop, presumably hoping I would go back home, but I just followed her, crying. I have no idea whether she would have got on the bus if it had come along but thankfully she had time to cool off before the number 24 put in an appearance.

The only time I can remember a major discord between my parents was an occasion where my dad, after shouting at my mum, slammed out of the house, got in his car and screeched off up the road! I was terrified that he was going to have an accident. I didn't have to fret for long as ten minutes later he pulled back into the drive in one piece – he had probably only been round the block!

I realise how fortunate I am to have had such an untroubled childhood, and when Chris and I took the decision to have children we both agreed that we wanted the same for them.

Of course we have had our disagreements over the years but if we can manage fifty-eight years together, like Mum and Dad, we'll be doing OK!

One Hundred

The 'hundred' is probably the best-known exercise in
Pilates and probably my least favourite.

Pilates is a method of exercising originally devised by Joseph
Pilates in the 1920s to rehabilitate injured athletes and
dancers. It has been favoured by celebrities through the years as
a way to strengthen and elongate muscles without building bulk.
Everyone talks about the importance of building 'core' strength
these days but this was the principle of Joseph Pilates's method
over ninety years ago.

I was first introduced to Pilates at QVC when we started
selling a product called the Pilates Performer. It was a home-use
version of the 'Reformer' piece of equipment used in Pilates
studios around the world. Basically it is a moving platform,
controlled by bungee cords, that you sit, stand or lie on and
perform various exercises. You adjust the cords for more or less
resistance and your own body weight also adds to the level of
resistance.

The guest and developer of this product is a lady called
Marjolein Brugman and I often tell her, quite truthfully, that by
introducing me to Pilates she changed my life.

I will be honest with you: the first few times I used my
Performer machine I didn't like it. When I lay down on the
moving platform I used to experience a kind of motion sickness.

However, I persevered and within three months of first using it I was a devotee.

I love what it has done to my body, strengthening and toning all my muscles and helping to maintain my natural flexibility. The only thing that was lacking from the original Performer machine was a way to work out aerobically.

Marjolein rectified this shortcoming when she developed the cardio board. It is a mini trampoline that slots into place at one end of the machine and allows you to bounce while you are lying down. This gives you an intense aerobic workout in only twenty minutes with the added benefit of engaging your core muscles every time you jump away from the trampoline, in order to keep your legs in the air. Genius! You know you hear those adverts that say, 'This is the only piece of exercise equipment you will ever need'? Well, in my opinion, unless they are talking about a Pilates machine with a cardio board, they may not be entirely accurate.

As well as using the machine a couple of times a week to maintain my fitness, I also do Pilates mat work after I have been on the treadmill or in the swimming pool.

The funny thing is, a large proportion of the exercises are remarkably similar to what I used to teach in my body-conditioning classes, and in the 1980s I had never heard of Pilates!

One Hundred And One

You must be wondering why there is a chapter 101, when this book is quite clearly called *One Hundred Lengths of the Pool*.

Well, something happened in April 2012, when I had just two chapters of the book left to write, that I felt I should include. I could have axed a chapter to include this one, as it would have been relevant for chapters 10, 12, 26, 55 or particularly 22, but as I wanted you to read the book as I had originally intended, I decided to add this chapter at the end.

On the 10th of April 2012, I went for a 360+ health check. I hadn't been feeling ill, apart from being a lot more tired than usual, which I just put down to getting older, but I thought an 'MOT' wouldn't be a bad idea.

All the tests I had done on the day were fine, apart from a slight concern over a high tri-glyceride count as part of the cholesterol levels check. I will be honest, this did surprise me slightly as I am a vegetarian so I have very little animal fat in my diet, and I don't eat a lot of sugar-rich foods or drink much alcohol, but I wasn't unduly worried. My heart was fine, lung capacity good, weight within normal parameters for my height, and one of my blood tests showed no sign of anaemia or any other problems. However, another sample of my blood had to be sent away for further analysis, which I was assured was fairly routine, and I would get the results within a couple of days.

Two days later, as I was finishing a meeting with my boss at QVC, my mobile phone rang. It was the doctor who had conducted the medical tests at my 360+ health check.

'Can you talk?' he asked.

'Yes,' I replied as I took a seat in the production office.

'We have had the blood test results back and they are showing a very high white blood cell count. It's probably nothing to worry about, but I think you should make an appointment to see a haematology consultant as soon as possible.'

'How high is very high?' I asked.

'Well, the normal levels are between 4 and 11, and yours is 38.4.'

'What do you think might be causing it?' I asked.

'It could be any number of things, including your body producing lots of white cells to fight a bacterial infection, but you have been advised to see a consultant haematologist to exclude chronic myeloid leukaemia.'

I hung up the phone in a mild state of shock, but had to put it to the back of my mind as it was already past 6 p.m. and I was on air at seven and eight and needed to get ready. I'm not really sure how I got through those two hours, after which I drove home and decided not to mention anything to Daniel until after I had spoken to Chris, who was out working.

Although I had to be up early the next morning to have a mammogram, which was the final part of my 360+ health check, I stayed up until Chris got home at 1 a.m. He was as shocked as me, but he tried to reassure me that it was probably nothing.

The following morning I rang the doctor from the 360+ health check again just to confirm that I had understood what he had told me the previous evening. He reiterated the importance of seeing the consultant haematologist as soon as possible and then told me that he would give my number to London Bridge Hospital for them to ring me and organise that appointment as a matter of urgency, and also appointments to see a couple of other consultants which were less urgent.

When Daniel came down for breakfast I filled him in on the bare bones of what I had been told, taking care not to alarm him, and I also sent a text to Sophie as she was at work.

I had my mammogram done, and then went in to work for my shows at five and six. While I was preparing for my shows my mobile phone rang. It was London Bridge Hospital, who were having difficulty organising me an appointment for the following week as most of the consultants were away at a conference. As it was apparently urgent, an appointment was made for me at University College Hospital for the Monday morning at 11 a.m. with the registrar to Professor Goldstone, who was also away at the conference.

Sophie came to our house straight from work and, Sophie being Sophie, she looked at all the possible things that the high white blood cell count might be that had nothing to do with cancer. By the time she had finished, she almost had me convinced that it wasn't going to be anything awful, although right at the pit of my stomach there was a little knot of dread.

It was a long weekend, but at least I was working so that kept my mind occupied and I only had to wait for a couple of days before my appointment.

On the Monday morning Chris and I got the train to University College Hospital in London. The registrar came to apologise that he was running a little late as he had had an emergency on his ward round. Chris asked if they would be taking a blood sample, and when it was confirmed they were, he suggested that I had that done while I was waiting for my appointment, which they did.

When I went in for my appointment they already had the results. The registrar started by asking me if I had been feeling unwell and I said no, just very fatigued. He checked my neck, under my arms and my groin for swollen lymph glands, and my abdomen just under my ribcage which I later learnt was to see if my spleen was enlarged. He was then very direct with me.

'Are you a person who likes to know everything up front, or would you prefer to wait until we have got all the test results back?' he asked.

'I am definitely the former,' I replied.

That was when he told me that the blood test that day showed an even higher WBC of 42.8 and that it was probable that I had chronic myeloid leukaemia, known as CML. To confirm his suspicions he said that I would need to have a bone marrow biopsy which he would prefer me to have done immediately in order not to delay the diagnosis any longer than necessary, and so begin treatment as soon as possible. I agreed to have the biopsy done straight away and then emailed QVC to say that I would not be available for my shift that evening.

I didn't know anything about the procedure for a bone marrow biopsy as I wasn't expecting to have one so hadn't read up on it. You can have it under local anaesthetic or, if the pain becomes unbearable, you can have a general anaesthetic. If I wanted it done that day it would have to be under local anaesthetic as I had eaten breakfast.

The technician who performed the biopsy was really kind. He explained that they would be taking the sample from the back of my pelvis, so I would be lying on my side. He said he would give me lots of local anaesthetic so that I wouldn't feel anything, and then amended his statement to say 'not much'.

In fairness, although it did hurt, it was no worse than having a baby and didn't take as long, but the sensation was horrible as not only do they take a 'plug' of bone marrow, they also take little bits of bone too. Chris stayed with me throughout the procedure and I remember squeezing his hand very tightly.

At one point I had to ask the technician to stop, not because of the pain, but because I thought I was going to throw up. When he had finished he dressed the wound, and then I had to lie still on my back for thirty minutes or so.

~~That was when I cried, not because of the experience or the~~ pain but because of something Chris said: 'I would give anything to be lying on that bed right now instead of you.'

When I got home I immediately Googled the bone marrow biopsy in conjunction with CML to find out what they were looking for. They look for the presence of something called the Philadelphia chromosome which is present in the bone marrow of ninety per cent of people with CML. If it is there, then the suspected diagnosis is confirmed.

Without going into too much detail, the Philadelphia chromosome is a mutation of chromosome 9 and chromosome 22. The bottom of each of the chromosomes breaks off and for some reason attaches itself to the bottom of the wrong chromosome. The bottom of 22 joins chromosome 9, making a very long but non-problematic chromosome 9, but when the bottom of chromosome 9 joins 22 it creates the mutated chromosome 22, also known as the Philadelphia chromosome. This causes problems as it triggers the body to overproduce white blood cells which, when mature, are normally useful for fighting infections. Unfortunately these mass-produced white blood cells don't mature so they don't fight infection, they just crowd all the other good stuff you need in your blood.

I was pretty uncomfortable for the next couple of days and I wasn't allowed to shower for fear of infection, so it's a good job I wasn't scheduled to work! When I did take the dressing off on the Wednesday evening the wound was healing well.

I went in to work on the Thursday for a customer event, which was a long and tiring day. I usually love meeting and talking to the QVC viewers but I was anxious about the diagnosis and also still uncomfortable from the biopsy. I was on my feet for most of the day so I was really glad to get home that night. I was working again on the Friday but then I had the weekend off.

I was back at work on the Monday for the start of a run of seven consecutive days. This was not normal, but I had agreed to cover a couple of extra shifts for one of our presenters who was going into hospital. On the Wednesday, before going in to work, I had an appointment with a different type of consultant, as at this point we still weren't sure of the cause of the high white blood cell count. Thankfully that appointment didn't flag up anything untoward.

The next day, the 26th of April, was D-Day. I had my appointment with the professor at UCH to get the results of my bone marrow biopsy, and so hopefully have a diagnosis confirmed. They took another blood sample when I arrived and after a short wait it was time for me to meet the professor.

If I'm honest, I think I already knew that this appointment was simply to confirm what the registrar I had seen ten days prior had already prepared me for. I would imagine they don't perform bone marrow biopsies unless there is good reason.

The professor smiled as he shook my hand and then said, 'Well, I have the results of your biopsy and it confirms that you do have chronic myeloid leukaemia.'

'OK,' I said. 'Is there any chance that there could be a mistake?'

'No,' he said, 'The Philadelphia chromosome is present in ninety-six per cent of the bone marrow sample that we took, and your WBC is now forty-eight.'

'Right,' I said, feeling surprisingly calm.

He continued, 'If I had been handing you this diagnosis ten years ago the treatment and prognosis would have been very different, but there has been a huge amount of research in this field and there is now what can only be described as a "miracle drug" to treat this condition. You may have to stay on it for the rest of your life but you should be able to lead a near-normal life. You are very unlucky to have CML but very fortunate to have it now rather than ten years ago. By the time I have finished with you, you will have the cleanest blood in London.'

He is right that I am unlucky to have CML. It is one of the rarer forms of leukaemia, with only around 600 cases diagnosed in the UK each year. It is more common in men than women and usually strikes people who are over sixty, although there are always exceptions.

The good news is that while it is one of the rarer types, it is also the most treatable with drug therapy. The other good news is that they caught it early.

'So what happens now?' I asked.

'We will start you immediately on a half dose of the "miracle drug", which is a targeted oral chemotherapy, to see how well your body tolerates it, and if all goes well we will increase it to the full dose when I next see you. You will also have to take a drug to help protect your kidneys, as they are going to be working very hard to get rid of the immature white blood cells that will hopefully be killed off.'

With that he handed me a prescription for the drugs and a sheet produced by Macmillan Cancer Support, listing the most common possible side effects of the drugs. He warned me that I should be prepared to take some time off work, armed me with several telephone numbers to contact if I experienced any of the aforementioned side effects over the weekend, and booked me an appointment to see him four days later.

The pharmacist who handed over the drugs was very kind and helpful. She told me I would need to drink at least three litres of water a day to help my kidneys and to keep side effects to a minimum, and she also recommended nibbling on a ginger biscuit if I felt nauseous. She said I should stop taking my vitamin supplements, apart from the Bs, and that I shouldn't drink green tea, which is fine with me as I hate the stuff! And that was it.

I left University College Hospital that day the same person, but knowing that from that moment my life would be a different kind of normal.

Epilogue

As far as I know the treatment for my chronic myeloid leukaemia is going well, although I did have a bit of a setback recently.

I have to visit the hospital on a very regular basis to have my blood checked. All the blood tests had indicated that everything was progressing according to plan, but when I had a test called bcr/abl and a second bone marrow biopsy the results weren't as good as they should have been.

I had a nervous couple of weeks worrying that maybe I had become resistant to the drug or, worse still, that I had a mutation that would prevent the drug from working. The professor was of the opinion that the dose of the 'miracle drug' I was taking was too low so he doubled it to what is considered a normal dose. Unfortunately I couldn't tolerate it so we are now trying a three-quarter dose, which I am tolerating, but I won't know until I have my next bcr/abl test in a month or so whether it is working sufficiently well on my condition.

If it is, I will continue with this drug until I reach remission and then stay on it for at least two more years or possibly for the rest of my life. If this dose isn't working adequately I will have to change to a different drug and hope that I can cope with any side effects that may cause.

The early side effects I experienced on my current drug of intense bone and muscle ache and debilitating tiredness had lessened as the professor had me on a reduced dose of targeted chemotherapy. I am hoping that the recent increase in medication won't make those effects worse again.

One side effect that I can't seem to get rid of though is a blocked sensation that is sometimes in the back of my throat and sometimes lower down in my oesophagus. At times it is not too bad but other times I feel my throat constricting, making it difficult to breathe. I have had tests, including an endoscopy, to make sure that nothing untoward is going on with my digestive tract, but everything seems to be in order. The professor is certain that my medication is causing it but is loath to change anything in case I experience worse side effects on a different drug. It is uncomfortable but not intolerable at the moment.

I still feel quite tired a lot of the time and a little bit breathless so it is more difficult for me to exercise as much as I would like. This has had the knock-on effect of me gaining a little weight, which I am not too happy about, but at the moment it is the least of my concerns.

Recently I have noticed that my hair is thinning. When I mentioned it to my hairdresser he simply said, 'It is, but you still have sixty per cent more hair than most people I see and it is thinning evenly rather than in a patchy manner.'

I am lucky I had such an abundance of hair to start with, and if I need to adopt a shorter style for a while it's not the end of the world.

I've also had a touch of oedema around my eyes, making them puffy, particularly in the mornings if I've been sleeping on my front, and most recently cramp in my fingers, which makes it a bit tricky to fasten jewellery clasps when I'm live on air at QVC!

All in all though I know I am in safe hands with Professor

Goldstone and I am sure that my positive attitude will help me to beat this latest adversity in my life.

As I said in *chapter 37*:

'That which does not kill us makes us stronger.'

Short Story Writing Competition

The Foundling

It was a warm sunny day, not a cloud in the sky. I was trotting through the wood with my mistress, when I heard the padding footsteps that were to become so familiar to me. I turned around and peered at a golden animal. Its beauty was so stunning; to me a fellow dog, it was an attractive cocker spaniel. It whined and my mistress stopped and turned around. She stroked and petted the whining spaniel, but still it would not cease following us. My mistress in gazing down at the spaniels silky paws, found that she had trodden on a porcupine and some of its stinging pines were stuck in her paw. My mistress picked up the poor whimpering bundle and carried her home. The spaniel was lain on one of our best cushions, taboo for me, and my mistress bathed her paw. Then she phoned for the vet who was taking his surgery, but he promised to call and see our new pet after his surgery.

The vet lives in Ottawa, as we do, the capital city of Canada. I live with my mistress, the servants and a few cats, in a large mansion on the outskirts of the busy city. My master had died a few years previously, leaving my mistress with the large house and its extensive grounds. The house was called 'The Willows', my mistress is 'Lady Angelica Barton' and my name is simply Ean. We later named the new arrival, for she was to stay with us, Mandy. My master owned a small copper mine in Northern Rhodesia where unfortunately he was killed by a landslide, caused by the blasting in the mine, the week before Northern Rhodesia became Zambia. Still enough of my history. When the vet arrived he said Mandy would be fully recovered in several days. My mistress promised to take good care of her until the vets next visit; this however was impossible, as you will now see.

Early the following morning mistress received an urgent telegram from her uncle in the U.S.A. She read the brief note with a most disturbing facial expression. The hustle and bustle of the next few hours completely confounded me, I was forgotten. My mistress and the servants were running around, and it was only later that I found out that her aunt had been taken gravely ill. Her uncle was flustered and had sent for mistress to organise the kitchen staff at his house during his wife's illness. I heard the door of the shooting-brake slam shut and listened as mistress drove the car into the distance.

Then one of the servants, a genial French-Canadian woman, remembered me and opened a tin of some rather tasty dog meat (she was not one of the kitchen staff and had given me some tinned chicken.) After that I was miserably alone and went to find Mandy; she was asleep, huh women! When she awoke it seemed that she did not want her dogmeat, so I obligingly caught her a rabbit. She preferred this, but I made a mental note not to make a habit of running and fetching for her — she could do it for me when she was a little better.

The next few days followed quietly, me catching her food. There had been several telegrams and letters from my mistress; her aunt was improving, the domestic staff were entirely unruly, she would be returning home in about a week, and how was Mandy? Not a word about me! This dog is going to be tiresome I thought. Her leg was healing and the vet pronounced her fit and well — well enough to catch her own food! Then a rather cunning plan entered my well trained doggy brain; next day, action!

Mandy wished to know which was the most fruitful hunting place, aha chance! I promised faithfully to show her, the following day. Seven 'o'clock the next morning the sun was streaming in through the windows and a light breeze ruffled the branches of the weeping willows in the garden, causing them to dip their arms into the cool water of the pond, in which swam many coloured fish, a source of amusement on lazier days. I set off somewhat slowly that morning on account of Mandy's paw not being perfectly healed. She limped rather apologetically behind me, not really wishing to hinder my progress. However, we trudged for approximately three miles, following a stream which wound appreciatively under the trees, as the day became hotter. Then I began to run, I crossed the stream, bounded up the hillside opposite and over the top of the hill, toward a shortcut I knew to get home. I stopped several times en route to celebrate. I had lost Mandy, she was taking the attention and interest of everyone from me, and now she would never return! Not that I disliked her, she was very beautiful; that was probably the reason why I resented her; I am a rather overfed Labrador, sort of blackish in colour, and very affectionate to humans who fuss over me and give me sweets and chocolates.

Suddenly I could see the white towers of 'The Willows', I bounded playfully round the fishpond, up on to the terrace, wandered around the veranda and into the drawing room. I heard the cook whistle me – ooh dinner, I thought, and bounced into the kitchen. I stopped dead in my tracks, for what I saw gave me the fright of my life; my dinner was there all right but so was Mandy, licking her paws after a most satisfying dinner of rabbit she had obviously caught herself. She regarded me with a look of surprise; why was I refraining from eating the dinner she had caught for me? I recovered my composure and went to sniff at my dinner. The smell was gorgeous, but I could not eat it after she had humiliated me like that. I turned away which really broke my heart, still cook would give me something else. It was only later, after Mandy had eaten my dinner, that I realised that cook was not going to give me anything else, and I should have eaten the rabbit while it was there. I spent a hungry, cold night, whereas Mandy slept like a log. So ended my first attempt to get rid of Mandy.

During the next few days Mandy mentally tormented me, by giving me teasing glances and uttering peculiar sounds which sounded like a human giggling. I consoled myself by ignoring her. I usually watched television in the evenings, and it was one night as we were watching the news that we made up our disagreement. I was seated on the couch watching the news, this did nothing to cheer me up as I listened to all the fighting. The Americans fighting the communists in Viet-Nam, the Chinese demonstrating against the Russians, the Chinese fighting each other, Israel against Jordan, and now India against Pakistan. This being the case I was totally miserable and left the T.V. for more congenial surroundings.

I trudged up to the boxroom unaware that Mandy was close behind me. I had just settled down on the rug in the corner, when she came and nuzzled up to me, her soft brown eyes looked really forgiving, then she settled down too. I knew then that she had forgiven me, and the days ahead would be happy ones. But I was wrong, we soon encountered trouble again, but it was not between Mandy and I.

Two days later mistress returned, we were all very pleased – to begin with that is. Dear, ill, aunt Agatha had come with her. Poor aunt Agatha, simply half dead she was. She marched into the house pushing mistress out of the way, 'Angelica, Angelica, there are two horrible looking dogs asleep in the lounge of all place!' 'Um' replied mistress giving us a knowing wink.

'Well they must be moved, and immediately.' Mandy and I took the hint and retired inconspicuously. The next few days were literally unbearable, aunt Agatha shouted at us all day long. Mandy and I spent less time in the house and more time doing a circular tour of the estate. On one of these wanderings we discovered a hollow in a tree trunk in an old oak tree, on the far side of the park. After a brief discussion we decided that this seclusion should be our future home until aunt Agatha returned to her undisciplined staff, though how they could be undisciplined with her around I do not know. That night we spent many hours lining the inside of the hole with blankets and rugs from our own baskets, then we returned to the house and settled down for the night. The next day we ate as much food as possible, and then I went to catch food for our store, while Mandy raided the larder.

It was later that day when we moved into our new home. Mistress and aunt Agatha were watching the T.V. that night, so they did not notice our absence. We spent the night in our tree, it was very comfortable and warm. As we had plenty of food we decided to remain in the tree until the dragon left; there would be no need to return to the house prior to this event. During the day we would go out hunting in the surrounding countryside; nobody came to look for us, they probably never even noticed that we had gone. We lived this kind of life for approximately a week. Then, one day we heard the ecstatic roar of aunt Agatha's limousine which she had sent for to take her home. Our joy knew no bounds, and we rushed cheerfully back to the house. Mistress was recovering on the veranda, and Mandy and I settled comfortably beside her a homely picture.

Acknowledgements

I always think of acknowledgements in books as a bit like an acceptance speech when you receive an award. With that in mind, I will try and keep this brief.

Firstly I have to thank my partner Chris, the most patient man on the planet, for his unending support and also for helping me to remember some of the things that we have shared over the past thirty-five years that appear in this book. He is my rock. Thanks to my children, Daniel and Sophie, who I love with all my heart, for their encouragement and for giving me the space to write even when they 'wanted to talk'. Thank you to my mum, the only person I allowed to read the first fifty chapters of my book when it was still a work in progress, for the positive feedback she gave me, and to my dad, who, although no longer alive, has been the driving force for me to finish this book.

A big thank you to Debbie McNally at Random House for having faith in me, and also to my copy-editor, Justine Taylor, for checking my punctuation and grammar without 'meddling' with what I had written (her words not mine).

And lastly thank you to all the people who have been a part of my life and feature in this book – without you there would be no stories to tell.

Picture Credits

Be-Ro cookery book cover reproduced by kind permission of Sharon Waller at Premier Foods.

First day at QVC by kind permission of Sue Leeson at QVC.

All other photographs are the personal property of the author.

Index

(the initials JR in subentries refer to Julia Roberts)